# THE BIBLE
## IN ITS ANCIENT AND
## ENGLISH VERSIONS

Edited by
### H. WHEELER ROBINSON
**M.A., D.D.**

Sometime Reader in Biblical Criticism in
the University of Oxford
Principal of Regent's Park College, Oxford

## GREENWOOD PRESS, PUBLISHERS
### WESTPORT, CONNECTICUT

The Library of Congress cataloged this book as follows:

Robinson, Henry Wheeler, 1872–1945, *ed.*
    The Bible in its ancient and English versions. Edited
by H. Wheeler Robinson. Westport, Conn., Greenwood
Press ₁1970₎
     vii, 337 p.  23 cm.
     Reprint of the 1940 ed.
     CONTENTS.—Introduction, by the editor.—The Hebrew Bible, by
the editor.—The Greek Bible, by W. F. Howard.—The Syriac Bible,
by T. H. Robinson. — The Latin Bible, by H. F. D. Sparks. — The
English versions (to Wyclif) by W. A. Craigie. — The Sixteenth-
century English versions, by J. Isaacs.—The Authorized version and
after, by J. Isaacs. — The Revised version and after, by C. J.
Cadoux.—The Bible as the word of God, by the editor.—Bibliography (p. ₁303₎–316)
     1. Bible—History.  2. Bible—Versions.  3. Bible.  English—Ver-
sions.   I. Title.

BS445.R66  1970        220.4            76–109832
ISBN 0–8371–4323–3                     MARC
Library of Congress       70 ₁7₎

Originally published in 1940 by Claredon Press, Oxford

Reprinted in 1970 by Greenwood Press, Inc.,
51 Riverside Avenue, Westport, Conn. 06880

Library of Congress catalog card number 76-109832
ISBN 0-8371-4323-3

Printed in the United States of America

10  9  8  7  6  5  4  3  2

# CONTENTS

# INTRODUCTION

Books about the Bible have Legion for their name (and some of them deserve a Gadarene destiny). Any new-comer to the throng should be challenged to justify his coming. He should either bring new knowledge or make old knowledge more accessible. The contributors to the present volume are chiefly concerned to make the latter claim, though incidentally their researches may have added something to the common stock. They have written both for the professional student (at the outset of his studies) and for the reader of general education. Their combined aim is to present the history of the Bible from its first origins and in its ancient versions, and then to continue that history along the line which specially interests the reader of the English Bible. The story is a fascinating one, and it is our hope that the present telling of it, involving a good deal of technical detail, has not wholly obscured that fascination. The closing chapter is of a different order, dealing as it does with the Bible as Revelation. Its present justification is that but for this claim, there would have been no story to tell. The enormous amount of detailed work lavished on the Bible by scholars of many generations has been inspired by the belief that this is a unique book, through which God still speaks uniquely to man.

Within this general scheme, the fullest liberty has been given to the different contributors, and no systematic attempt has been made to co-ordinate their views on those points of detail on which scholarship may legitimately show variance. The variety of method in different chapters springs partly from the differences of the material to be handled, and partly from the natural idiosyncrasies of the writers. The same considerations apply to the varying length of the Bibliographies (to each chapter) collected at the end of the book. But, for the most part, these have been kept as brief as possible, and are intended to serve simply as indications of further and more specialized material for study, without any attempt at completeness.

From such a book as this, exhibiting such great variety of translation from a common original, one topic of particular literary interest emerges. This is the difficulty and subtlety of the art of faithful translation. Readers familiar with a single version only, who have never had occasion to translate for themselves, may be puzzled by the great variety of renderings which this book illustrates. But there can be no finality in translation, since no one rendering can ever fully and faithfully reproduce its original. Even when the two languages possess words of identical meaning, there are characteristic differences of context in thought and culture, which introduce subtle varieties of meaning. The words *'ish, anthropos, barnasha, homo, man,* all refer to the same object, yet how different have been the conceptions of physiology and psychology linked with each! How far from the thought of the ancient world are modern ideas of human personality! Apart from such differences, for which the translator must wholly depend upon his reader's knowledge, the translator has to choose between the 'literal' rendering, reproducing vocabulary and idiom as closely as possible, and the rendering of *ideas* in the idiomatic form natural to the language into which he is translating. He is further handicapped, in regard to a version of sacred Scriptures, by the prescriptive rights of some familiar rendering, any change in which is apt to be resented. The result, as will often be seen from the following pages, is apt to be a compromise, perhaps less satisfying to the translator himself than to anybody else.

Each version, therefore, is, in some degree, a new book, and has a subsequent history of its own. We can see this best from our own Authorized Version, which has attained classical rank in English literature. Whatever its faults of translation—and they are many—when considered as a reproduction of the original (itself often obscure or debatable), however much it has added to, or subtracted from, that original, the Authorized Version remains by common consent one of our most splendid literary monuments. The generations to come are not likely to displace it. Even if its intrinsic literary qualities could be ignored, it has served itself heir to so much from the versions of its past, and has written its own language so deeply on the literature of its future, that it can never be forgotten.

On the other hand, there will always be the need for more accurate and (because of archaisms) more intelligible translations. Our knowledge of both the form and meaning of the original text increases with the passage of time. Obsolete words and phrases become a real stumbling-block. This applies to every version.

The Revised Version to-day itself calls for revision, and one of the possible services of the book now offered to the English reader will be to create an informed understanding of the need, and to help those students whose further studies may perhaps contribute to the satisfaction of the need.

I am grateful to the Regius Professor of Hebrew in the University of Oxford, for reading the typescript of Chapter I, to my colleague, the Rev. A. J. D. Farrer, for similar help in regard to Chapter IX, to the Rev. Professor H. H. Rowley, for reading the proof of the Bibliographies, and to my colleague, the Rev. L. H. Brockington, for reading the whole proof, and for compiling the Indexes. The careful and expert proof-reading carried out at the Press itself should also be gratefully acknowledged.

H. W. R.

OXFORD,
Michaelmas, 1940.

# I

# THE HEBREW BIBLE

### SYNOPSIS

Characteristics of the Hebrew language (vocabulary and syntax, prose, and poetry). Survey of the growth of Hebrew literature (early songs and stories, history, laws, prophecy, psalms, wisdom, apocalyptic). Parallel, but later, growth of a 'Canon' (Torah, 'Prophets', Writings: the law-books of Josiah and Ezra). Distinction of the Hebrew from the Greek Bible.

Printed Editions. Manuscript sources (writing materials, work of the Masoretes, the extant manuscripts). Why the Masoretic text requires criticism (obscurity, variants, evidence of early versions). Problems for the translator.

## 1. *The Hebrew Language*

ANY one unacquainted with Hebrew who opens an ordinary Hebrew Bible will notice certain peculiarities. He sees rows of heavily printed lines, of which the letters seem top-heavy, since they are mostly thicker at the top than the bottom; he sometimes wonders whether he is looking at the book upside-down. Underneath these letters (the consonants) he will see more lightly printed a number of dots and strokes (the vowels) and he may wonder again at this apparently artificial division of the elements of a word. But, if he were looking over the shoulder of the reader of the 'Torah' (the Pentateuch) in a synagogue service, he would see written (not printed) on the skin roll the consonants only, and be left to wonder still more at the feat of memory which can reproduce the complete sounds from the consonants only. This, however, is no more, indeed much less, than is done by the skilled shorthand reporter who reads off his consonantal outlines fluently enough, even when the subject-matter is new to him. Both the reader of the Hebrew text and the reporter might be in doubt about a single consonantal outline removed from its context. Thus, the consonants *d–b–r* in Hebrew mean 'word', 'pestilence', or 'he said', as in English they

4512

B

might stand for 'dabber', 'Deborah', or 'debar'. But in both cases the context usually removes all risk of ambiguity.

The use of a purely consonantal text in the synagogue service is, like the use of the written roll instead of the printed book, an example of that reverent conservatism which so often characterizes religion. As a matter of fact, the vowels were not inserted at all in the older writing of Hebrew; they were not added to any Hebrew text of the Bible, even in their most primitive form, before about the sixth century A.D. This vowel-less character of the script is found also in other 'Semitic' language (this being the name of the group to which Hebrew belongs). We can see it in the Phoenician inscription on the tomb of Ahiram belonging to the thirteenth century B.C., or on the Moabite Stone of the ninth century B.C., or on the potsherds of the sixth century B.C., recently found at Lachish. But the consonants in these and in many other similar scripts are considerably different in form from those of the printed or written Hebrew Bible, which in this respect is less conservative than the Samaritan Pentateuch. The Samaritan script is modelled on that of those ancient 'North-West Semitic' languages already indicated.

Besides this 'North-Western' group, in which numerous varieties of Aramaic are also now usually included,[1] there is an 'Eastern' or Accadian group (Babylonian and Assyrian) and a 'Southern' group (Arabic and Ethiopic). As may readily be understood, the study of these cognate languages throws much light on both the vocabulary and grammar of the Hebrew language. This help is the more necessary for historical exegesis because the meaning of words in post-Biblical Hebrew has often developed considerably from that of their use in the Biblical texts, e.g. the Biblical ṣedākāh = 'righteousness' has come to mean also 'alms'.

The primary place of the consonants in Hebrew (as in other

---

[1] Including the Aramaic which replaces Hebrew in Ezra iv. 8—vi. 18, vii. 12–26, Dan. ii. 4b—vii. 28; cf. Gen. xxxi. 47, Jer. x. 11.

Semitic languages) is seen in the fact that its vocabulary is built up chiefly by the vocalic modification of the consonantal root. Thus, in the example already given, *d–b–r* can be pronounced *dābār* as meaning 'word', *dibber*, 'he spoke', or *dōbēr* 'one speaking', whilst the apparently remote meaning, 'pestilence', which belongs to the pronunciation *déber*, links up with the Arabic development of the meaning of the root. The tri-literality of the root is a marked feature of the Semitic languages, though there are indications of an earlier bi-literal stage. The Semitic alphabet has a number of peculiar sounds, notably in its gutturals and emphatic dentals and sibilants; 'in the Arabs all parts alike of the mouth and gullet are organs of speech'.[1]

The Hebrew vocabulary is concrete and therefore picturesque. Hebrew 'psychology' attributed psychical qualities to the physical organs—heart, bowels, hand, eye, ear, &c., and would therefore say 'without heart', when it meant 'without understanding' (Hos. vii. 11), or 'he that planted the ear' (Ps. xciv. 9) instead of 'the creator of audition'. The same kind of realism extends throughout the language, and matches the quality of the think-ing. To 'start on a journey' is (originally) to 'pull up' (tent-pegs); an altar is 'a slaughtering-place'; worship is 'prostration'; the word for 'morning' (*bôḳer*), when the light 'ploughs through' the darkness, is linked to that for 'cattle' (*bāḳār*) who do the ploughing. No doubt, this is more or less true for all language, and we all use words of whose original picturesqueness we have become unconscious. But the point is that Hebrew is nearer its origins and, through the structure of the language, likely to be more conscious of them. Its living speech was helped out by many dramatic gestures (note the frequency of 'behold!') and its very words often epitomized an action, as in the examples given. The emphatic 'tone', or stress of the voice, in Hebrew words, and its effect on the unstressed syllables, illustrate the vigorous character of the utterance.

[1] A remark made to C. M. Doughty by an Arab (*Arabia Deserta*, i. 154).

The Hebrew syntax matches the vocabulary by its simplicity and directness. It prefers co-ordination to subordination in the structure of sentences. A literal translation of the Hebrew would become monotonous to us by the multiplication of the word 'and'. Hebrew is as poor in connective particles as Greek is rich. Yet Hebrew has many simple ways[1] of expressing its finer shades of meaning, such as variation in the order of words, circumstantial clauses, the repetition of words for emphasis, the brief preliminary indication of a person or thing before it is wrought into the structure of the sentence (*casus pendens*). Its paucity of adjectives finds compensation either by apposition of nouns (e.g. 'the cords, the gold' for 'the golden cords') or by the peculiar relation known as 'the construct' (e.g. 'pot of my washing', for 'my wash-pot').

An example of Hebrew narrative prose will perhaps convey an impression of Hebrew style better than any further generalizations. It is taken from the story of Rebecca encountered at the well by Abraham's servant. The translation is purposely made as baldly literal as possible, to convey the form, as well as the meaning of the Hebrew (Gen. xxiv. 15 ff.):

And—it—was, he not—yet has—finished to—speak, and—behold! Ribqah going—out (she—was—born to—Bethuel ben Milcah wife—of Nahor, brother—of Abraham) and—her—jar on her—shoulder; and—the—girl good—of appearance exceedingly, a virgin, and—a—man not has—known—her, and—she—went—down to—the—fountain and—filled her—jar and—came—up, and—ran the—servant to—meet—her and—said 'make—me—swallow, pray, a—little—of water from—thy—jar and—she—said 'drink, my—lord' and—she—hastened and—she—let—down (i.e. quickly lowered) her—jar on—her—hand and—she—let—him—drink: and she—

[1] In past time, a great deal of subtlety has been found in the Hebrew verbal system, with its 'perfect' and 'imperfect', with and without the conjunction *waw*, and relatively small indication of temporal distinctions. Comparative study now seems to make probable the mixed origin of these forms, the peculiarities being due to the syncretism of different usages from different sources, Accadian, and Aramæan: cf. G. R. Driver, *Problems of the Hebrew Verbal System*; D. W. Thomas, in *Record and Revelation*, p. 379.

finished to–let–him–drink and–she–said, 'also for–thy–camels I–will–draw until they–have–finished to–drink: and–she–hastened and–emptied her–jar into the–drinking–trough, and–she–ran yet to the–well to–draw, and–she–drew for–all his–camels: and–the–man gazing at–her, keeping–silence to–know whether–has–prospered Yahweh his–way or not.

Here may be seen in particular the repeated co-ordination of clauses, just as a child might tell the story taking one detail at a time, whilst swiftly moving from each to the next in the series. This circumstantiality of narrative is characteristic of the Hebrew prose style and gives to it much of its dramatic power, as well as the facility afforded for translation into other languages. We note also the preference for direct speech in place of the 'oblique oration'.

This example of prose narration needs to be supplemented by one of poetic style, for which we may take Ps. cxxvi, a fine example of the more elaborate Hebrew lyric:

> At Yahwéh's túrning the–fórtunes–of Zíon,
>> We–wére as–dréamers.
> Thén was-fílled–with láughter our-moúth,
>> And–our–tóngue with ringing–crý.
> Thén they–saíd among–the–nátions,
>> Gréatly hath Yahwéh dóne with–thése.
> Gréatly hath Yahwéh dóne with–us,
>> We–wére rejoícing.
> Túrn, Yahwéh, our–fórtunes,
>> As–chánnels in–the–Négeb.
> The–sówers with–téars,
>> With–ringing–crý, shall réap.
> Góing shall–one–gó, and–wéeping,
>> Béaring the–trail–of séed:
> Cóming shall–one–cóme, with–ringing–crý
>> Béaring his-shéaves.

Here two characteristics of the Hebrew poetical style are obvious, viz. its parallelism, or balanced repetition, contrast, or completion of an idea, and its rhythm, dependent on the accented syllables (usually the last) of each word or combination of words. In this poem the stresses of the voice run in three pairs (2 +2 +2) for each of the first four couplets (except that the third, as it now stands, has 3 +2 +2), and in triplets and pairs (3 +2) for the last four (except that the sixth, as it now stands, has 2 +2). The most frequent Hebrew rhythm is that of the triple stress, and the most frequent kind of parallelism is that of simple repetition of the same idea (e.g. Deut. xxxii. 1, 2). In Ps. cxxvi both the rhythm and the parallelism are more elaborate, the change of rhythm between the first and second stanzas probably corresponding with the change from a grateful remembrance of divine help to a new prayer for it. The parallelism of the last two couplets is specially effective, picturing as it does the whole contrast between the autumn toil and the harvest joy, with something of the effect of Millet's 'The Angelus'. This effect is produced with true art, because with the minimum of words:

> Hālók yēlék ubākóh
> nōs'é meshek-hazzára'
> Bó' yābó' berinnáh
> nōs'é 'ălummōtháw

Naturally, there are many varieties of style in the Old Testament, as we should expect from a literature extending over a millennium, and by no means all of its writings reach the artistic simplicity of some of the patriarchal narratives, or preserve the simple art of those religious lyrics which were Israel's supreme aesthetic achievement. The Hebrew language is, indeed, specially suited for poetry, for it stirs the emotions by its suggestions, rather than informs the mind by a complete and analytic statement.

## 2. *The Hebrew Literature*

A survey of the contents of the Hebrew Bible must begin by emphasizing the difference between the Hebrew 'Canon' in its

present form (with which the following section will be concerned) and the actual origins and nature of the literature from
which that 'Canon' was drawn, which is the subject of the
present section.

It cannot be proved that any of the literature which has come
down to us was written before the settlement of the Hebrews in
Canaan. The possible use of written records at an earlier date,
as by Moses, is not, of course, to be denied, for writing had been
known in the Near East for many centuries before this. But,
in the nature of things, it is highly improbable that a nomadic
people, struggling to establish themselves as invaders of the
cultivated lands, would have any interest in 'literature' or any
opportunity, or even capacity, for producing it. At this stage of
development we must think rather of oral traditions, in the form
of oracles, maxims, stories, and especially songs, which are most
easily remembered. Thus the 'Song of Lamech' (Gen. iv. 23,
24) evidences its nomadic origin by the unrestricted character
of its demand for blood-vengeance, and the 'Song of the Ark'
(Num. x. 35, 36) may well be a memory from the time of
Israel's desert wanderings. The earliest piece of Hebrew literature which we possess is generally admitted to be the 'Song of
Deborah' (Judges v), describing a memorable struggle of the
recently settled invaders against the Canaanite inhabitants of the
land. David's laments over Saul and Jonathan (2 Sam. i. 17–27)
and over Abner (2 Sam. iii. 33, 34) are generally recognized as
his own, and the 'Court History of David' (2 Sam. ix–xx,
1 Kings i, ii) is probably the earliest historical narrative we
possess. This is especially worthy of study, as illustrating Hebrew
prose at its best—Hebrew prose as the gradual product of a long
discipline in oral story-telling. To a date not long after this we
may ascribe the collection of tribal songs now known as 'The
Blessing of Jacob' (Gen. xlix). That such collections of songs
were made at an early date we know from the references to 'The
Book of Jashar' (Joshua x. 13, 2 Sam. i. 18, 1 Kings viii. 13 in

the Septuagint text), and to 'The Book of the Battles of Yahweh' (Num. xxi. 14), neither of which, unfortunately, has been preserved. The stories of heroes told in Judges (though not their much later setting) also go back to this period, and some of the tales told about Saul and David (1 Sam. ix ff., xvi ff.) must be quite early. In the ninth century the earlier collection of stories about the patriarchs (J) began to be made and it was paralleled in the following century by a later collection (E). 'The Blessing of Moses' (Deut. xxxiii) may be dated somewhere about 800 B.C., as also the stories about Elijah and Elisha. Thus a considerable number of detached songs and stories had come into written existence before there was any thought of the more systematic presentation of 'history', and these provided the material for subsequent 'editors', such as those who shaped the present Book of Judges, and compiled 1 and 2 Kings. Long after these books came the work of the 'Chronicler' (*c.* 300 B.C.) making use of the earlier histories, the contemporary evidence of Haggai and Zechariah, the memoirs of Nehemiah and Ezra; on this basis the history was rewritten in accordance with contemporary conceptions of it. We may usefully contrast the much more reliable narrative of 1 Maccabees (*c.* 100 B.C.)

Another and still longer line of development, eventually destined to claim the foremost place in Israel's literature, was that of 'law'. From the nomadic days law, in the primitive form of ruling custom, the verdict of the sheikh, the decision of the sacred oracle (Urim and Thummim, cf. Deut. xxxiii. 8), was a necessary part of the life of the community. Early oral decisions became precedents, and were collected into such a form as 'The Book of the Covenant' (Exod. xx. 22—xxiii. 19), the earliest code of Hebrew law we possess, and one that presupposes an agricultural community. This is usually dated under the early monarchy; the next code we can date (621) is that of Deuteronomy (xii–xxviii) which is largely an expansion of it. The third, formulated probably in the exilic period, is that known as

'The Code of Holiness' (most of Lev. xvii–xxvi). It is not until the exile and the enforced detachment from the performance of the ritual, that we get those great compilations of priestly law which bulk so largely in the Pentateuch. More will have to be said of these in relation to the 'Canon'. Here it should be noted that the dates at which these successive strata of 'law' were codified gives no further indication of the time of their origin than is afforded by a *terminus ad quem*. Many of the items must, by their nature, go back to a remote period, such as the very primitive 'Ordeal of Jealousy' (Num. v. 11–31), or the rite of the scape-goat for Azazel (Lev. xvi. 8 ff.), which are fossil survivals in much later strata. It should also be remembered that 'law' is a very inadequate rendering of the Hebrew word 'torah', which meant originally an 'instruction' or 'direction', such as was given by the sacred oracle; 'torah' came eventually to mean practically 'revelation', the whole revelation of God in the Pentateuch.

From the Christian, though not from the Jewish, standpoint, the most important part of the Hebrew literature is undoubtedly the prophetic. Christianity is conceivable without the Law, but not without the Prophets. In the teaching of its Founder, and in the subsequent interpretation of His work, it went back to make new contacts with those perennial sources of inspiration which the traditional interpretation of the Law ('the tradition of the elders') had so largely obscured. Prophecy, like the other lines of development in Hebrew literature, had humble beginnings. The psychical phenomena of the primitive *nabi'* (of the dervish type) were little more than the equivalent of the physical 'casting of lots' by the sacred oracle. But values are measured by results, not by origins. The resort to psychical phenomena, as a means of knowing the will of the gods, had in it the germ of mediation through Hebrew prophecy, for which human personality in all its wide and deep range became the organ of divine revelation. The earliest prophetic 'visions'

which have come down to us in the Hebrew records are those of
Micaiah (1 Kings xxii. 17, 19 ff.). On the eve of battle he sees
the already scattered host of Israel. Another vision of his explains the deception of the optimistic prophets, by the activity
of 'a lying spirit in the mouth of the prophets' for which Yahweh was responsible. These particular 'visions' are fragmentary
remembrances preserved by their incorporation in the story of
the battle in which Ahab was killed. In the next century the
prophets became so prominent that their disciples began to make
and collect the independent records of their oral utterances which
now bear the names of the prophets of the eighth century and
onwards—Amos, Hosea, Isaiah, Micah, Zephaniah, Jeremiah,
and Habakkuk ('Nahum' has a literary character of its own).
We can see the transition from oral to written prophecy being
made in the case of Isaiah (viii. 16, xxx. 8) and of Jeremiah
(xxxvi), to whom Baruch acted as professional 'scribe'. We must
not think of these prophets as authors composing literature.
They were men of action who flung their contribution into
the melting-pot of contemporary politics, though themselves far
from being mere politicians. Their concern was not a book, but
a practical utterance, 'the word of Yahweh'. For them and for
their disciples it was a secondary matter to whom amongst men
a particular oracle might be ascribed, if it was recognized as
coming from Yahweh. One result of this attitude was the great
freedom with which additions were made by later generations to
.the original record. Probably every prophetic writing includes
later expansions, and adaptations to new circumstances; the
original prophet is the nucleus of the prophecies rather than their
author.

The changed circumstances of the Exile not only provided
the occasion and opportunity for much of this expansion of the
writings, but led to the production of the more 'literary' prophecy,
such as we see in Deutero-Isaiah (xl–lv) and Ezekiel. The
chaos of the first year of Darius (520) led to new political hopes

on the part of the small community in Jerusalem, recorded for us in Haggai and in Zechariah (i–viii). Malachi gives us a glimpse of the disillusionment which followed. But the great period of prophecy which began with Amos about 760 B.C. ended with Deutero-Isaiah about 540 B.C. The literary records of this period contain some of the noblest and most influential examples of Hebrew literature, the more impressive because produced for other than literary ends. Even when we have allowed for the obscurities of an unfamiliar idiom, of an often corrupt text, and of historical references to which we no longer have the key, they hold a unique place in the literature of the world and remain a permanent source of fresh inspiration. The prophetic consciousness of Israel brings us nearer than does anything else to those supreme moments of time in which man has believed that he makes genuine contact with eternity—though the Hebrew prophet characteristically puts it the other way round, as the self-revelation of God to man.

The religion of the prophets was never the religion of Israel. Yet, from the first, they began to exercise a profound influence upon that religion, which shows itself in the subsequent literature. This is notably the case in the codification and presentation of earlier law, such as we find in Deuteronomy (reflecting the influence of Hosea and other prophets of the previous century) and in the 'Law of Holiness' (which has points of contact with Ezekiel). Prophetic ethics find notable expression in Lev. xix, which ranks with Job xxxi as affording a compendium of Old Testament morality at its best. The purification of the ritual from its less worthy elements, either by their elimination or by their sublimation into higher meaning, was largely due to the prophetic teaching, and the priestly assimilation of this teaching robbed the prophets of some of their glory as pioneers, as soon as the whole 'Law' was ascribed to Moses. We may trace the prophetic influence also along the three other lines of development which have chiefly contributed to the

Hebrew literature, viz. those of the Psalms, of 'Wisdom', and of apocalyptic.

The Book of Psalms is to be regarded historically as the collection of 'praise-songs' (*t*ᵉ*hillim*, the Hebrew name for it) rendered by Levitical choirs to simple melodic music in the worship of the second Temple. The close relation to the cult, explicit in the titles, is frequently apparent in the Psalms themselves; thus the burnt-offerings figure in lxvi. 13–15, the libation in cxvi. 13, the aspersion with hyssop in li. 7, the processions in xlii. 4 (*R.V.* mar.), the blowing of the horn in lxxxi. 3. In xx, for example, the actual sacrifice may have come between verses 5 and 6; in cxxxvi the liturgical refrain of the congregation has been retained throughout. By no means all the psalms were of this public character; xlii and xliii (originally one, as the refrain shows) form a private 'lament'; xlix is a 'Wisdom' poem, and so on. But the majority of the psalms were either used in the cult or bear upon it. Behind the present five 'books' there is ample evidence of earlier collections from which these were drawn.

The attempts made to date the individual psalms are generally as futile to-day as they were when the psalm-titles were added. There is every probability that some of the Psalms go back to the times of the pre-exilic temple (e.g. xxiv), though even this hardly admits of individual demonstration. The early existence of psalms in Babylonia and Egypt confirms this probability; in fact, civ appears to be modelled on the 'Hymn of Ikhnaton' (*c.* 1370 B.C.). Modern study of the Psalms (with which the names of Gunkel and Mowinckel are specially connected) has worked on the classification of them by 'types'. The best way to appreciate the Psalms as literature is to take our stand with those who chanted them in the courts of the second temple, and to follow the thoughts of the Psalms as a compendium of post-exilic religion, to which the teaching of the great prophets has clearly contributed (cf. l with Isaiah, lv with Jeremiah). This is a sufficient background, and it may be made vivid by reading the enthusiastic description of worship in Ecclus. l. As we stand with the psalmists on the temple mount, we are taught to look backward on history (cv, cvi) and forward to the eschatology of the kingly rule of God (xciii, xcvii). We look up to the sun (xix) and the stars (viii) as the creation of God, and see His handiwork both in the storm (xxix) and the quieter operations of nature (lxv), as well as in all living creatures (civ). We are made conscious of a cause to be maintained against the ungodly (lxix) as well as of the strife within the heart that calls for forgiveness and spiritual renewal (li). As we study the psalms sympathetically in this fashion, we may discover the secret of their universal appeal and of their far-reaching use for public liturgy and private devotion. It is the triple secret of simplicity, catholicity, and intensity, and these qualities have been achieved partly by the gradual adaptation of the originals by successive generations to the needs of public worship and private prayer and meditation.

The Wisdom literature forms a second realm in which the influence of prophetic teaching can be seen, especially in the cardinal doctrine of moral retribution, already systematized in the Book of Deuteronomy. Here, again, as with the Law and the Psalms, we have to think of the incorporation of many earlier elements in the final literary results. The Hebrew idea of 'Wisdom' was rather that of practical sagacity (Gen. xli. 33, cf. 1 Kings iii. 16 ff.) than of intellectual knowledge, and this practical quality continues throughout down to the characteristic appeal to 'experience' made by the Wisdom teachers. These we may regard as a voluntary and informal 'Board of Education' dealing with the instruction of the young and morally immature. They already existed as a class in the middle period of Israel's development (Isa. xxix. 14, Jer. ix. 23, xviii. 18), and we may suppose that a considerable part of their material consisted of maxims and adages of the past, the traditional shrewdness of the generations, expressed in proverb (Jer. xxxi. 29, Ezek. xviii. 2), fable (Judges ix. 8–15, cf. 2 Kings xiv. 9), parable (2 Sam. xii. 1–6), and allegory (Ezek. xxiv. 6). But this native stock of traditional 'Wisdom' was reinforced and extended by resort to the copious international material which is illustrated by the Wisdom literature of Babylonia and Egypt. In some instances the literary relation is demonstrable (e.g. Prov. xxii. 17—xxiv. 22 and *The Teaching of Amen-em-ope*). The widespread *Story of Ahikar*, containing much Wisdom material, was found in Aramaic amongst the documents of the Jewish colony at Elephantine.

The Wisdom books of the Old Testament are Proverbs, Job, and Ecclesiastes, and with these must be grouped the two Apocryphal books, Ecclesiasticus and the Wisdom of Solomon. There are also scattered Wisdom passages elsewhere (e.g. Ps. xxxvii, Baruch iii. 9 ff.), and this class of literature is continued in the post-Biblical book known as *The Sayings of the Fathers*, which belongs to the Mishnah. The canonical Proverbs avowedly consists of a number of collections with special titles; it seems to have taken its present form in the early Greek period. Ecclesiasticus, 'The Wisdom of Ben Sira', written about 180 B.C., continues the general outlook of Proverbs, though the unifying hand of a single author is here apparent. The canonical Ecclesiastes, with its pessimistic outlook on life and its denials of either moral retribution or a life beyond death, represents 'Left Wing' Wisdom, as the 'Wisdom of Solomon' may be said to represent the 'Right Wing'; the latter has been stimulated by many Greek ideas, such as those of the un-Hebraic doctrine of the immortality of the soul, or of an immanent and pervasive Logos. The Book of Job claims a place of its own, as giving the orthodox theory of moral retribution, together with a pungent criticism of this from the standpoint of an innocent sufferer. It contributes the suggestion, explicit in the Prologue (hidden from Job himself), and implicit in the speeches of Yahweh, that there *is* a divine purpose in innocent suffering, however unexplained to the sufferer. By the courage of its criticism, the brilliance of its descriptions of nature, and the depth of its insight into one of the greatest human problems, the Book of Job deservedly takes a foremost place, not only in Hebrew literature, but in the literature of the whole world.

The third development of the prophetic teaching is that in the apocalyptic books. Whilst this is in form the most direct continuation of prophecy, so that apocalyptic has been described as the product of unfulfilled prophecy, there are important differences of character. Whereas the prophets announced to their contemporaries a direct 'word of Yahweh', the apocalyptists ascribe to some great figure of the past, such as Abraham or Enoch, the far-off vision of that imminent end of human history which the age of the writer is to expect. Whereas the prophets, by their demand for repentance, invite man's co-operation with God, the apocalyptists unfold a deterministic scheme of history in which the issue is decided by supranatural means. Whereas the prophets look for the Kingdom of God to be established on this earth, as a restoration of this present life to what it should be, and is so far from being, the apocalyptists largely (after 100 B.C.) place the future in a realm beyond this world and this life, a world to which resurrection is the door of entrance, whilst they are utterly pessimistic as to the present order. The Book of Daniel, the chief representative of this class of literature in the Old Testament, is one of the earliest of a long series of such works which flourished in the following two centuries. It was preceded, however, by such writings as Joel (*c.* 400 B.C.), the apocalypse in Isa. xxiv-vii (*c.* 300 B.C.), and the later chapters of Zechariah, which represent prophecy in transition to apocalyptic. The literary form of apocalyptic, especially its fondness for excessive symbolism, is unattractive to us. But we must not ignore the undoubtedly great service of this literature in maintaining faith through troubled generations. Neither must we miss that conception of the unity of history under the hand of God, seen in the fulfilment of His purpose, which brings to clear expression the doctrine of the prophets and underlies the Christian philosophy of history. In this respect, apocalyptic is a legitimate and logical issue of the conception of history which dominates the Old Testament.

### 3. *The Hebrew Canon*

As was stated at the outset of our review of the literature, its origins and historical nature form a separate topic from that of the recognition of its authority as revelation, to which we now turn. The actual or assumed *religious* character of all the contents of the Hebrew Bible as it lies before us must not obscure the fact that there was other Hebrew literature of what we should call a secular character. This is evidenced, for example, by David's laments over Saul and Jonathan and over Abner, and especially by the 'Song of Songs', which has probably been incorporated only because its allegorical interpretation converted it into a history of Israel from the Exodus to the Messianic restoration, in terms of Yahweh's love for His people. We cannot claim to possess more than a selection from the Hebrew literature as it once existed, a selection obviously made in a religious interest. What has been the process of this selection?

From the very beginning, the strong religious faith of this people and its application to the whole of life would tend to give a religious character even to narrative told for its own sake, such as 'The Court History of David'. Further, the origins of 'law', regarded as divine 'instruction' (torah) given through the sacred oracle (Exod. xviii. 15 ff.), of which the authority was extended to other legal decisions, would prepare the way for the supreme place given to 'Torah' by the later Judaism. The oracles of the prophets claimed a divine origin from the very beginning, and this claim was continued in apocalyptic. Liturgical poetry used in worship would easily acquire a sacred character by association.

Even 'Wisdom' could claim to be truly, if less directly, inspired (cf. Prov. viii. 12 ff.) and could be ultimately identified with the sacrosanct Torah (Ecclus. xxiv. 8 ff., 23). Thus there were many preparations in the religious life of Israel for the further and distinct claim that the literature which recorded this life was itself authoritative, as being divinely inspired, and as being the permanent revelation of divine truth.

A starting-point for the discussion of the Canon has often been found in the division of the Hebrew Bible into the three parts, known as the Law (Pentateuch), the Prophets (Joshua, Judges, 1 and 2 Samuel, 1 and 2 Kings, Isaiah, Jeremiah, Ezekiel, and 'the Twelve'), and the Writings (Psalms, Proverbs, Job, Song of Songs, Ruth, Lamentations, Ecclesiastes, Esther, Daniel, Ezra, Nehemiah, 1 and 2 Chronicles). There is some evidential value in this division and order, such as the priority of the Prophets to the Writings, and the late grouping of Daniel (not with the Prophets, as in the English Bible) and of Chronicles. But the growth of the Canon (as such) was much more complicated and indeed obscure than this triple grouping might suggest, and no valid evidence exists for the formal recognition of any one of these divisions. The ascription of the whole Torah to Moses (including the oral tradition of its interpretation, cf. the opening words of *The Sayings of the Fathers*) is a late product of Jewish theology. Its significance is measured by the claim that the Prophets and the Writings had nothing to add to the Torah, and that, in fact, if Israel had not sinned, nothing but the Torah (and Joshua) would have been necessary.[1] In our review of the growth of the literature, it has been assumed (on sound literary and historical evidence) that the Prophets were the real pioneers in the higher religion of Israel, though Moses, himself a 'prophet', laid the foundation for their work by his proclamation of Yahweh as the God who had brought Israel out of Egypt.

[1] Strack-Billerbeck, *Kommentar zum Neuen Testament*, i. 246; iv. 446.

The first point in the history at which we can assert the recognition of a sacred book as authoritative falls in the seventh century B.C. This book was the basis of the reformation of religion carried through by Josiah in 621 B.C. (2 Kings xxii. 8 ff.) and is now identified by the great majority of Old Testament scholars with the central part of our present Book of Deuteronomy. In almost every detail, the reforming measures correspond with the requirements of that book. The influence of its style and teaching on the subsequent period is generally admitted, both in regard to the editing of the history (Judges, 1 and 2 Kings) and the religious outlook (Malachi). Deuteronomy, then, can be regarded as substantially the first contribution to the ultimate *corpus* of authoritative literature.

A second notable point in the history is the public reading of a law-book by Ezra the scribe (Neh. viii. 1 ff.) which we may date in 397 B.C.[1] This, too, was accepted as authoritative and apparently as something new, previously unknown to the hearers. The consequent celebration of an eight-day Feast of Tabernacles, at a fixed point in the calendar, points to Lev. xxiii. 39, and therefore to the Law of Holiness, rather than to the already known Deuteronomy (cf. xvi. 13 ff.), and this inference is confirmed by the use of 'booths' (Lev. xxiii. 42) of which the Deuteronomic form of the commandment says nothing. Further, the payment of 'the tithe of tithes' by the Levites to the priests (Neh. x. 38) follows the Priestly Law of Num. xviii. 26 and not the Deuteronomic Law (xiv. 22 ff., xxvi. 12 ff.). These points suggest that Ezra's law-book, brought by him from Babylon, was some part of the Priestly Law (including the Law of Holiness), and not Deuteronomy. On the other hand, it is not likely to have been the completed Pentateuch, for much of this would hardly have been the programme for a restoration of religion, and it is far too long for Lev. xxiii to have been reached

[1] I have summarized the evidence for this date (in place of the traditional 458) in *The History of Israel; its Facts and Factors*, p. 151.

on the second day' (Neh. viii. 13). It is no valid argument to say that the Samaritan schism proves the completion of the Penta-teuch before this date, on the undeniable ground that the Samaritan Pentateuch is virtually identical with the ·Hebrew. The fact is that we do not know when the final separation of Jews and Samaritans took place, and Josephus (though with some confusion) brings it down to the time of Alexander.

We may assume, however, that by the middle of the fourth century the Pentateuch existed practically in its present form, and was accepted as, in some sense, an authoritative book. ' The two law-books previously accepted (D and some parts of P, including H) formed the nuclei; to these had been added (to D during the exile?) the previously existent literature which told of Israel's origins and ancestors and those redemptive acts of Yahweh to which the prophets and psalmists ever appealed. This literature (JE) was already old by the fourth century, and for an unsophisticated people antiquity easily becomes authority. The combined material was set in a framework of history (as conceived by the priestly school of writers) from the creation onwards, to form our Pentateuch.

But other literature of the past, with intrinsic claims on attention and reverence, was also long since in existence. There were the historical books and the records of the earlier prophets. They could not claim the same place as the stories of Israel's ancestors and the primary revelation now believed to have been given through Moses, but they were treasured and read. In course of time they came to form a *corpus* of their own, though we have no information as to the exact process. All we can say is that by about 200 B.C. they existed largely as we now have them, since soon after this date Ben Sira (Ecclus. xliv ff.) has them under his eye in their present order. He makes no refer-ence to Daniel—which confirms the conclusion otherwise established that this book was composed some fifteen years (165 B.C.) after Ben Sira wrote. The Book of Daniel itself shows (ix. 2) that by this time the Prophets have acquired quasi-canonical authority; they are being studied as authoritative revelation.

As for the third group, the 'Writings', these are mentioned rather vaguely and variously in the Prologue to Ecclesiasticus, written by the grandson of Ben Sira, but not so as to enable us to define the group. In fact, it remained a disputable quantity till the beginning of the second century A.D. At the (Jewish) Council of Jamnia (A.D. 90) the right of Canticles, Ecclesiastes, and Esther to a place in this group could still be challenged, and in the following century Rabbi Akiba still thought it necessary to defend Canticles. But in the list given by Josephus (*contra Apionem*, i. 37–41), writing at the beginning of the second century A.D., the contents of the group were those of our Hebrew Bible.

It will be seen from this review of what is known how unsystematic and gradual was the establishment of the Hebrew Canon, even though it was virtually completed by the time of the New Testament writers. These do not cite the three disputed books and only one of them (Jude, verses 14–16) passes explicitly beyond the Hebrew Canon, to cite 'Enoch'.[1] In the actual process of recognition we must give a large place to the usage of the synagogues, which existed a long time before the New Testament times, and mediated the transition from the religion of the Temple to the religion of the Torah. In regard to the books now included in the Apocrypha, which were never recognized in the Palestinian Canon, though they formed part of the Greek Bible (as will be seen in Chapter II) we may conjecture that various reasons prevented their inclusion in the group of accepted writings, such as the fact that some of them were not written in Hebrew, and some of them belonged to that apocalyptic school from which the Palestinian Jews turned away the more firmly because they were popular with the Christians.

[1] Cf., however, 1 Cor. ii. 9, Eph. v. 14.

We may also notice the fact that Josephus regards the divine inspiration of literature as having ceased in the time of Artaxerxes, so that no book acknowledged to be of later date could be regarded as inspired (e.g. Ben Sira's, which *was* written in Hebrew, but made no claim to have been written earlier, as did Ecclesiastes).

## 4. *The Printed Editions*

The long process by which these canonical Scriptures have been transmitted to us is not less difficult to trace than the formation of the Canon. Our earliest manuscripts (other than fragments) belong to the end of the ninth and the beginning of the tenth century, and our knowledge of the transmission in the previous centuries is scanty and largely a matter of inference from the final results. It is therefore advisable to begin with some account of the chief printed editions (from the fifteenth century onwards) and then to go back to the period of written record.

The first part of the Hebrew Bible to be printed was the Psalms in 1477, with Kimchi's commentary (probably at Bologna). The first complete Hebrew Bible was printed at Soncino in 1488. It has vowels and accents, but no commentary. The third edition of this (published at Brescia in octavo, 1494) was used by Luther for his translation of the Old Testament. In 1516–17 Daniel Bomberg issued the first of the Rabbinic Bibles, in four folio volumes (and also a quarto edition). The standard text, which subsequent editions have more or less followed, was that of Jacob ben Chayyim (Venice, 1524–5), in four folio volumes. This incorporated a very large amount of work on the Jewish Masora (§5*b*), and gave the *Targums* and certain Jewish commentaries. A well-known Rabbinic Bible was that of Joh. Buxtorf (Basle, 1618–19), and another was that of Moses of Frankfort (1724–7). A page of Buxtorf's Bible gives the Hebrew text on the left, with the *Targum* on the right. Between is the Masora Parva; below and above the

Masora Magna. Surrounding these are famous Jewish commentaries by ibn Ezra, Rashi, Kimchi, ben Gerson.

The first of the four great Polyglot Bibles was the Complu-
tensian, published by Cardinal Ximenes in 1514–17 at Alcala.[1]
This gives the Vulgate in the centre of the page flanked by the
Hebrew on the left and the Septuagint (with Latin translation)
on the right; thus, as the editors remark concerning this first
Christian edition of the Hebrew text, 'in the middle between
these (the two columns) we have set the Latin translation of
Blessed Jerome, as though between the Synagogue and the
Eastern Church, putting them like the two thieves one on each
side, but Jesus, that is the Roman or Latin Church, between
them'. In the lower part of the page the *Targum* is given on the
right (for the Pentateuch only) and a Latin translation of it on the
left. The quality of the work is severely criticized by Ginsburg.

The second of the Polyglots is that of the Plantin press at
Antwerp (8 vols., 1569–73). The third is that of Paris (9
vols., 1629–45), which gives not only the Vulgate, the Septuagint, and the *Targums*, but also the Syriac, Arabic, and Samaritan (the last, of course, for the Pentateuch only). The best-known
Polyglot in this country is that edited by Brian Walton, and
published in six volumes in 1657, followed by Edmund Castell's
lexicon in two volumes in 1669. (This Polyglot added Ethiopic
and Persian to the previously named versions.) An opening of
the Pentateuch volume is impressive,[2] for it gives at a glance in
the upper half of the two pages and in columns from left to
right: (1) the Hebrew text, with interlinear Latin translation;
(2) the Vulgate; (3) the Septuagint, with Latin translation;
(4) the *Targum* of Onkelos, with Latin translation; (5) the
Samaritan text in the old Semitic script; and (6) a Latin translation of the Samaritan (Aramaic) version. On the lower half

[1] A page facsimile is given by A. S. Geden (*Introduction to the Hebrew Bible*,
opp. p. 78).
[2] A two-page facsimile is given by Geden, op. cit., between pp. 82 and 83.

of the pages there are given the Syriac and the Arabic versions, and their Latin translations. Brian Walton had been ejected from his livings in 1641 and imprisoned in the following year; when released he withdrew to Oxford and devoted himself to Oriental languages, so that this great piece of work represents the quietly growing harvest of troublous years (he became Bishop of Chester at the Restoration).

Of many subsequent editions of the Hebrew Bible, all that need be mentioned here are those of Joseph Athias (1659–61), and of E. Van der Hooght (1705), A. Hahn (1833), as well-known manual forms. In more recent times, Baer's critical editions of separate books (1869–95) covered all except Exodus–Deuteronomy, and were the best form of text for the student at the time. Paul Haupt's *The Sacred Books of the Old Testament* consisted of editions of the separate books in an emended text (1893–1904) and did not include Exodus, Deuteronomy, The Twelve, or Megilloth. C. D. Ginsburg, on the basis of a very great amount of work on the Masora, published the first edition of his Hebrew Bible in 1894. In 1905–6 the first edition of R. Kittel's *Biblia Hebraica* appeared, with critical footnotes largely based on versional readings (second edition, 1909). The third edition (1937) has special significance, as its text (edited by Professor P. Kahle) reproduces that of the earliest complete and dated Hebrew manuscript which we possess. More will be said of this later. Already by the time of the Mishnah (*c.* A.D. 200) the Torah was divided into sections know as *parašiyyoth*. The division into chapters was derived from the Vulgate, and was first adopted in a printed Hebrew text in the Complutensian Polygot (1514–17).[1] The present numeration of verses was first introduced by Arias Montanus in 1571, and not by Athias in the following century, as is sometimes stated.[2] But verse-division, as distinct from numeration, naturally belonged to the original accentual system.

[1] Ginsburg, *Introduction*, p. 26.   [2] Ibid., p. 107–8.

### 5. *The Transmission of the Written Text*

We turn to consider the long period prior to the Printed Editions, in which the transmission of the text depended on writing. Here we shall notice: (*a*) the writing materials, (*b*) the work of the Masoretes, (*c*) the extant manuscripts.

(*a*) We know that papyrus was used in Palestine from an early date, since we hear of a supply of 500 rolls of it being brought to the king of Gebal (Byblus) about 1100 B.C. Papyrus was made of strips of the pith of the papyrus plant, which grew in the Nile. These were laid transversely and glued together, one sheet being fastened to another to make a continuous roll of the required length. The dry climate of Egypt has allowed the preservation of many papyri, but we could not expect this to occur in Palestine. The most detailed reference to writing materials in the Old Testament is that found in Jer. xxxvi. 23, which describes the destruction of the roll of prophecies which Jeremiah had dictated to Baruch. The writing was in some dark fluid (cf. Ezek. ix. 2), presumably with the usual reed pen (Ps. xlv. 1) and probably on one of these papyrus rolls, in successive 'columns' (*R.V.* mar.) As every three or four of these were read out to the king, he seized the roll, slashed them off with the scribe's pen-knife, and flung them into the brazier which warmed the winter-house. Documents of this kind were stored in earthenware vessels, as were the deeds of Jeremiah's property at Anathoth (Jer. xxxii. 14). Broken earthenware was itself used for records, as we know from the potsherds ('ostraka') discovered at Samaria (stewards' accounts of the ninth century) and at Lachish (letters). For engraving on hard material, such as the Moabite Stone or the rock of the Siloam tunnel, an iron stylus would be used (Job xix. 24, Jer. xvii. 1). The clay tablets on which so much of the literature of Mesopotamia has been preserved are paralleled by those of Tell el-Amarna, which throw so much light on the state of Palestine about 1380 B.C., and by those of Ras Shamra, rendering similar service for Canaanite mythology before Israel's settlement in Canaan.

Another material used from an early date was the skin of animals, of which Egyptian specimens exist which are ascribed to 2000 B.C. That this material was used by the Jews is suggested by the fact that the synagogue rolls of the Torah are still of this nature. Some authorities think that Jeremiah's roll was written on leather; at any rate this holds for the copies of the Torah from which the Greek translation known as the Septuagint was made in the third century B.C. The 'parchment' or 'vellum' of later periods is simply a finer leather made from the skins of sheep, goats, and calves, and used for its durability. But the climate of Palestine and the fortunes of history have not allowed any of the more ancient texts of the Old Testament to come down to us. In fact, as already stated, our earliest manuscripts (apart from papyrus fragments) fall as late as the tenth century A.D.

(*b*) We have hardly any direct information about the transmission of the text in the Old Testament period. It is, however, natural to suppose that the professional 'writers' (the early 'scribes', i.e. *sōph'rīm*) were its agents. They certainly existed as a class in the time of Jeremiah, and his companion, Baruch, was one of them (Jer. xxxvi. 26). Jeremiah refers to 'the false pen of the scribes' writing falsely (viii. 8), and the reference is often taken to be to the writing of Deuteronomy. A couple of centuries afterwards Ezra, who was also a priest (Ezra vii. 11), is characterized as a skilled scribe in the Torah of Moses (verse 6); this shows the natural transition from the copyist to the expert in the subject-matter. Many centuries later we have Talmudic traditions of the work of these *sōph'rīm*,[1] which show their part in the necessary revision of the text. We have always to remember that the text was purely consonantal

---

[1] e.g. Nedarim, 37 *b*, 38 *a*, quoted in H. L. Strack's article in Hastings's *Dictionary of the Bible*, iv. 731, and by Ginsburg (with the Hebrew text), in his 'Introduction', pp. 307 ff.

(except for the *matres lectionis* mentioned on p. 30) until the work of the Masoretes (*c.* sixth century) and that the words were written continuously or divided only by a dot (as in the Moabite and Siloam inscriptions), so that errors in copying were even easier than at a later date. The writing was in the ancient Semitic script, at least until the date of the Samaritan schism, towards the end of the fourth century B.C. After this it was changed into the 'square' or Aramaic script which the founts of type in our printed editions resemble.

After the destruction of the Jewish state in A.D. 70, it obviously became necessary to ensure the preservation of this consonantal text and the correct tradition of its pronunciation. This became ultimately the work of the *Masoretes*. The name 'Masoretes' is derived from the Hebrew word *Masora*, in the sense of 'tradition'. These 'traditionalists' may be regarded as continuing the work of the *sōph'rīm*, from the first to the tenth century A.D., though our knowledge of their work comes from the latter and post-Talmudic part of this period. It is to them that we owe from about the sixth century the creation of the systematic vocalization and accentuation of the consonantal text, and the consequent creation of a *textus receptus*. (The Masora, denoting their corpus of textual criticism, must not be confused with Midrash, denoting the exposition of the text.)

The development of the representation of the Hebrew vowels seems to have taken place independently in both Palestine and Babylon, the two chief spheres of Jewish learning and tradition. An earlier and more primitive 'Palestinian' system preceded that of Tiberias which is found in the ordinary Hebrew Bibles. By dots or strokes, placed beneath the consonants which they follow (except for *o*), the quality (not the quantity) of the seven fundamental sounds (*i*, *e*, *ä*, *a*, *å*, *ō*, *u*), is distinguished, though *a* is short and *ä* and *ō* are long. Combinations of these signs with a half-vowel (*S'wā*) give the *hātēfs*, or 'hurried' sounds, denoting minuter distinctions of pronunciation, chiefly due to

the influence of thé gutturals. In the less differentiated Babylonian vocalization, signs different from the Western are used, and
these are written *above* the consonants they follow. The oldest
form of this vocalization, consisting only of dots, suggests
connexion with the Eastern Syriac vowel system.[1] In a later
form, somewhat different signs were developed (distinguishing
*ā* and *a*), and with the same sign for the unaccented vowels and
again for their occurrence before *Daghesh forte* (the doubled
consonant).[2] But the Western method of vocalization prevailed
over the Eastern, so that the A.D. 916 manuscript of the prophets,
though Babylonian, has the vocalization of Tiberias.

In our Hebrew Bibles there are to be found other symbols—
one for each word—which are called 'accents'. This is not the
best of names for them, since the indication of the tone-syllable
(over or under which they usually stand) is not their only or
even their original purpose. They were designed to indicate the
'cantillation', or musical recitation of the scriptures in the
worship of the synagogue, though their original values in this
connexion are no longer known. They also indicate the logical
structure of the sentence, like our own marks of punctuation.
To the modern student they render valuable service in this
connexion, as well as in indicating the tone-syllable, the place
of which usually affects the vocalization. These 'accents' fall
into two groups according as they distinguish the logical parts of
the sentence ('disjunctives') or link words together ('conjunc-
tives'). The system is highly complicated, and varies in Psalms,
Proverbs, and Job from that of the other books. For the
accentuation, as well as for the vocalization, there was an
independent development in Babylonia.

In addition to the vocalization and accentuation, the work of

---

[1] P. Kahle, 'Der Alttestamentliche Bibeltext', in *Theologische Rundschau*, 1933,
p. 233. The *names* of the vowels in Hebrew, Syriac, and Arabic are closely linked;
cf. Bauer-Leander, *Historische Grammatik der Hebräischen Sprache*, i, p. viii.

[2] Ibid., p. 235.

the Sopherim and Masoretes extended in a number of other directions. The most familiar illustrations of this are to be found in the differences between the *K͏ᶜthībh*, or written text, and the *Q͏ᶜrī*, that which was to be read. There are said to be between thirteen and fourteen hundred examples of such differences, though many of them do not affect the sense, as when in Ruth ii. 11, for example, the 'Easterners' inserted (the sign of the direct object) *'eth* before the word *kōl* ('all'). Sometimes the *Q͏ᶜrī* substituted a euphemism for (public) reading, e.g. in 2 Kings xviii. 27, where the text has 'their dung' and 'their urine', the reader is directed to use Hebrew words meaning 'their filth' and 'the water of their feet'. The substitution of *Ādonai* (Lord) for *Yahweh*, to avoid any risk of blaspheming the Name, is indicated by the vowels of the former word being added to the consonants of the latter, so giving rise to the false form, *Jehovah*. But some of the readings amounted to what we should call textual criticism, though no alteration was made in the consonantal text. All that was done was to add the vowels of the new word to the consonants of the old. As examples we may take Jer. xxxi. 38 and li. 3. The former enjoins the addition of a word which the Hebrew text obviously requires, viz. 'come' after 'days', as is given in both the Authorized and Revised Versions. The word was accidentally omitted by some copyist through the resemblance of two Hebrew words. Jer. li. 3 omits (in reading) a word which has been accidentally repeated by a copyist, viz. *yidrōk*, 'he will bend'. The omission is confirmed by manuscripts and ancient versions and is accepted by the Revised Version, whilst the Authorized Version shows what difficulties the retention of the mistake must make.

Another, though very small, group of emendations seem to have actually been made in the consonantal text. These are the *Tiḳḳūnē Sōphᶜrīm*, 'the corrections of the scribes'.[1] Thus in

[1] The full list of 18 instances is given and discussed by Ginsburg, op. cit., pp. 352–62.

Gen. xviii. 22, where we now read that 'Abraham stood yet before the Lord', we are told that the original text was 'The Lord stood yet before Abraham', which the context requires. Obviously, it was felt unseemly that God should be represented in the attitude of a servant. Alterations of this kind must have been much more extensive than the few instances recorded; we have an example of them in the change of the term 'Baal' into 'Bosheth' ('shameful thing') in some proper names (cf. Meribba'al of 1 Chron. viii. 34 which in 2 Sam. iv. 4 has been altered to *Mephibosheth*). In fifteen instances words or clauses have dots above them (the *puncta extraordinaria*), to indicate erasures, as in Greek and Latin manuscripts.[1] Thus in Ezek. xlvi. 22 the closing Hebrew word, meaning 'made with corners', is dotted; that it should be removed is confirmed by its absence from the Greek, Syriac, and Vulgate versions. Ginsburg regards these dots as the oldest element of the *Masora*.[2] There are also other textual readings (*sᵉbhīrīm, 'iṭṭūrē hassōphᵉrīm*) which may be regarded as special classes of the *Qᵉrī*.

But all such instances of textual correction on the part of the Masoretes are the exception that proves the rule: viz. that in general they were meticulously careful guardians of the consonantal text *as it reached them*. This is seen from the general character of the Masora, i.e. the textual notes which are found written above, below, and in the margins of Biblical manuscripts, as well as in separate treatises. These are largely concerned with the indications of *hapax legomena*, or of the number of instances in which a particular form occurs. Everything countable seems to be counted, and if such work seems to us often futile, it was not so to men deeply concerned with the literal accuracy and the 'plenary inspiration' of the Scriptures; moreover, its practical usefulness for copyists is apparent. The Talmud records an incident in connexion with the statement that the Hebrew word *gāḥōn* in Lev. xi. 42 contained the middle letter of the Torah,

[1] Op. cit., p. 321.    [2] Op. cit., p. 834.

viz. *wāw* (= *ō*). A Rabbi asked to which side the *waw* belonged, whereupon another offered to count. Accordingly a Torah was brought and they remained until they had settled the point by counting.[1] Minute classifications of the results of such work were made, such as an alphabetical list of words occurring twice in the Old Testament, once without and once with the conjunction *waw*; since the first example was the word *ochlah*, a treatise which began with this list was *Ochlah we-Ochlah*. A further point of interest was that of the occurrence or absence of the *matres lectionis*, the four consonantal letters (*wāw, yōdh, hē*, and *āleph*) which were used from a very early date to give some indication of long vowels and diphthongs; these have often become established in the consonantal text. When they occur, the instance is known as a *scriptio plena*, when they are absent, as a *scriptio defectiva*. It is clear that such a difference has become purely orthographic, but orthography was a major interest with the Masoretes. The Rabbinic commentaries known as the Midrashim often extract important truths from such minutiae. A stock example is in regard to Hag. i. 8, where the Hebrew verb rendered 'I will be glorified' is written without the final letter *Hē*. Since this letter of the alphabet has the numerical value 5, the Talmud[2] says that it is absent because five things were absent from the second temple which had been found in the first, viz. the ark, the holy fire, the Shechinah, the Holy Spirit, and the Urim and Thummim.

(c) From the hands of the Masoretes there have come to us the manuscripts from which the Hebrew printed texts are ultimately derived; hence the name 'Masoretic text' given to the *textus receptus*. Until recent times all our Hebrew Bibles followed the text of Jacob ben Chayyim (printed in 1524–5). Professor Paul Kahle, however, the leading scholar in Masoretic studies on critical lines at the present time, has pointed out that

---

[1] *Kiddushin*, 30 *a*, quoted in *Hasting's Dict. Bible*, iv. 729.
[2] *Yoma*, 21 *b*, quoted op. cit., p. 730.

the text of ben Chayyim's edition is that of manuscripts not earlier than the fourteenth century.[1] But there are now available manuscripts from the end of the tenth and the beginning of the eleventh century which more correctly represent the Masoretic text. He has therefore chosen the earliest complete manuscript, that known as B 19A (in Leningrad), dated A.D. 1008, for the text printed in the third edition of Kittel's *Biblia Hebraica*, published in 1937. With the text he has also been able to give the smaller Masora in the margin, so that this is the best edition for the modern student, and successfully answers Ginsburg's claim that any deviation from the ben Chayyim text must justify itself. The manuscript employed professes to be an exact copy of the codex of ben Asher, now in the possession of the Sephardic Synagogue in Aleppo, which was not itself available. Other early manuscripts of about the same period are a codex of the 'Prophets', in Cairo, dated 895, and another codex of the 'Prophets', in Leningrad, dated A.D. 916. There is also a manuscript of the Pentateuch in the British Museum (Or. 4445) for which Ginsburg claims a ninth-century date.[2] It may seem strange to the reader that there are no earlier manuscripts than these, but the peculiar history of the transmission of the text must be borne in mind. Quite apart from the long line of persecutions and massacres suffered by the Jews through the centuries from the Maccabean age onwards, in which countless manuscripts have perished, there is the Jewish treatment of all such texts as became worn-out by use or were deemed unsuitable. Reverence prevented their immediate destruction, but they were withdrawn from use, and placed in the 'Geniza'[3] (*ganaz* = 'conceal'), a sort of lumber-room belonging to the synagogue. At the necessary clearance of this from time to time

[1] See his article, 'Der Alttestamentliche Bibeltext' in *Theologische Rundschau*, 1933, pp. 227–38, also his preface to Kittel, ed. 3; from these the information given above is chiefly derived.

[2] Op. cit., pp. 469–74, where a facsimile page is given showing the Masora.

[3] Cf. W. Bacher's article, 'Genizah', in *Ency. Rel. & Ethics*, vi. 187–9.

the contents were ceremonially buried. It is only when the Geniza has accidentally escaped this treatment (as at Cairo) that its contents have yielded those earlier manuscripts which the scholar so eagerly desires. So far, no complete copies of the Hebrew Scriptures earlier than those already named have been found, but in recent years a large number of fragments of both Palestinian and Babylonian manuscripts have come to light. The Cairo fragments, extending from the sixth to the ninth century A.D., yield the genuine Babylonian tradition.[1] But, as Professor Kahle points out, all this earlier evidence is too late to show any important amount of variation in the *consonantal* text; for this we should need Geniza fragments four or five centuries older, and such have not yet been discovered. That important variations must have existed and that there was a pre-Masoretic period when the transmission of the text was without any such care for literal accuracy as the Masoretes displayed, will be evident from the following section.

### 6. *The Criticism of the Masoretic Text*

We have already noticed some of the signs of textual criticism as exercised by the Masoretes themselves. But it is impossible for the modern scholar, with a far greater critical apparatus, to stop where they did. The ancient Versions, as the following chapters will show, carry us back to forms of the Hebrew text earlier by many centuries than its finally established Masoretic form. The science of comparative philology and the scientific study of Hebrew grammar have made it impossible for us to be content with some of the traditional meanings and interpretations. The Masoretic text itself calls for criticism on the three chief grounds of (*a*) the impossibility of rendering some of the Hebrew words and phrases, in their present context, (*b*) the existence of parallels within the Masoretic text, showing variant

[1] Cf. Kahle's list of manuscripts, with many facsimiles, in *Zeitschrift f. d. alttest. Wissenschaft*, 1928, pp. 113 ff, and his preface to Kittel, ed. 3 (1937).

readings, though professedly going back to the same original, (c) the evidence of the Versions to the existence of a preferable Hebrew text at an earlier date. These three groups of evidence may be briefly illustrated. As examples of intrinsic proof that corruption has occurred, we may take the following. In 1 Sam. i. 5, the Hebrew reads 'to Hannah he used to give one portion, *'appaim'*, where the word *'appaim* (meaning elsewhere 'nostrils', 'face', and 'anger') admits of no translation in this context. The Revised Version 'double' is not justified by vocabulary or grammar (see mar.) and the Authorized Version 'worthy' is an ancient guess going back by way of the Genevan Version to the *Targum*. But the Septuagint evidently read *'ephes* = 'but', so that we read properly 'but he loved Hannah' (though he gave her only one portion). In 1 Sam. vi. 18 the Revised Version (mar.) acknowledges that the Hebrew has 'meadow' (*'ābēl*) and not 'stone' (*'eben*) which the context requires. In 1 Sam. xiii. 1 the Authorized Version is an impossible rendering of the Hebrew and the Revised Version acknowledges that a word has dropped out, though we cannot be sure whether the missing word was 'thirty', as supplied by the Revised Version from Greek evidence. The Hebrew says, 'The son of a year was Saul at his reigning', which means 'one year old'; the *Targum* gets out of the difficulty in a characteristic way by rendering 'as the son of a year in whom there are no sins was Saul when he reigned'. Another evident omission is that of Gen. iv. 8, 'And Cain said to Abel his brother'. The Hebrew verb suggests a statement of what was said just as much as does the English, and the lacuna is supplied in the Septuagint, Syriac, Old Latin, and Samaritan by the words 'Let us go into the field'. The *Targums* have 'Come, let us go out of doors' (cf. the Vulgate). Sometimes it is clear to the critical reader of the Hebrew text that the consonants, once written continuously, have been wrongly divided into separate words. A generally accepted example of this is to be found in Amos vi. 12, where we have *'im yaḥărōš babbᵉḳārīm*, meaning 'does one plough with oxen?' to which the answer in those days was clearly 'yes'. But by redividing the consonants (and adding the proper vowels) we get *'im yĕḥārēš bᵉbāḵār yām*, meaning 'is the sea ploughed with oxen?' the required parallel to the corresponding line 'do horses run on crags?' and equally requiring the (proper) answer 'no'. In some instances the consonants have been transposed by the copyist; thus in Ps. xlix. 11 (12) the Hebrew reads 'their inwards (*ḳirbām*) are their houses for ever', where clearly something is wrong. But if two consonants of *ḳirbām* are transposed, we should get those for *ḳibrām* or *ḳᵉbārīm* meaning 'their grave' or 'graves', either of which gives an intelligible sense. As a matter of fact, this is the reading of the Septuagint, the Syriac, and the *Targum*.

Another line of proof that the Masoretic text suffered many changes in the pre-Masoretic days is afforded by the comparison of passages of which a double tradition exists within the Old Testament itself. Thus, in the three verses of a prophecy now assigned to both Isaiah (ii. 2–4) and to Micah (iv. 1–3) the former passage has one word not found in the latter, and the latter has four words not found in the former, whilst three words show variation and the order of the words varies in three instances. There are three differences of orthography and Micah has an additional couplet of eight words, which seem to be required by the structure of the poem. (There are further differences in the Septuagint.) A more extensive comparison could be made of Ps. xviii and the same psalm as found in 2 Sam. xxii. Thus in Ps. xviii. 42 (43), we find *'ărīḳēm*, 'I empty them out', whilst in 2 Sam. xxii. 43 *two* variants of this are found, viz. *'ădiḳḳēm*, 'I pulverize them' *'erḳāʿēm*, 'I stamp them down'. For the prose tradition we may compare 2 Kings xviii ff. and Isa. xxxvi ff. Thus in Isa. xxxvii. 18 we have 'the lands and their land' and in 2 Kings xix. 17 'the nations and their land', the latter obviously being required.

The importance of the ancient versions for the criticism of

the Masoretic text and the restoration of a much earlier one will be indicated and illustrated in the following chapters, dealing with the Greek, Syriac, and Latin Bibles. The proper use of them requires an elaborate scholarship, since they vary in character and quality from book to book and even within the same book. Allowances must, of course, be made for the use of paraphrase and the influence of the particular object for which the translation was made. It is not necessary here to attempt even the briefest characterization of them, but something should be said of the *Targums*, to which no separate chapter has been allotted (though some reference to them will be found in Chapter III). The *Targums* were never a 'Bible' in the sense in which we can speak of the Greek, Syriac, and Latin Bibles. They are the late written form of the much earlier oral translation of Hebrew books into the Aramaic vernacular, when the Hebrew was no longer understood by the ordinary worshipper in the synagogue. As is natural from the circumstances of their origin, they are often paraphrastic and homiletically expansive, and they frequently modify the text to suit current religious ideas and to avoid anthropomorphisms. Thus in Gen. iv 14. the words 'from thy face I shall be hid', appear in the *Targum* of Onkelos as 'from before thee it is impossible to be hid'. For Exod. xxiv. 10, '(they saw) the God of Israel', the *Targum* has 'the glory of the God of Israel' (cf. Septuagint, 'the place where stood the God of Israel'). The *Targum* of Jonathan to Judges v. 31 reads 'Like Sisera so shall perish all haters of thy people, Yahweh, and his lovers shall be destined to shine with the shining of his glory, for one three hundred and forty three (times), as the going forth of the sun in his might'. Here the esoteric number is derived from the exegesis of Isa. xxx. 26 (interpreted to mean seven times seven weeks). There are *Targums* to all the books except Daniel and Ezra-Nehemiah (of which our original text is partly Aramaic). The two *Targums* already quoted (of the Pentateuch and of the Prophets) seem to have been put into their present form in Babylon in the fifth century A.D. There are not a few places in which the evidence of the Versions does not enable us to restore a plausible text, though the Masoretic text gives every sign of being corrupt, e.g. Deut. xxxii. 5. In such places there is often legitimate scope for conjectural emendation and some conjectures may win general acceptance, as in regard to Amos vi. 12, named above. But conjectural emendation on the scale practised by some modern commentators has little more value than an academic exercise. In recent years there has been a growing reaction against such subjectivity. Even when, as must often be the case, the Masoretic text does not satisfy us, it is there to be explained in the best way possible as the only accepted text we have, or are ever likely to have.

## 7. *The Task of Translation*

When scholarship has done all it can to establish the original Hebrew text, the task of the translator begins and he has many difficulties to face. In the second century B.C. the grandson of ben Sira discovered this when seeking to translate his grandfather's Hebrew into Greek. He asks the indulgence of his readers for any failure to render the wording of the original, for, as he remarks, 'those things said originally in Hebrew have not equal force when they are transferred into another tongue'. This is a difficulty which faces every translator, even when he is rendering one *modern* language into another. But the difficulty is greatly increased when an ancient language is being rendered into a modern tongue. Then, the two worlds of life and thought, of speech and art, lie immeasurably farther apart. The undertones and overtones of each written word—all the associations it calls up to one who uses it familiarly—are necessarily wanting in the foreign word which replaces it, often with a very different set of associations. As we have seen (§ 1), the Hebrew vocabulary and syntax are simple enough, and it is usually not difficult.

except in the case of rare words or a corrupt passage, to know what is meant. In regard to verse, the Hebrew parallelism constantly helps to reveal the sense. But it is frequently impossible to find an English word with content adequate to the corresponding Hebrew term. The terms usually translated 'covenant' (*b'rīth*), 'loving-kindness' (*ḥesed*), 'holiness' (*ḳodheš*) 'judgement' (*mišpāṭ*), 'law' (*tōrāh*), 'soul' (*nephes̆*), and a host of others are quite inadequately rendered by these English words—and it is impossible to find any that are fully adequate.

All translation is therefore a compromise. On the one hand, we may attempt to follow the original as closely as possible, and trust to the reader to put as much of the meaning as he gathers from the context into the English equivalents. On the other, we may follow the general sense rather than particular words and try to give the equivalent meaning by something of a paraphrase. Fortunately, reverence for the Scriptures has usually led to the adoption of the more literal method. Fortunately—because the Authorized Version, for example, has thus acquired a simplicity and clarity, indeed a dignity, which it could hardly have possessed if written more paraphrastically in seventeenth-century English. We have only to compare the preface written by its translators with the text of their translation to feel the difference and to realize how much the virtues of the English Version are really Hebrew in origin.

We must not, however, forget that every established translation enters into a history of its own, which is quasi-independent of the original. That which is lost is, for better for worse, replaced by something else. New doctrinal meanings and new literary associations gather round the often quoted—or misquoted—words, whilst the translation itself has enshrined particular beliefs which may be far removed from the original text. Few Hebrew scholars would defend the translation and Messianic implication of 'Until Shiloh come' (Gen. xlix. 10), or the rendering 'a virgin shall conceive' (Isa. vii. 14), or the association of faith in immortality with 'I know that my redeemer liveth,' &c. (Job. xix. 25); yet how great a wealth of new association have such translations gathered to themselves!

Perhaps there will always be room for two kinds of translation of sacred Scriptures—the classical version to be used in public worship, even though antiquity has obscured some of its meaning, and the modern vernacular (and more exact) version which can help the private reader to come as near as is possible to the original. But the majesty, dignity, and impressiveness of that original can be felt in their fullness only by the diligent student of the Hebrew text.

H. WHEELER ROBINSON

### Note on the Samaritan Pentateuch.

This is not a version, but a particular form of the Hebrew, written in a script directly descended from the Old Semitic (see p. 26). It has many minor variations—the number noted in Kittel's text is said to be about 6,000—from the Masoretic Text, and the Septuagint agrees with 2,000 of these (so Eissfeldt, *Einleitung in das Alte Testament*, p. 709). But few of these are of importance, and its chief value is to show the substantial agreement of the text of the Pentateuch about 300 B.C. with our present text. This Hebrew Pentateuch in the Samaritan script (*Textus Hebraeo-Samaritanus*) is to be distinguished from the Aramaic Targum (*Versio Samaritana*); both are given in Walton's Polyglot.

# II

# THE GREEK BIBLE

## SYNOPSIS

I. The Old Testament

  A. The Septuagint
   i. Its origin.
   ii. The legend of the seventy translators of the Law.
   iii. The completion of the Greek translation of the Old Testament.
   iv. The books of the Greek Apocrypha.

  B. Before and After Origen
   i. The later versions : reasons for their production. (a) Aquila. (b) Theodotion. (c) Symmachus.
   ii. Origen and his Successors. The Hexapla and the Tetrapla. Consequent corruption of the Septuagint. Pamphilus and Eusebius. Lucian of Antioch, Hesychius.
   iii. The printed text. Complutensian; Sixtine; Holmes and Parsons; Tischendorf; Swete's Cambridge Manual Septuagint; Larger Cambridge Septuagint; Rahlfs.

  C. Value of the Septuagint.
   i. For textual criticism.
   ii. For literary criticism.
   iii. For theological outlook. (a) Hebrew ideas modified in Greek translation. (b) Greek words stamped with special religious meaning.

II. The New Testament

  A. Growth of the New Testament Literature and Canon
   i. Appeal to authority in Early Church: (a) Old Testament. (b) Words and example of the Lord Jesus.
   ii. Rise of the new literature.
   iii. Formation of the Canon. Church's defence against (a) Marcion, (b) Montanism. Anti-Marcionite prologues. Muratorian Canon. Views of Serapion, Clement, Tertullian, Origen, Eusebius, Athanasius. Apostolicity the criterion. Evidence of great codices of 4th and 5th centuries.

  B. Chief Manuscripts and the Printed Text
   i. History of the Greek Bible in manuscript. (a) Ancient book production. (b) The more important manuscripts : papyri, uncials, cursives.
   ii. The printed text. Complutensian Polyglot, Erasmus, Aldus, Stephanus, Elzevir, Walton's Polyglot, Mill, Wells, Mace, Bengel, Wettstein, Griesbach, Lachmann, Tischendorf, Tregelles, Westcott and Hort, Eberhard and Erwin Nestle, Souter.

C. Estimate of the Value of the Textual Tradition

    (a) Doctrinal influence on text slight and never universal.
    (b) Harmonization in Synoptic Gospels. How far due to Tatian?
    (c) Peculiarities of Codex Bezae and its allies.
    (d) Influence of Marcion on text.

D. Bearing of Recent Discoveries on Textual Theory

    Importance of local centres. Five main groups of textual authorities now recognized: (a) Byzantine (late), (b) Alexandrian, (c) Caesarean, (d) Western, (e) Syrian.

## I. THE OLD TESTAMENT

### A. *The Septuagint*

#### i. *Its Origin.*

THE translation of the Old Testament into Greek was due to two great movements in the ancient world which were secular rather than religious—Alexander the Great's conquests and the Jewish Diaspora. When Alexander's brief and splendid career came to a sudden end his empire fell into fragments, but he bequeathed to posterity the world of Hellenism. From the shores of the Mediterranean to the banks of the Indus his victorious pathway is marked by new cities which he founded. His armies were recruited from every part of the Greek world, and they not only learned to speak a common dialect but also introduced this Greek *Koiné* (as it was called) into the conquered territories. Whatever the fate of this linguistic legacy may have been in the Middle East, it became the established language of the kingdoms over which his generals and their successors ruled. Macedonia, Pergamum, Syria, Egypt, all became spheres of Hellenistic culture. The Antigoni, the Attalids, the Seleucids, and the Ptolemies were not only heirs of Alexander's conquests, they were diffusers of Hellenism. At the same time another movement was spreading with remarkable rapidity. The Jewish Dispersion began with the transportation of entire populations to Nineveh and Babylon when the Northern and Southern kingdoms were overrun by Assyrian and Babylonian empire builders near the end of the eighth and the beginning of the sixth centuries before Christ. After the destruction of Jerusalem by Nebuchadrezzar there was a considerable migration to Egypt, and when Alexander founded his famous city at the mouth of the Nile Jews were incorporated among the first citizens. Nor was forcible transportation or enrolment in a foreign legion the only method of dispersion. The lure of trade carried members of this commercial race to all the cities which fringed the Mediterranean Sea, and Jewish synagogues were to be found from the pillars of Hercules to the shores of the Euxine. For a while the Hebrew scriptures were read in Hebrew and expounded in Aramaic. But after two or three generations the Aramaic mother tongue was forgotten, and the Jews who lived in lands to the west of Palestine spoke only the Greek *Koiné*, the lingua franca of the Mediterranean world.

It was in Alexandria that the need of a Greek translation of the Jewish scriptures was first felt. All through the Ptolemaic period the Jews must have increased in this city both in numbers and in importance. Three and a half centuries after its foundation we learn from Philo that about two-fifths of the population of Alexandria were Jews, and that the race numbered more than a million in Egypt. Moreover, Alexandria soon became under the Ptolemies the foremost centre of culture in the Hellenistic world. Here Judaism was to come into closest touch with Greek modes of thought, and in the writings of Philo to see Moses reappear in the garb of Plato. But the first step in what Deissmann has called 'the hellenizing of Semitic monotheism' was taken when the Hebrew Pentateuch was translated into Greek.

## ii. *The Legend of the Seventy.*

The name Septuagint (or LXX), by which the Greek Old Testament is generally known, goes back to a legend which is found in the Letter of Aristeas, a pseudonymous document of uncertain date, probably written some time in the second century

B.C. According to this story, King Ptolemy Philadelphus, prompted by Demetrius of Phalerum who wished to include in the royal library at Alexandria manuscripts of the Jewish Law with copies of all books known to the world, sent a letter to Eleazar, the high priest at Jerusalem. In this the king described his recent release of more than a hundred thousand Jewish captives, and, declaring his wish 'to show favour to these men and to all the Jews throughout the world and to those who come after them', he revealed his purpose that their Law should be translated from the Hebrew tongue into Greek 'so that these writings also might belong to us in our library along with the other royal books'. The high priest was asked to select six elders from each tribe, 'men of the best manner of life who are versed in the Law and able to translate, that from the majority it may be found wherein they agree, because the investigation relates to matters of high importance'. This letter was sent by the hands of Andreas and Aristeas who carried dedicatory offerings for the Temple. Eleazar in his reply commended Ptolemy's 'reverent piety for our God', and, though confessing that the project was 'contrary to nature', he overcame his religious prejudice 'as a sign of friendship and affection', and in gratitude for the king's 'unforgettable benefits for our countrymen'. He sent the seventy-two elders with a copy of the Law. The translators were fêted on their arrival and delighted the king by the wisdom with which they replied to all his questions. They were then conducted to a restful spot on the island of Pharos, where a house had been specially prepared for their use. Here they set to work, 'making the results agree by comparisons with one another's findings'. By a happy coincidence the translation was completed in seventy-two days. Demetrius, who had been sent by Ptolemy to arrange for the transcription of their work, then 'assembled the Jewish people in the place where the translation had been made and read it over to all in the presence of the translators'. The seventy-two elders and Demetrius were applauded, the accuracy of the translation was attested, and a curse was invoked upon any who should henceforth tamper with the text. The translation was read to the king, who marvelled greatly at the mind of the lawgiver, and gave orders that the book should be guarded with due reverence. He then bade farewell to his guests and sent them back loaded with presents for themselves and for Eleazar.

In course of time the legend gathered accretions. Thus the translators were said to have worked in separate cells and by miraculous aid to have produced identical versions. Later on they were credited with the translation of the scriptures as a whole, and were endowed with an inspiration not inferior to that which produced the Hebrew originals. But even the story as told by Aristeas is legendary. Professor H. B. Swete and Dr. H. St. John Thackeray extracted from it the following elements of truth. (1) The Pentateuch was translated first as a whole and has a unity of style which distinguishes it from the later translation of the Prophets and the Writings. (2) The language is that of the vernacular papyri found in Egypt and contains Egyptian words. The translators were almost certainly Alexandrian, and not Palestinian, Jews. (3) Quotations from Genesis and Exodus in Greek are found before 200 B.C., and the constructions can be paralleled from the earlier Ptolemaic papyri. The date must therefore be placed in the third century B.C. (4) The homogeneity of the translation makes it improbable that so large a number as seventy were at work on the Pentateuch. A rabbinic version of the story gives five. The tradition of the larger number may have been influenced by the story of the seventy elders who were with Moses on the holy mount. (5) The Hebrew rolls were possibly imported from Palestine. (6) Ptolemy Philadelphus as a patron of literature may have encouraged the enterprise. But the popular style, unlike the literary Hellenistic to be looked for in a work prepared for the royal library, fits in rather with the closing statement that the entire translation was read to the people and approved by them before it was presented to the king. The Greek rendering of the Law was the authorized version of the synagogue rather than the version prepared by royal command.

### iii. *The Completion of the Greek Old Testament.*

The Law was translated into Greek in the third century B.C. The other two sections of the Hebrew scriptures, the 'Prophets' and the 'Writings', were translated gradually during the next two centuries. It has been suggested, with great probability, that a beginning was made with select passages prescribed in the lectionary for the festivals and special sabbaths. This was soon followed by the translation of the books as a whole, beginning with Jeremiah, Ezekiel, and the Twelve Prophets, after which Isaiah and the 'Former Prophets' (i.e. the historical books) were also dealt with by companies of translators. In the year 132 B.C. the grandson of Jesus ben Sira came to Egypt and found a Greek translation of 'the law itself, and the prophecies and the rest of the books'. As a Palestinian Jew this writer of the Prologue to Ecclesiasticus would know the second part of the Hebrew scriptures, which was evidently already current in a Greek rendering. It seems that some of the Hagiographa also were then already known in Egypt in translations. From various indications we may infer that by the beginning of the Christian era the Greek version of the Hebrew Old Testament was complete.

### iv. *The Greek Apocrypha.*

It is in its scope that the Greek Old Testament differs most remarkably from the Hebrew Bible. In addition to those books which ultimately found acceptance in the Jewish canon, our oldest manuscripts of the Septuagint contain a number of other writings which must have enjoyed a wide circulation in the Diaspora, and were accepted by the Christian Church as part of its sacred inheritance. Most of these were written originally in Hebrew or Aramaic, but have survived only in their Greek translation. Others, composed in Greek, are the product of Alexandrian Judaism. At the beginning of the Christian era the third division of the Hebrew Bible was in a fluid state, and there were a number of books that were regarded with favour as deserving a place among the Hagiographa. It is also clear from the evidence of the Septuagint that the text of the prophetical books had not yet reached a final form when they were translated. There was no canon of Scripture in the Greek Diaspora, and even the earliest surviving Greek bibles of the Christian Church are not in complete agreement regarding the books to be included.

Generally speaking, however, the Septuagint may be said to exceed the Hebrew Bible by including the following writings.

*1 Esdras* (which appears under the same title in the English Apocrypha but is called 3 Esdras in the Vulgate) is another recension of the account of the Captivity and Return. The book opens with an extract from 2 Chronicles (xxxv. 1—xxxvi. 21). Passages from Ezra in a disturbed order, with an interpolation (iii. 1—v. 6) from an unknown source, coming between Ezra iv. 24 and Ezra ii. 1, are followed by Neh. vii. 73*b*—viii. 13*a*, which gives an abrupt ending to the book. This is strangely followed by *2 Esdras*, a translation of Ezra-Nehemiah (chs. i–x Ezra, chs. xi–xxiii Nehemiah), and this must not be confused with the book bearing that name in the English Apocrypha, which is not found in the Greek Bible. In later Latin texts 4 Esdras of the Vulgate (English 2 Esdras) appears as three books, chs. i–ii being called 2 Esdras, chs. iii–xiv —otherwise known as the Ezra Apocalypse—bearing the name 4 Esdras, and chs. xv–xvi becoming 5 Esdras.)

*The Wisdom of Solomon* and *Ecclesiasticus* (or *The Wisdom of Jesus, son of Sirach*) are examples of that Wisdom literature of Judaism which is represented in the Old Testament by Job, Proverbs, and Ecclesiastes. But whereas Pseudo-Solomon was an Alexandrian Jew who wrote in Greek, ben Sira was a Palestinian Jew who composed his book in Hebrew. In recent years considerable portions of a Hebrew text of Ecclesiasticus have come to light. But some reason, perhaps its relation to an acute sectarian controversy, kept it out of the Jewish canon.

*Baruch*, a composite book, was published in its present form soon after the fall of Jerusalem in A.D. 70. The original Hebrew, in which parts of it were certainly written, has entirely disappeared, possibly because the liturgical use which it once served had come to an end.

*The Epistle of Jeremy*, which forms the last chapter of Baruch in both the Latin and the English Bible, is thus found in some Greek manuscripts, but in most others it is given a place of its own, following Baruch and Lamentations, which are treated as supplements to Jeremiah. This was written in Hebrew at the end of the fourth century B.C. and translated into Greek about a century and a half later.

*Tobit*, a romance of the exile, written towards the close of the third century B.C., combines folk-lore and Persian angelology and demonology with an ardent devotion to the Law.

*Judith*, a novel in which the Jewish struggle for religious and political liberty under Jonathan the Maccabee is thinly disguised in the form of a narrative set in the times of 'Nebuchadrezzar king of Assyria', can be dated with comparative confidence in the mid-Maccabean period. The same epoch-making revolt gave rise to the four very different books which are generally given a place at the end of the Septuagint, although none of these was included in the great Vatican codex B, and only the first two were admitted to Jerome's Vulgate and to the English Apocrypha. Four books bearing the title Maccabees are found in a number of manuscripts of the Septuagint, but they are not connected with one another except in so far as they deal with the persecution of the Jews during the period of the Ptolemaic and Seleucid suzerains.

*1 Maccabees* is a Greek translation of a Hebrew history of the Jewish nation from the attempt of Antiochus Epiphanes to hellenize the land until the death of John Hyrcanus in 104 B.C. It is our best authority for the events of that stirring epoch in Jewish history.

*2 Maccabees*, on the other hand, is a Greek composition, probably in part an epitome of the history of Jason of Cyrene. It is generally dated in the earlier half of the first century B.C., and regarded as of doubtful historical value, but useful as a specimen of Pharisaic propaganda in this period.

*3 Maccabees* has nothing to do with the Maccabean family, but describes the profane attempt of Ptolemy IV (Philopator) to enter the Holy of Holies after his victory at Raphia (217 B.C.). Foiled by the priests at Jerusalem, he returned to Alexandria determined to work vengeance on these recalcitrant Jews throughout Egypt. He was thwarted by divine providence and afterwards became the friend of the race which he had tried to destroy. The story is composite, for the writer seems to have combined a tradition of Philopator's attempted desecration of the Temple with a story preserved by Josephus of a persecution of Egyptian Jews by Ptolemy IX (Physcon) nearly a century later. The book is marked by a florid style, and there is good reason for thinking that it was written in Alexandria in the first century B.C. as an apology for orthodox Judaism.

*4 Maccabees*, an Alexandrian treatise on the control of the passsions by the reason, is famous for the lurid description of the tortures inflicted upon Eleazar and upon the heroic mother and her seven martyr sons in the persecution under Antiochus Epiphanes. The story is based upon the episode related in 2 Maccabees, chs. vi–vii. In praising the steadfast faith of these martyrs the writer is the first to enunciate the doctrine of vicarious atonement by the suffering of the righteous. This probably won for the book its place in the Christian Old Testament, but as Jerome, following Eusebius, attributed the book (quite wrongly) to Josephus, we can understand its exclusion from the Latin, and therefore from the English, Apocrypha.

Apart from these additional books the Septuagint varies from the Hebrew Bible in the additional matter contained in certain books which are common to both. The two most remarkable examples are the additions to Esther and to Daniel. The English Apocrypha supplies *The Rest of the Chapters of the Book of Esther*, following Jerome, who gathered at the end of canonical Esther all the Greek additions which in the Septuagint are distributed in large sections through the entire book, and increase by 107 verses the 163 verses of the Hebrew text. The places which these six additions occupy in the Greek version are indicated in the margin of the English Revised Version. There is no linguistic evidence to show that they have been translated from a Hebrew original, and as Esther was one of the last books to gain a place in the Hebrew canon it is not surprising that this popular story gathered round it further embellishments, partly to give it a deeper religious character and partly to amplify the narrative.

The book of *Daniel* receives three supplements. (*a*) In the English Apocrypha *The History of Susanna* is prefaced with the words: 'Set apart from the beginning of Daniel because it is not in the Hebrew, as neither the Narration of Bel and the Dragon.' This refers to the place which Susanna has in the great uncials, where it comes immediately after the title 'Daniel'. In this they follow Theodotion's version. In the one manuscript which preserves the text of the Septuagint for Daniel Susanna follows the rest of Daniel as chapter xiii, which is also its position in the Vulgate. (*b*) *Bel and the Dragon* in most manuscripts comes immediately after Daniel xii, without a title. But in the one manuscript of the Septuagint the heading reads: 'From the prophecy of Habakkuk the son of Jesus of the tribe of Levi'. (*c*) The English Apocrypha gives to a long insertion of 67 verses the title *The Song of the Three Holy Children*, with the heading: 'Which followeth in the third chapter of Daniel after this place,—*fell down bound into the midst of the burning fiery furnace* —verse 23. That which followeth is not in the Hebrew, to wit, *And they walked*—unto these words, *Then Nebuchadnezzar*— verse 24.'

Before we leave the Greek Old Testament Apocrypha three other books claim a brief mention because of the place given to them in some printed editions of the Septuagint.

*The Prayer of Manasses*, which was admitted into the English Apocrypha, has a strange literary history.[1] There is no evidence that this Prayer ever formed part of the text of Chronicles, and its preservation is entirely due to its liturgical use in the Christian Church.

*The Psalms of Solomon*, eighteen in number, were written in Hebrew in the middle of the first century B.C. This original is lost, and the book would have perished had not its Greek translation found favour in Christian circles. The title comes immediately after that of the Second Epistle of Clement at the end of the Books of the Old and New Testaments in the catalogue at the beginning of the Codex Alexandrinus. The text may have been lost with the missing leaves of this codex which contained the last part of 2 Clement. But it is preserved in some late cursives, either after the Psalter or among the Wisdom books.

*The Book of Enoch* never formed part of the Septuagint, but its quotation in the Epistle of Jude shows that it was regarded as almost canonical in the early Church. For a century past the book has been known from an Ethiopic translation. The lost Hebrew original was mainly a Palestinian work of the second century B.C. In 1886 a small vellum book was found in a Christian grave in Upper Egypt containing fragments of the

---

[1] *The Apocrypha and Pseudepigrapha of the O.T. in English*, i. pp. 612 ff. (H. E. Ryle and R. H. Charles).

E

Gospel and Apocalypse of Peter and the first thirty-two chapters of Enoch in Greek. In 1930 some leaves of a papyrus codex came to light containing chapters xcvii. 6–civ, cvi–cvii.

## B. *Before and After Origen*

### i. *The Later Greek Versions.*

The Septuagint came into existence to answer the needs of the Jewish Dispersion in Egypt and the lands adjoining the Mediterranean. From the middle of the first century it became the Bible of the Christian Church, whose missionaries went from synagogue to synagogue 'proving from the scriptures that the Messiah was Jesus'. Their armoury of proof-texts, or *Testimonia*, was drawn from the Greek Old Testament, and in the long controversy between the Church and the Synagogue effective use was often made of passages which could not have been employed if the Hebrew original had formed the basis of discussion. It was but natural that the *Auctor ad Hebraeos* should find a prophecy of the Incarnation in the words of Ps. xl.

> Sacrifice and offering thou wouldest not,
> But a body didst thou prepare for me;
> In whole burnt offerings and sacrifices for sin thou hadst no pleasure:
> 'Then said I, Lo, I am come
> (In the roll of the book it is written of me)
> To do thy will, O God'.                          (Heb. x. 5–7.)

In vain would the Jewish disputant reply to such arguments (even if he had the knowledge) that the Hebrew text makes no reference to the preparation of a body but reads, 'Ears hast thou pierced for me'. The Septuagint was the only bible read in the synagogues of the Diaspora. Justin Martyr's *Dialogue with Trypho* (A.D. 155–61) furnishes several examples of the charges and counter-charges which Jew and Gentile brought against one another in their textual polemics. Trypho rightly protests (lxvii) against the argument from prophecy which Christians based on the word παρθένος in the Septuagint of Isa. vii. 14 (cf. Matt. i. 23).[1] On the other hand, Justin (ibid. lxxii f.) accuses Jews of cutting out from the Septuagint passages which Christians had applied for apologetic purposes.[2] One is from an account of the passover celebrated by Ezra, but the words quoted are found in no manuscript of the Greek Bible, though Lactantius cites them in Latin as from Ezra. A second is Jer. xi. 19, which is found in all known manuscripts of the Septuagint. The third is a passage attributed to Jeremiah, for which there is no manuscript authority, though Irenaeus quotes it sometimes as from Isaiah and elsewhere as from Jeremiah. The fourth is the well-known Christian gloss on Ps. xcvi. 10 (LXX), 'Tell it out among the nations: the Lord reigned from the tree'. This may have crept into some manuscripts of the Septuagint by a glossator's marginal reference to Ep. Barnabas viii. 5.

It is not surprising that the appropriation of the Septuagint by the Church as the Christian Bible caused a Jewish reaction. With the destruction of the Temple in A.D. 70 Judaism was thrown back upon the Sacred Book as its unique possession, and more attention began to be paid to the preservation of the true text of the books now recognized as forming the Palestinian Canon. The school of Rabbi Akiba is associated with this textual revision, and it was a pupil of his who produced the first of a series of new Greek translations of the Old Testament.

(a) *Aquila*, a proselyte born at Pontus, devoted himself to an extremely literal Greek rendering of the newly established Hebrew text. It was his aim to reproduce every word in the original and to translate the derivatives of a Hebrew root by

[1] The Hebrew word עַלְמָה means young woman, whereas בְּתוּלָה is the Hebrew for 'virgin'. The three second-century revisers of the Septuagint, Aquila, Theodotion, and Symmachus, naturally translated the Hebrew word by νεᾶνις.

[2] For full details see A. Lukyn Williams's footnotes in his translation of *The Dialogue with Trypho* (S.P.C.K., 1930), pp. 150–5.

derivatives from the corresponding Greek root. The best-known example of the barbarous Greek produced by this well-meant fidelity is his consistent rendering of the Hebrew word ETH (which is sometimes a particle indicating the direct object and at other times a preposition meaning 'with') by the Greek preposition σύν. The very defects of this curious experiment make it invaluable for the recovery of the underlying Hebrew text. But, apart from citations (as in Field's *Hexapla*) only a few fragments of Kings and of Psalms xc–ciii survive. These were discovered in 1897. Aquila's work is dated in the second quarter of the second century.

(*b*) *Theodotion*, a native of Ephesus and a convert to Judaism, produced his version during the reign of Commodus (A.D. 180–92). It was a revision of the Septuagint by comparison with the contemporary Hebrew text rather than an independent translation. There are two remarkable features of this version; its longer recension of the book of Job (containing one-sixth more than the Septuagint), and its text of Daniel, which is entirely different from that of the Septuagint. This raises an important problem, for Theodotion's version has been substituted for that of the Septuagint in every known manuscript of Daniel with two exceptions. On the other hand, the text represented in Theodotion is quoted in several New Testament passages, in Barnabas and Clement of Rome, and by Justin and Irenaeus—all before his time. It is therefore not improbable that there were two early Greek translations of Daniel, one of which was revised by Theodotion. This became the recognized text, whilst the other, presumed to be the Septuagint version, survived in its completeness in a solitary manuscript.[1] Theodotion

---

[1] This is the cursive 87, dating from the ninth or eleventh century, in the Chigi library at Rome, which contains the Major Prophets. In 1930 the sensational discovery of the Chester Beatty Papyri brought to light, amongst many other biblical treasures, portions of a codex containing Ezekiel, Daniel, and Esther, and written in the first half of the third century. The considerable fragments of Daniel represent the original Septuagint text, without the Hexapla additions. This text of Daniel

accepted the apocryphal additions to Daniel, but does not seem to have included other books outside the Hebrew canon.

(c) *Symmachus*, an Ebionite, probably wrote shortly after Theodotion. His method was the opposite to that of Aquila, for his aim seems to have been to free the translation from the trammels of Hebraic idiom. His Hebrew text, like those of Aquila and Theodotion, must have closely resembled that known to us.

ii. *Origen and his Successors.*

The supreme name in the history of the Greek Old Testament is that of the great scholar *Origen* (A.D. 186–253), pupil and successor of Clement in the catechetical school of Alexandria. About the year 240, while living at Caesarea, Origen produced the *Hexapla*. He had acquired a knowledge of Hebrew and tested the various Greek versions with the current Hebrew text. The result of his comparative study was an arrangement of the Old Testament in six columns to each page. In the first stood the Hebrew text in use among Origen's Jewish teachers in the early part of the third century. The second column gave a transliteration of the Hebrew words in Greek characters. The third, fourth, and sixth columns presented the versions of Aquila, Symmachus, and Theodotion, whilst the fifth column offered a new text of the Septuagint. This was not a new translation so much as a critical text. Its chief characteristics were these. (*a*) The order is determined by that of the Hebrew in the first column. (*b*) Where the Septuagint is missing the passage is supplied from Theodotion, or more rarely from Aquila or Symmachus. (*c*) A system of diacritic signs indicated additions. Thus, insertions in the Greek text, where there was nothing in the Septuagint corresponding to a passage in the Hebrew column, were introduced by an

also underlies the Syriac translation of the Septuagint of the Hexapla made by Paul of Tella at Alexandria (A.D. 616–17).

asterisk and closed with a metobelus. (*d*) In the poetical and prophetical books sometimes a reading was inserted in additional columns from other Greek versions of uncertain origin, called the *Quinta* and the *Sexta*.

Unfortunately Origen did not preserve in his fifth column the best attested form of the original Septuagint, but attempted to bring his text into closer harmony with the Hebrew. He appears also to have issued a *Tetrapla*, that is, a shorter edition in four columns of his great work. In this the first two columns based upon the Hebrew were omitted, as well as all reading from the Quinta and the Sexta. These prodigious labours won great respect for Origen's text, though the enormous size of the book in both its editions must have made its duplication extremely difficult. But until the capture of Caesarea by the Saracens, nearly four centuries after the death of Origen, this monument of learning was consulted in the famous library there by Christian scholars. Chief among his successors were *Pamphilus* and *Eusebius*, who worked at Caesarea half a century after his death. They published the Hexaplaric text of the Septuagint, and attempted to preserve his critical symbols. Unhappily many who followed in their wake simply reproduced this text without the signs, so that a hopelessly mixed text gained currency as the pure form of the Septuagint. Two editors of the Greek text of the Old Testament had a far-reaching influence upon its later manuscript history by reason of the authority which their editions enjoyed in certain great Christian centres.

*Lucian*, who like Pamphilus was a martyr in the persecution of 309–12, worked at Antioch where his revision of the Septuagint gained official favour, and whence in due course it was adopted in the Church of the imperial capital at Constantinople. Lucian's method was that of conflation, blending divergent readings, and so many ancient readings are preserved in his text which would otherwise have been lost.

*Hesychius*, another martyr in this persecution, represented the school of Alexandrian scholarship, and his revision probably represented the manuscripts current in Egypt before the time of Origen.

We have now reached the period when, with the State recognition of Christianity, the great uncial manuscripts of the Greek Bible were prepared, and the textual history of the Septuagint becomes merged in that of the Greek New Testament.

### iii. *The Printed Text.*

The earliest printed edition of the Septuagint was the Complutensian Polyglot (1522, see below, pp. 74 f). Next came the Sixtine (1587) which Cardinal Carafa prepared for Pope Sixtus V., depending largely upon the great Vatican manuscript, Codex B.

A critical edition, in which a diligent use was made of numerous manuscripts, versions, and patristic quotations, was produced at Oxford between 1788 and 1827 by R. Holmes and J. Parsons.

Tischendorf brought out four editions of his manual text of the Septuagint between 1850 and 1869. In his final edition he printed a revision of the Sixtine text, whilst his critical apparatus recorded variants from Codex A, from his own facsimile of Codex C, from his own discovery Codex ‫א‬, and from Cardinal Mai's edition of Codex B.

This held the field until H. B. Swete edited the manual Cambridge Septuagint in three volumes (1st ed., 1887–94, 4th ed., 1909). In this the text of B is printed, and where this is defective Codex A takes its place, or the uncial manuscript which stands nearest in age or importance. The apparatus gives the variants in the more important uncials. In 1906 the larger Cambridge Septuagint began to appear. While the text is practically the same as that of the manual edition there is a full critical apparatus prepared by the late A. E. Brooke, N. McLean, and the late H. St. John Thackeray. At present the work has advanced as far as the Octateuch, Kingdoms, Chronicles, 1 and 2 Esdras, Esther, Judith, and Tobit.

In 1935, about a week before the editor's death, the Württemberg Bible Society of Stuttgart produced in two handsome volumes, beautifully printed, a text of the Septuagint prepared by A. Rahlfs and based upon the three best codices, B, ℵ and A, with occasional reference in the apparatus to other authorities.

## C. *The Value of the Septuagint*

### i. *For Textual Criticism.*

As the great uncial manuscripts of the Septuagint are five hundred years nearer to the date when the latest book of the Old Testament was written than our oldest Hebrew manuscript their evidence should be of great value in restoring the original text. Many of the recently discovered papyrus texts of the Septuagint belong to the fourth, third, and even second centuries A.D., whilst part of a papyrus roll in the Rylands Library containing a number of verses from Deuteronomy was actually written in the second century B.C. But merely documentary priority does not prove the superiority of the Septuagint text to that of the Hebrew. Nevertheless, the Greek translation often preserves a text which has suffered corruption in the Hebrew and enables us to see how that corruption came about. Two examples may illustrate this.

In 1 Sam. xix. 22 the Hebrew text reads: 'Then went he also to Ramah, and came to the great well that is in Secu.' The Septuagint reads: 'to the well of the threshing floor that is in the Sephei.' This is almost meaningless, but it supplies the clue. The Greek translators, baffled by the Hebrew word *S<sup>e</sup>phī*, simply transliterated it. The word means a 'bare height', a natural site for the village threshing floor. A Hebrew scribe misread the word HGRN as HGDL, and SPY as SKU.

In 1 Sam. xiv. 41 the Hebrew text reads: 'Therefore Saul said unto Yahweh, the God of Israel, Give Thummim. And Jonathan and Saul were taken by lot, and the people escaped.' The Septuagint reads: 'And Saul said, O Yahweh, God of *Israel*, why hast thou not answered thy servant this day? If the iniquity be in me or in my son Jonathan, Yahweh, God of *Israel*, *give* Urim; but if thou sayest thus, The iniquity is in thy people Israel, *give* Thummim. And Saul and Jonathan were taken by lot, but the people escaped.' The scribe skipped from the first 'Israel' to the second, and from the first 'give' to the second.[1]

## ii. *For Literary Criticism.*

A more complicated set of problems is raised by the marked difference in contents and arrangement between the Hebrew and the Greek forms of several of the books. Thus Job in the Greek text current in Origen's time was nearly 400 lines shorter than the Hebrew, and the gaps were supplied from Theodotion; whilst the Greek text of Jeremiah varies from the Massoretic text in excess, in defect, and in extensive transposition.

Two books in the Apocrypha present specially interesting textual phenomena, which suggest theories regarding their literary history. Ecclesiasticus was known to be a translation from a Hebrew original but this was lost until fragments began to reappear in 1896. From a comparison of this recovered Hebrew text with the various forms of the Greek text it has

---

[1] S. R. Driver's *Hebrew Text of the Books of Samuel* supplies many examples for the student of the original text. The English reader will find numerous examples in the footnotes to Kennedy's 1 and 2 Samuel in the *Century Bible* and to S. R. Driver's *The Book of Job* (Oxford, 1906). The last-named book (p. xxvii) gives references to passages in other books where the margin of the Revised Version supplies the reading of the Septuagint or the Syriac. A study of Josephus's *Antiquities* and of Philo's works in the Loeb Classical Library, with the editors' footnotes, will bring to light many interesting points in the textual criticism of the Old Testament.

been inferred that an original Hebrew text was translated by ben Sira's grandson. Later on the Hebrew text was revised in the interest of a spiritual Pharisaism, and this revised text was translated into Greek. The two recensions are represented in two groups of Greek manuscripts, though many of these have been corrected in either direction at many points.

Tobit cannot be compared with its Semitic original, since no trace of that has ever been found. But the wide divergence between the two recensions preserved in the manuscripts ℵ and B shows that considerable freedom was possible in the transmission of the story. The most probable theory is that the ℵ recension represents the earlier form of the book as it was composed in orthodox circles in Egypt before 200 B.C., whilst the B recension shows how it was revised about A.D. 150 in Jewish circles of the Dispersion which were in agreement with the official Judaism of Palestine.

These two books were never in the Hebrew canon. But their history may suggest a similar freedom in the editorial handling of the prophetic books and the hagiographa before they had received canonical authority.

iii. *For Theological Outlook.*

The Septuagint was not a transcription but a translation of a Semitic book into the language of the Hellenistic world. This involved interpretation. In the result Hebrew ideas underwent a measure of transformation, and Greek words received a stamp which gave them a new theological significance.

(*a*) The most important change of all was in the rendering of the Divine name. It is well known that the sacred tetragrammaton YHWH was never pronounced in the synagogue, but the word *Adonai* was substituted. It would have been in keeping with Septuagint usage simply to transliterate ᾿Αδωναί (as the translator of Ezekiel did according to the text of A). But by the translation Κύριος the book was liberated from the tribal traditions of Israel and given a world-wide significance. Aquila and Symmachus in their Jewish reaction adopted the meaning-less form ΠΙΠΙ, which is simply made of the Greek letters in outward appearance most like the Hebrew letters for YHWH. Again, though the Hebrew title (Lord) of Hosts is sometimes transliterated Σαβαώθ, the Septuagint came nearer to the Greek mind with (Κύριος) τῶν δυνάμεων, and nearer still with (Κύριος) παντοκράτωρ. Another feature of the Septuagint is the modifica-tion of what might seem to be crude anthropomorphisms, such as 'hand' for 'power' of God, His 'robe' for His 'glory' (Isa. vi. 1). Platonic terms creep in at Gen. i. 2 (ἀόρατος καὶ ἀκατασκεύαστος), and a Stoic word (ἡγεμονικός) at Ps. li. 12 (LXX l. 14).

Such transformations (and many more might be adduced) justify the statement that without the Septuagint a Philo would have been impossible. Still more important is the effect upon the vocabulary and the theological ideas of the New Testament due to such a book as the Wisdom of Solomon.[1]

(b) On the other hand, many Greek words found in the theo-logical vocabulary of the New Testament owe their special meaning to the associations of the Septuagint. Thus the im-portant Hebrew word bᵉrīth, 'covenant', is translated by διαθήκη not by συνθήκη, the ordinary Greek word, as that might suggest a contract between equals. The word διαθήκη in everyday Greek meant 'will' or 'testament', and only the context can determine its use in any passage in the New Testament. Again, the words ἱλάσκομαι, ἱλασμός, ἱλαστήριον come from a root which in Classical Greek suggests the placation of an offended deity. The Septuagint is determinative for the New Testament, and shows that in every instance the meaning is that of expiation not of propitiation.[2]

---

[1] Cf. Wisd. vii. 26 with Heb. i. 3, and Col. i. 15.

[2] Cf. C. H. Dodd, *The Bible and the Greeks*, in which the religious vocabulary of Hellenistic Judaism is studied in its bearing on the interpretation of the New Testa-ment.

## II. THE NEW TESTAMENT

A. *The Growth of the New Testament Literature and Canon*

i. *Religious Authority in the Early Church.*

(*a*) *The Old Testament.* Primitive Christianity knew but one sacred book, the writings of the Old Covenant. The Gospel was proclaimed against a background of Scripture. St. Paul, in recalling to the Corinthians the outline of the saving truth which he had preached to them, writes: 'For I delivered unto you first of all that which I also had received, how that Christ died for our sins *according to the scriptures*; and that he was buried; and that he was raised on the third day *according to the scriptures*; and that he appeared to Cephas—' (1 Cor. xv. 3 ff.). The words attributed by St. Luke (xxiv. 44 f.) to the risen Lord faithfully reflect the belief and the faith of the earliest apostles: 'These are my words which I spake unto you, while I was yet with you, how that all things must needs be fulfilled, which are written in the law of Moses, and the prophets, and the psalms, concerning me. . . . Thus it is written that the Christ should suffer, and rise again from the dead the third day.' The preaching recorded in Acts (ii. 14–36, iii. 18–26, viii. 35, x. 43, xiii. 29), St. Paul's definition of the 'gospel of God' at the opening of the Epistle to the Romans (i. 1–4), and the catena of quotations which forms so important a part of the argument in the Epistle to the Hebrews and the First Epistle of Peter, show how fundamental the Old Testament was both to the preaching and to the apologetic of the early Church. The argument from prophecy, which led to the widespread use of *Testimonia* or messianic proof-texts, was the Christian answer to the scandal of the cross. The life and death of Jesus were part of the providential design.

So long as the Church remained on Palestinian soil the appeal would naturally be to the Hebrew scriptures read in the synagogue and expounded in Aramaic. But, with the extension of the Christian mission to the regions beyond, it was the Septuagint that was read every sabbath day to which the Apostle appealed. Even after the schism which separated the Church from the Synagogue the public reading of the Septuagint in Christian worship must have continued, for St. Paul assumes that his readers are familiar with these scriptures. While the Law and the Prophets were invested with a special authority, the New Testament supplies evidence that the third section of the Old Testament—the Writings—was elastic in its compass. Not only has Wisdom left a deep mark on the Epistle to the Hebrews and upon Romans, but Paul (according to Origen) quotes from an Apocalypse of Elijah (1 Cor. ii. 9), James (iv. 5) from the lost Book of Eldad and Modat, and Jude from the Book of Enoch.

But more important than such occasional quotations is the authoritative use of the Old Testament as the word of God. The individuality of the ancient prophet or psalmist was of small account. So the writer who introduces a citation from Ps. viii with the words 'Someone has somewhere said' (Heb. ii. 6) also declares that 'God who of old time spoke to the fathers in the prophets by divers portions and in divers manners has at the end of these days spoken to us in a Son' (Heb. i. 1). The revelation of the Old Testament was occasional and fragmentary, but it was the God and Father of our Lord Jesus Christ who spoke in those inspired men.

(*b*) *The Lord Jesus.* Great as was the reverence shown in the early Church for the ancient scriptures, greater still was the reverence for the voice and example of Him to whom they bore witness. When a word of Jesus could be quoted (Acts xx. 35) it gave irresistible force to an apostolic appeal, or settled out of hand a question in dispute (1 Cor. vii. 10, ix. 14). But even more determinative for the life of the Church was the living example of His character and the sense of the presence of His Spirit in their fellowship.

ii. *The Rise of the New Literature.*

The needs of the missionary Church called forth its earliest writings. The Messianic Testimonies may well have been the first written collection. The story of the Passion and Death of Christ, sayings and parables of Jesus, and incidents in His life, must have formed the staple of the oral tradition, proclaimed by apostles and taught by catechists. Gradually, as the first generation of eye-witnesses passed away, their reminiscences and teaching in a more or less stereotyped shape assumed a written form.

Probably a collection of Sayings of Jesus was one of the first to be committed to writing. The preface to St. Luke's Gospel gives us a fair account of the way in which one Christian of the second generation set about his task. Those to whom we owe these written records were not biographers but evangelists. The earliest of them heads his work 'The beginning of the good news of Jesus Christ (the Son of God)'.

The mother tongue of Jesus was Aramaic, and His sayings would be recorded in that language. The eye-witnesses of His ministry were Aramaic-speaking Palestinians, and the first narratives of the life, death, and resurrection of Jesus must have been transmitted in that tongue. But with the spread of that Gospel to the Graeco-Roman world all was translated into the Greek *Koiné*. It is in that dialect of Greek that the Gospels have been handed down. It may be doubted whether any one of our Gospels was ever written in Aramaic. But Aramaic idioms and Latinisms of vocabulary and syntax are curiously mingled in the Greek of St. Mark, thus lending colour to the ancient tradition that this Gospel was written in Rome by one whose home in early life had been Jerusalem. There is an Aramaic tinge in the sayings of Jesus reported in all the Gospels. Many scholars think that the Gospel according to St. John either was written by one who thought in Aramaic, or else embodies sources that have been translated from Aramaic into colloquial

Hellenistic. St. Luke's style is remarkable, for the writer, whilst one of the most cultivated Greek writers in the New Testament, models his style on the peculiar idiom of the Septuagint, and his pages abound in Hebraisms. This becomes progressively less noticeable in Acts, and almost disappears when the narrative leaves the soil of Palestine.

The earliest Christian writings of which we have direct evidence are a number of letters written by the Apostle Paul to the Churches in the four Roman provinces where he had laboured, and to the Church in the imperial capital which he had not yet visited. A number of other letters in due course, some of them bearing apostolic names, came to be treasured in the Churches which had received them, and gradually gained a wider circulation. An early Christian leader of great influence in proconsular Asia wrote seven letters to the principal Churches in that province. In the year A.D. 96 Clement, Bishop of Rome, wrote a letter to the Corinthian Church. Towards the end of the second decade of the second-century Ignatius, Bishop of Antioch, while on his way to execution at Rome, wrote letters to seven Churches. Polycarp, Bishop of Smyrna, with whom the martyr stayed on his last journey, sent copies of these seven letters, together with a covering note, to the Church at Philippi. This may supply an illustration of the way in which some early admirer of the Apostle Paul visited the Churches in the Pauline sphere of influence and copied such letters of his as survived. There is some internal evidence that Paul's correspondence with Corinth was in a fragmentary condition, and that our 2 Corinthians embodies parts of three distinct letters.

Fragmentary survivals of Gospels and quotations in early Fathers from others that are completely lost are some indication of the literary activity of the generations that followed the close of the Apostolic Age.

Besides epistles and gospels, another kind of writing arose in response to the necessities of the persecuted Church, and in line with the tradition of 'Zion in her anguish'. Hebrew prophecy had been followed by Jewish apocalyptic. This large literature was represented in the Old Testament canon by the book of Daniel, a 'tract for the times', arising out of the crisis provoked by Antiochus Epiphanes (168 B.C.). During the last decade of the first century, in the reign of Domitian, the Christians of proconsular Asia suffered severe persecution. A Christian prophet named John was sent to a penal settlement on the island of Patmos, from which he wrote letters to seven Churches and composed an apocalypse. This wonderful book draws upon the imagery and language of Jewish apocalyptic, combines with this allusions to the Roman empire and the imperial cult, and transfuses the whole with exultant prophecies of the victory of the slaughtered Lamb of God. This is the supreme example of a Christian apocalypse, but we have a fragment of one which bore the name of Peter, and must at one time have enjoyed wide popularity. The Revelation of John contains portions that were originally written in Hebrew, and the Greek of the whole is unlike anything else within the covers of the New Testament.

iii. *The Formation of the Canon.*

By the middle of the second century a prolific Christian literature had appeared, but as yet there was no thought of any book to rival the sacred scriptures of the Old Testament. The first step in the direction of the formulation of a Christian canon came from Marcion, a man of vigorous character and eccentric mind, whose early home was at Sinope in Pontus, where his father is said to have been a bishop. The young heresiarch visited the Churches of proconsular Asia,[1] where his views were denounced, and then arrived at Rome. There he propounded his doctrine of the irreconcilable opposition between the God of justice known from the Old Testament and the unknown God of mercy, revealed for the first time in Jesus Christ. Marcion carried the

---

[1] Harnack, *Marcion*, (2nd ed.), p. 24.

Pauline antithesis of law and gospel to such an extreme that he renounced the Old Testament entirely, and attempted to separate every trace of it from the teaching of Christianity. After a colloquy with the presbyters of the Church at Rome, Marcion was excommunicated in July 144 and formed a secession Church which rapidly spread to every province of the Empire. He issued a canon of Christian scripture consisting of Gospel and Apostle. The former was an edition of St. Luke mutilated to agree with Marcion's views. The 'Apostle' was an expurgated edition (with brief introductions) of ten Pauline epistles, excluding the Pastorals. There can be little doubt that 'Laodiceans' in his list is the circular epistle which bears the title 'Ephesians' in our New Testament. This canon, together with Marcion's *Antitheses*, a treatise showing the incompatibility of the Old Testament with Christianity, formed the bible of the heretical Marcionite Church. The orthodox Christian Church was compelled to meet the challenge. The fourfold Gospel was the reply. It is probable that we have the introduction to the earliest Gospel canon of the Catholic Church in the Anti-Marcionite Prologues.[1] That to St. Matthew is entirely lost. That to St. Luke has survived in its original Greek form. Those to St. Mark and St. John are extant in an early Latin rendering in a number of manuscripts of the Latin Gospels. The date when this first 'Introduction to the Gospels' (as we might term it) was written is uncertain, but it lies between the years 160 and 180, for Irenaeus seems to have known it. 'The Apostle' was also edited to present what was regarded as the true text not of the ten epistles only, but of the thirteen which had been known from the end of the first century. Marcion's Prologues were retained (for their heretical implications were not recognized) and special ones were added for the three Pastoral Epistles.

[1] See De Bruyne, 'Les plus anciens prologues latins des Évangiles', *Revue Bénédictine*, xl. 193–214 (July 1928); Harnack, *Die ältesten Evangelien-Prologe und die Bildung des N.T.* (1928); also *Expository Times*, xlvii. 534 ff., xlviii. 188.

Three points deserve attention. (*a*) This is not the first recognition by the Church of the value of these writings, but their publication as an authoritative standard, as a counterblast to Marcion's new Bible. (*b*) Acts and Revelation are expressly mentioned in the Prologue to the Gospels with obvious reference to Marcion's rejection of them, but they were not yet published in this canon, as the Church was for the present only concerned with counteracting the defective contents and unsound text of the Marcionite Bible. (*c*) By this time the codex was replacing the roll for Christian writings, and for the first time it was possible to include all four Gospels or all thirteen Pauline Epistles in one volume.

The next stage in the determination of the Canon is found in the Muratorian Fragment, a Roman document of about A.D. 200. This names after the fourfold Gospel the 'Acts of all the Apostles', the thirteen Pauline Epistles (denouncing as Marcionite forgeries those to the Laodiceans and to the Alexandrians), the Epistle of Jude, two Epistles of John, and the Wisdom of Solomon. Three apocalyptic books are acknowledged with different degrees of approval. The Apocalypse of John is accepted simply, that of Peter with the qualification, 'which some of our friends will not have read in the Church'. The 'Shepherd', written by Hermas during the Roman episcopate of his brother Pius (i.e. about A.D. 145), should only be read in private, for it is too recent to rank as of apostolic authorship whereas the prophetic books were fixed and closed (in the Old Testament). The fragment closes with a significant paragraph directed against the Gnostic heretics, Basilides and Valentinus, and the Phrygian Montanus, just as Marcionism is attacked earlier in the catalogue.

Thus the position at Rome at the end of the second century was fortified against heretical assaults on two fronts. Marcion's arbitrary limitation of apostolic writings in one direction, the Montanists' recognition of unlimited inspiration in the other, had to be countered by the rule of apostolicity. The canon was not closed, for it was still open to the Church to receive as authoritative any other writings recognized as apostolic in origin. But no claim of prophetic inspiration would admit a book which could not point to an apostle, or a man in close association with an apostle, as its author.

The application of this rule raised some interesting issues. About this time Serapion, Bishop of Antioch (190–216), forbade the public reading of the Gospel of Peter in the neighbouring Church of Rhossus because of its Docetic taint. 'For our part, brethren, we receive both Peter and the other apostles as Christ, but the writings which falsely bear their names we reject, as men of experience knowing that such were not handed down to us.'[1] Clement of Alexandria, whose range of reading was far wider than that of the Romans, when quoting a logion says, 'We do not find this saying in the four Gospels *that have been handed down to us*, but in that according to the Egyptians'.[2] His contemporary, Tertullian of Carthage, representing the Church in the province of Africa, quotes from the four Gospels as having come from actual apostles of the Lord, or from those closely associated with them. This explains the order in which the Gospels were arranged in the Western Church: Matthew, John, Luke, Mark. Tertullian accepted the Epistle to the Hebrews as from Barnabas, Origen (185–255) accepts it as Pauline, while recognizing the difference in style. Both Tertullian and Origen accept 1 Peter, the latter also accepts James, 2 Peter, and 2 and 3 John, though recording the dissent of some. The Church of Alexandria was less rigid than that of Rome, and we find Origen regarding Ep. Barnabas as one of the Catholic Epistles, the Shepherd of Hermas as scripture, and the Didache (or Teaching of the Twelve Apostles) as canonical. But he records that the claims of the last two are disputed and that the Gospel according to the Hebrews is not accepted outside the Jewish Christian communities.

[1] *Apud* Eusebius *H.E.* VI. xii. 3.       [2] *Stromateis*, iii. 13.

Eusebius of Caesarea (265–340), whose mastery of the whole field of early Christian literature gives a special value to his report, offers a threefold classification of the New Testament writings: (*a*) Acknowledged throughout the Church are the four Gospels, Acts, the Pauline Epistles (including Hebrews), 1 John, 1 Peter, and the Apocalypse; (*b*) disputed, but generally recognized are James, Jude, 2 Peter, 2 and 3 John; (*c*) disputed, but spurious, are the Acts of Paul, the Shepherd of Hermas, the Apocalypse of Peter, the Epistle of Barnabas, and the Didache. Eusebius, whose dislike of millenarianism explains his attitude, places the Apocalypse of John in both the first and the third categories, with the addition each time, 'If that should seem right'.

When Athanasius wrote his 39th Festal Letter at Easter 367 he named the twenty-seven books of our New Testament as alone canonical. Here and there doubts were still expressed about the Apocalypse, and in the East both it and the Catholic Epistles were only slowly received. As we have seen, the criterion was apostolic authorship. To the mistaken critical judgement of the ancient Church we owe the presence in the New Testament of not a few books. The most striking instance is Hebrews, which was certainly not written by Paul. *O felix culpa!*

In the second quarter of the fourth century the Christian Church entered upon a new stage in its history. No longer persecuted and obscure, but enjoying imperial patronage, it provided vellum codices for its scriptures instead of the perishable papyrus copies upon which it had relied until now. The two great Greek Bibles in our possession which go back to this date contained the entire New Testament, though the Vatican Codex in its present mutilated condition is without the last part of Hebrews, the Pastoral Epistles, and the Apocalypse. The Sinaitic Codex has the New Testament intact, but in addition contains the Epistle of Barnabas and the Shepherd of Hermas.

The two great codices of the fifth century, the Alexandrian Codex and Paris Palimpsest (Codex Ephraemi Rescriptus) both contained the whole New Testament, but the former also has the Epistle of Clement of Rome to the Corinthians and the homily written in the middle of the second century wrongly known as the Second Epistle of Clement. Thus the official copies of the New Testament agreed in what they contained, but differed in what they excluded. In that great age of theological controversy there must be a written authority of unquestioned validity. A penumbra of less authoritative writings was allowed for purposes of edification.

### B. *The Chief Manuscripts and the Printed Text*

i. *The History of the Greek Bible in Manuscript.*

(*a*) *Ancient book production.* The period from the translation of the Pentateuch into Greek until the invention of printing covers seventeen centuries. For the first six centuries papyrus was the material on which manuscripts were written. From the beginning of the fourth to the end of the thirteenth centuries A.D. vellum was used, after that paper gradually took its place.

Papyrus was obtained from the pith of the papyrus plant, a reed which grew abundantly near the Nile. Strips of this pith were placed together vertically; other strips were laid across these horizontally. After being moistened with Nile water and glue, pressed and polished with ivory rollers, and dried in the sun, the sheets thus prepared were fastened together at the sides and formed into rolls. The maximum length of a roll for ordinary use was rather less than 35 feet, which would just contain one of the longer Gospels or the Acts of the Apostles. A church which possessed the four Gospels and the Epistles would keep the several rolls in a cylindrical box (Latin, *capsa*). Thus when the proconsul Saturninus asked Speratus (one of the

martyrs in the persecution at Scilla in North Africa, A.D. 180)
'What kind of things have you in your case?' the reply was
'Books of the divine law and letters of Paul, a just man'.[1]

Recent discoveries have shown that by the middle of the
second century Christian writings began to take the form of a
codex, or book made up of folded leaves (or quires).

With the State recognition of Christianity under Constantine
the copying of the Christian scriptures entered on a new era.
Henceforth vellum, a far more durable material than papyrus,
was used. We have it on the authority of Eusebius[2] that the
emperor ordered fifty copies of the Scriptures on vellum for the
churches in his newly founded capital, whilst Jerome tells us
that Acacius and Euzoius replaced the damaged books in the
library which Pamphilus had gathered at Caesarea by copies
inscribed on parchment (about A.D. 350).[3]

The papyrus period coincides with the era of the great
persecutions. The external prosperity of the Church which
brought in the use of vellum made possible the use of professional
scribes. The textual variations in our existing manuscripts for
the most part go back to a time when unskilled copyists transcribed the Christian writings for their own use. The most
carefully prepared copies were those made for reading in the
churches, and these would be the first to be destroyed when
persecution broke out against the Christians.

Within the vellum period a distinction is made between the
majuscules written in large uncial letters without division of
words or sentences, and the minuscules written in the small
cursive script. During the ninth and tenth centuries uncial and
cursive manuscripts are found side by side. From the eleventh
century onwards only the cursive style of writing is used. Paper
(manufactured in Asia as early as the eighth century) became so

---

[1] '*Quae sunt res in capsa vestra?*' See 'Passio Sanctorum Scilitanorum', in *Texts and Studies*, i. ii. 114.    [2] *Vita Const.* iv. 36.

[3] *Epist.* xxxiv, vol. i, p. 155 (Migne, *Patr.* xxii. 448).

general in Europe in the thirteenth century that many copies of the scriptures were written on it. But the superiority of vellum for beautiful craftsmanship kept it in use until the invention of printing brought the age of manuscripts to a close.

(*b*) *The more important manuscripts.* The chronological order, papyri, uncials, cursives, is exactly reversed when we turn to consider the order of discovery since the recovery of the original text engaged the attention of modern scholars.

In the year 1897 intense excitement was aroused when Grenfell and Hunt published a scrap of papyrus, found at Oxyrhynchus, dating from the third century and containing some 'Sayings of Jesus'. Another similar fragment, found near the same spot and dating from a later decade of the same century, was published seven years later. Fragments of apocryphal Gospels have come to light from time to time, the most important of which was found in 1934. Its importance lies in its date (A.D. 130–65) and the fact that the original work, which must have been written not later than about A.D. 110–30, draws from all four of the canonical Gospels.

The most important evidence for the text of the New Testament is obtained from the following papyrus manuscripts.

𝔭 5 (third century) has some verses from the first and twentieth chapters of St. John, written on a single-quire papyrus codex which originally contained the entire Gospel.

𝔭 13 (late third, or fourth century) has some considerable portions of the Epistle to the Hebrews.

𝔭 38 (fourth century) has a number of verses from Acts xviii and xix.

𝔭 45–7 are the famous Chester Beatty papyri, the most important addition to our New Testament manuscripts made within living memory.

𝔭 45 (early third century) is about one-seventh of what was once a complete codex of all four Gospels and the Acts. Portions of all five books are represented.

𝔭 46 (early third century) is the greater part of a codex which originally contained all the Pauline Epistles except the Pastorals. The order is of interest. Romans, Hebrews, 1 and 2 Corinthians, Ephesians, Galatians, Philippians, Colossians, 1 and 2 Thessalonians.

𝔭 47 (third century) is part of a codex of Revelation, containing in a mutilated form ix. 10—xvii. 2.

𝔭 48 (third century) contains twelve verses from Acts xxii.

𝔭 52 (first half of second century) is the earliest fragment of any part of the New Testament and contains five verses from John xviii, showing that in the early part of the second century the Gospel was already in circulation.

The value of these fragments of papyrus is that they show the kind of text that was current in their own locality at the time when they were written. Expert palaeographers can offer a rough estimate of their dates. But for the text in anything like a complete form we still depend upon the great uncial manuscripts. The most important are here named.

‫א‬, *Codex Sinaiticus* (early fourth century) is now in the British Museum. Part of it was discovered by Tischendorf in the monastery at Mount Sinai in 1844, and the rest was secured by him and placed in the royal library at St. Petersburg (Leningrad) in 1859. This manuscript originally contained the Greek Old and New Testaments, with the Epistle of Barnabas and the Shepherd of Hermas.

A, *Codex Alexandrinus* (early fifth century) contained originally both Testaments, together with 1 and 2 Clement.

B, *Codex Vaticanus* (early fourth century) originally contained both Testaments, but the last part of Hebrews, the Pastoral Epistles, and the Apocalypse have been lost.

C, *Codex Ephraemi Rescriptus* (fifth century), a palimpsest, contained both Testaments, but in the twelfth century the writing was expunged, and some writings by the Syrian Father, Ephraem, were copied upon it instead. By the use of chemical reagents it has been possible to recover the original text. Unfortunately the manuscript is sadly mutilated.

D, *Codex Bezae* (fifth century), a bilingual manuscript of the Gospels and Acts, has the Greek and Latin texts on opposite pages. It was rescued from the monastery of St. Irenaeus by Theodore Beza, the French Reformation scholar, when Lyons was being sacked by the Huguenots in 1562, and presented to the University of Cambridge in 1581. It is notable for many curious additions to the text, especially of Luke and Acts.

L, *Codex Regius* (eighth century), a copy of a much earlier original, is notable for containing both the longer and the shorter endings of Mark. This manuscript of the Gospels, almost complete, is in the Bibliothèque Nationale in Paris. Though badly written, it is valuable for its frequent support of readings found in Codex B.

W, *Washington Codex* (late fourth or fifth century), was obtained by an American, Mr. C. L. Freer, in Egypt in 1906. The text is of an unusually mixed character, and the manuscript is remarkable for a long insertion between the fourteenth and fifteenth verses of Mark xvi, in the longer ending of that Gospel.

Θ, *Koridethi Codex* (eighth century), is an uncial manuscript of the Gospels which was once in the monastery at Koridethi at the eastern end of the Black Sea, but was discovered in a remote valley of the Caucasus. Then it disappeared for thirty years. It is now at Tiflis, and its complete text was published in 1913.

For the Pauline Epistles where the Codex Bezae is not available D2, *Codex Claromoytanus* (sixth century), a bilingual Graeco-Latin manuscript, serves in its place.

For the Apocalypse, which is missing from B, an important witness is 046, *Codex Vaticanus 2066* (eighth century).

The Minuscules, though of so late a date, in many instances are copies of early but lost Uncials. Chief among these are:

1 (twelfth century), 118 (thirteenth century), 131 (thirteenth

century), **209** (fourteenth century), forming a group whose close relationship has been investigated by Professor Kirsopp Lake, so that they are sometimes known as the 'Lake group'.

**13** (twelfth century), **69** (fifteenth century, **124** (twelfth century, **346** (twelfth century) are known as the 'Ferrar group', after W. H. Ferrar, the Irish scholar who first proved their common ancestry. The manuscripts of this group are remarkable for placing the story of the woman taken in adultery (found in some late manuscripts in St. John between vii. 53 and viii. 12, and printed there in our English versions) after Luke xxi. 38. **346** is famous for the reading, otherwise found in the Curetonian Syriac text of the Gospels, in Matt. i. 16, 'Joseph, to whom was betrothed Mary the Virgin, who bare Jesus, who is called the Christ'.

**33** (ninth century), a remarkably fine manuscript containing the Gospels, Acts, and Pauline Epistles, was called by Eichhorn 'the Queen of the Cursives', and was highly regarded by Hort as having in the Gospels a text closely resembling that of B.

**81** (A.D. 1044) contains Acts only, in an exceptionally fine text.

**700** (twelfth century) is remarkable for having a reading in Luke xi. 2 which appears to have been in Marcion's text, and to have been known to Tertullian and to Gregory of Nyssa. Instead of 'Thy kingdom come' the manuscript reads, 'Thy holy spirit come upon us and cleanse us'.

ii. *The Printed Text.*

The first complete book to be printed was a Latin Bible in the year 1456. Three years before this date the fall of Constantinople started the flight to western Europe of Greek scholars who brought their Greek manuscripts with them. But nearly half a century went by before there was any thought of printing a Greek New Testament. The honour must be shared between Cardinal Ximenes, whose splendid achievement is the Complutensian

Polyglot,[1] and Erasmus, whose Greek Testament was the first to see the light. The Cardinal conceived his plan in 1502. The New Testament, with the Greek and Latin Vulgate in parallel columns was finished by 1514, the Old Testament was ready in 1517, but as the six volumes only appeared in 1522, Erasmus was first in the field with the small Greek New Testament which he prepared with great rapidity for the Swiss printer Froben of Basle. The first edition was published in March 1516, and was followed by successive editions in 1519, 1522, 1527, and 1535.

Unfortunately the earliest printed Greek Testaments were based upon a few late minuscules and were in no sense a return to the primitive text of the New Testament. Even the Greek text of the Complutensian (which was prepared with infinitely more care than Erasmus gave to his), though manuscripts were sent by the Pope, made no use in the New Testament of the earliest and most precious treasure in the Vatican library, Codex B. But the work thus begun was bound to go on until a Greek text was produced that deserved to supplant the Vulgate.

For some time the history of the Greek Testament lies with the great printing houses on the Continent. The famous firm of Aldus at Venice brought out a beautifully printed text of the whole Greek Bible in one volume in 1518. The great Paris house of Stephanus published a series of editions which provided a text still in general use in this country till sixty years ago. Robert Étienne, with the help of his son Henri, produced three small duodecimo issues in 1546, 1549, 1551, and a folio in 1550. The text was substantially that of Erasmus, but this folio stands out for two reasons. A number of readings are supplied in the margin, with symbols to indicate the manuscript authorities. Amongst the authorities consulted are those now known as Codex Bezae (D) and Codex Regius (L). The type was the beautiful Greek royal fount which Francis I had ordered to be

---

[1] Called after Complutum, the Latin name for Alcala, where it was printed.

cut. The following year Étienne brought out an edition of the Greek Testament with the Vulgate and the Latin translation of Erasmus in parallel columns. For the first time the chapters were divided into verses, numbered as in our modern bibles.

In 1624 the Dutch firm of the brothers Elzevir published a text substantially the same as that of Stephanus. In the second edition of 1633 the preface (virtually a publisher's puff) announced that this text 'had been accepted by every one', and so the term Textus Receptus has survived for the late and corrupt text which was standardized at this time.

For the next two hundred years the initiative passes from the bookseller to the critical scholar.

Brian Walton's great Polyglot Bible in eight volumes is notable in the New Testament volume (1657) for the variant readings from Codex A and several other newly examined manuscripts. John Mill's Greek Testament (1707) printed the text of Stephanus, with a critical apparatus using readings from many manuscripts, the ancient Versions, and the early Fathers. Edward Wells (1719) and Daniel Mace (1729) had the courage to abandon the Textus Receptus and print an emended text. Then for a century England yielded the primacy to the Continent. J. A. Bengel (1734), while reprinting the Textus Receptus, supplied marginal notes classifying variants according to their worth. J. J. Wettstein, expelled from Basle, published at Amsterdam in 1751 the Textus Receptus with critical notes and a wealth of parallels from classical, Jewish, and Christian writers. In his textual apparatus for the first time we meet with the system of designating uncials with capital letters and cursives with arabic numerals. J. J. Griesbach's edition of 1775–7 is famous for his development of the method, begun by Bengel and Semler, of grouping the authorities in families, the 'Alexandrian', the 'Western' and the 'Constantinopolitan'. The Berlin philologist, C. Lachmann, broke entirely with the tradition of the printed text, and in his two editions of 1830 and

1842–50 based his text upon the oldest Greek manuscripts and the Vulgate. Constantine Tischendorf published his first edition in 1841. His prodigious labours in visiting libraries and monasteries, and in discovering and transcribing and editing fresh manuscripts, and above all his discovery and editing of the Sinaitic Codex, give a special value to his eighth edition of 1869–72. This supplied the most complete critical apparatus available until von Soden's unwieldy edition came out forty years later. Meanwhile an English scholar, S. P. Tregelles, after travelling through Europe for the examination of numerous manuscripts, produced between 1857 and 1872 a revised text which suffered from two misfortunes. He was refused permission to see the Vatican Codex, and the text of the Gospels was published before the discovery and publication of the Sinaitic Codex.

All previous texts were superseded by the scientifically critical text of Westcott and Hort (1881). In 1898 the Württemberg Bible Society published a convenient pocket edition of the Greek Testament prepared by Eberhard Nestle, in which the text was determined by accepting the reading followed by any two of three well-known printed texts. A slightly revised edition of this was issued by the British and Foreign Bible Society in 1904. Alexander Souter edited for the Oxford Press a manual Greek Testament with a select apparatus in 1910, and Erwin Nestle in 1927 improved the Stuttgart edition of his father's text by adding a condensed apparatus at the foot of the page.

## C. *Estimate of the Value of the Textual Tradition*

Erasmus and his immediate successors were like the alchemists in their search for the philosopher's stone. Those medieval seekers with their retorts and crucibles were in quest of the unattainable but they prepared the way for the science of chemistry. The scholars of the sixteenth century thought that by turning from Jerome's Vulgate to Greek manuscripts they would recover the original text of the New Testament. This we now know to be impossible. But we have come immeasurably nearer to it during the last four centuries and have discovered on the way how rich and diversified is the history of that text. Textual criticism is a branch of Church History. In its early stages the history of the text is bound up with the history of the canon. The story of the versions is a fascinating chapter in the history of Christian missions. The writings of the Fathers, the lectionaries, the primitive liturgies, all bear their witness and make their contribution to the form of the sacred text.

(*a*) Doctrinal interests have sometimes affected manuscripts, but have never succeeded in corrupting the textual tradition as a whole. Two examples may be given. In the second half of the second century a difficult passage in the Prologue to St. John (i. 13) lent itself to slight alteration as a proof-text for the doctrine of the Virgin Birth. There is some evidence that Justin Martyr so took it, and the reading 'Who was born' for 'Who were born' is found in one Old Latin manuscript (b), and is so quoted in Latin three times by Irenaeus and twice by Tertullian.[1] Yet in the whole range of Greek manuscripts, and in the great majority of the versions, the temptation to support an article of the Creed and to elucidate a difficult text has been avoided. The other example is the notorious interpolation of the 'Three Heavenly Witnesses' in 1 John v. 7, 8. The story of this *Comma Joanneum* belongs to the history of the Latin Bible. Yet the Greek manuscript tradition resisted the inducement to incorporate so convenient an argument in favour of the doctrine of the Trinity. When Erasmus was preparing his third edition he was challenged by Stunica (one of the editors of the Complutensian Polyglot) on this passage, and pledged himself to insert the corrupt reading if his rival could produce a single Greek manuscript which contained it. An almost

---

[1] *Qui non natus est*; i.e. ὃς οὐκ ἐγεννήθη for οἳ οὐκ ἐγεννήθησαν.

contemporary manuscript[1], in which the words had been translated from the Vulgate, was shown him, and like Antipas,
sorrowfully, but for his oath's sake, he kept his word. Thus the
passage became entrenched in the Textus Receptus and in the
English Authorized Version. But textual criticism is justified of
her works, and no modern text or translation admits the intrusion.

(b) One of the great achievements of New Testament
criticism in the last fifty years has been to determine the relation between the Synoptic Gospels. This task was immensely
complicated by the state of the text. Harmonization of parallel
passages had in numerous instances obscured the true reading.
The recent discovery of a tiny fragment of Tatian's Diatessaron
in Greek so far East as Dura on the Euphrates, dating from about
A.D. 222, settles the question that this harmony of the four
Gospels was published in Greek as well as in Syriac. Even though
von Soden greatly exaggerated the influence of the Diatessaron
as a corrupter of the Gospel text, this may have been one of the
factors, though unconscious assimilation on the part of scribes
may account for much more. Fortunately there are generally
witnesses that have escaped this kind of corruption, and the
original text can be recovered.

(c) To many students the most fascinating of problems is that
concerned with the readings in Luke and Acts peculiar to the
Codex Bezae and a few allies. The story of the man whom our
Lord found working on the sabbath (Luke vi. 5) is an example
of the drifting piece of tradition which was anchored by some
scribe near to a saying in one of the canonical Gospels. (Such is
the story of the woman taken in adultery which Codex D with
many late manuscripts attached to John vii. 53, and which the
Ferrar group of cursives introduce quite appropriately at
Luke xxi. 38.) Such additions in Luke are generally regarded
with suspicion. Not a few leading scholars are inclined to

[1] Codex 61, the Codex Britannicus, or the Montfort MS., now in the library of
Trinity College, Dublin.

accept many of those in Acts, whilst others think that they bear the trace of a later hand, and are the result of extensive revision of the text by one with special knowledge of the districts referred to in the narrative.

(*d*) It has often been pointed out that the 'Western' Text finds much support in the writings of the Fathers in the later part of the second century. One of the most important tasks in deciding between the rival claims of the Alexandrian and the Western authorities is to discover how far the form of the text used in Rome was affected by Marcion in his edition of Gospel and Apostle. If Marcion's text agrees with one group against the other, the problem to be solved is whether Marcion has corrupted the original reading, or ecclesiastical considerations have substituted a more orthodox text for one which Marcion had faithfully transmitted.

### D. *The Bearing of Recent Discoveries on Textual Theory*

For a hundred and fifty years, from Bengel to Hort, criticism's main achievement was to group all the authorities in 'families', and to rule out one of these as negligible. Westcott and Hort recognized four such families. (*a*) The 'Syrian', so called because it was believed to be due to a revision at Antioch. This was an eclectic text which is represented in the quotations found in the works of John Chrysostom, who left Antioch to become Patriarch of Constantinople in 398, and in the mass of late manuscripts. This is now generally known as the Byzantine or Constantinopolitan text, and is universally acknowledged to be by itself of little value. (*b*) The 'Neutral', represented by ℵ and B, supported by 33 and the Bohairic version, and sometimes by Origen. This was regarded as the purest representative of the original text. (*c*) The 'Alexandrian' was a group of readings found in C, L, and sometimes in Origen, showing a scholarly revision of the Neutral text, mostly in verbal and grammatical points. (*d*) The 'Western', represented by D, the Old Latin and the Old Syriac versions, and in the quotations in Irenaeus, Tertullian, and Cyprian. This classification relates to the Gospels, and varies considerably for other parts of the New Testament.

In the last sixty years important discoveries have been made which have led to some modification of this scheme. First came the discovery of the Sinaitic palimpsest of the Syriac Gospels. Then the purchase of the Washington Codex, followed soon after by the publication of the text of the Koridethi. Finally, the constant succession of papyrus finds was crowned by the Chester Beatty collection.

It is now evident that no family can claim the title 'Neutral'. Further knowledge of the Sahidic version (the dialect spoken in Upper Egypt) shows that this carries us farther back than the Bohairic version (the dialect of Lower Egypt), and its readings, while often supporting the text of the earliest uncials, are sometimes in agreement with the Western group. The papyri also, though for the most part supporting ℵ and B, in some cases show that the Western text was known in Egypt. The distinction between 'Neutral' and Alexandrian has been abandoned. Most recently the study of the Koridethi Codex has shown that behind many of the readings in this late and unusual manuscript a text can be detected which also lay behind the two groups of cursives (families 1 and 13) called the Lake and the Ferrar groups. This is now known as the Caesarean text, because the Alexandrian scholar Origen, during his later residence at Caesarea, departs from the 'Alexandrian' type of text for one more closely resembling that arrived at by a comparative study of $\Theta$ and its allied group of cursives.

There is thus a renewed tendency to attach great importance to the influence of local texts. Alexandria and Rome were important centres in the second century and the types of text which we call Alexandrian and Western may have taken their special form there. The Old Syriac version represents a type of text current in Syria at the time that this translation was made, but it afterwards suffered from adaptation to other texts that were then dominant. Caesarea with the library collected by Origen, Pamphilus, and Eusebius, became an influential centre, as later on Constantinople ruled the textual tradition.

But there was no fixity in local textual traditions. The Western text found its most congenial home in the provinces of Africa and Gaul. Even the manuscripts themselves are not consistent in their loyalty to one local type. The Washington Codex is an astonishing example of heterogeneity. If, therefore, we can speak of five fairly well-marked groups into which our authorities fall, the Byzantine, the Alexandrian, the Caesarean, the Western, the Syrian, manuscripts which are classified under one of these may very well contain readings which are characteristic of any of the others. No one class can claim to have the monopoly of correct readings. But this does not mean that in the great majority of cases we are left in uncertainty. Speaking of St. Mark, to the text of which he had given the minutest examination, C. H. Turner wrote, 'Where B and k agree, we have perhaps the greatest security that any two witnesses can give us of external evidence for the recovery of the apostolic text'. That is to say, the best representative of the Alexandrian family and the best of the Western witnesses (African Old Latin), when in alliance, form an almost irresistible combination.

W. F. Howard.

# III

# THE SYRIAC BIBLE

## SYNOPSIS

The Syriac version of the Old Testament is, apart from the Septuagint, the oldest and the most important translation which we possess. It is not certain whether it was made originally by Jews or by Christians, but there is no doubt that it was used in Syriac-speaking Churches at an early period. It is not the work of a single translator, but it was all based on the Hebrew text current in Palestine at the beginning of the Christian era, though at times it shows traces of Septuagint influence. Later translations, based on the Septuagint, were issued by Philoxenus of Mabbogh (A.D. 508) and Paul of Tella (A.D. 616). The latter was a literal rendering of Origen's Hexaplar text, and is commonly known as the Syro-Hexaplar version.

Very early in the history of the Syrian Church we find Tatian's Diatessaron in use. No copy of this harmony of the four Gospels is known to have survived, but a commentary by Ephrem is extant in an Armenian translation. Almost contemporary with it—whether earlier or later is not certain—is the Old Syriac version of the separate Gospels, represented by two manuscripts only, but showing a text which is independent of the two main lines of early tradition followed by the Greek manuscripts. Its nearest affinities are with the 'African Latin', and with the recently discovered Greek Koridethi Codex (Θ), and it is thus of the highest importance for the textual study of the Gospels.

Under the influence of Greek texts commonly used in the fourth century, a new version was made by Rabbula, Bishop of Edessa (A.D. 412–35), which superseded the older versions completely, and is still the 'authorized version' of the Syriac-speaking Church. This included the whole of the New Testament as accepted by the Syrian Church, though it omitted four of the Catholic Epistles and the Apocalypse.

Philoxenus of Mabbogh included these books in his version of the New Testament, issued with his revised Old Testament, and the complete New Testament as accepted in the Greek Church was translated afresh by Thomas of Harkel in 616, as a companion work to the Syro-Hexaplar of the Old Testament.

While the Syriac versions are not in the direct line of descent through which the English Bible has come down to us, they, especially the Old Syriac Gospels, are very important for the determination of the original text of the Bible.

## The Syrian Church

THE command 'Go ye into all the world and preach the Gospel to every creature' was taken almost literally by the early Church. Our evidence suggests that every Christian was a potential evangelist, and the Church certainly spread widely through the agency of people whose very names are lost to us. We do not even know who founded the Church in Rome; we know only that it was in existence before St. Paul left Ephesus, and that he thought it large enough and important enough to be the recipient of his most elaborate and careful piece of theological writing. Still less do we know of the foundation of Churches which lay to the east, outside the world of Mediterranean culture. They existed, and existed from apostolic times, but we are dependent for information as to their origin on traditions which may be challenged at every turn. Thus we are told that Edessa, for many centuries the centre of a wide and vigorous Church, was evangelized by 'Addai', who is sometimes identified with the Apostle Thaddaeus, though Eusebius puts him among the Seventy, and not among the Twelve. The ancient Church of southern India claims to be the result of the labours of St. Thomas, and there is no good ground for discarding the tradition. It will be remembered that, according to Eusebius (*H.E.* v. 10), Pantaenus of Alexandria went on a mission to India, and found Christians already there, though, says the historian, the Church had been founded, not by St. Thomas but by St. Bartholomew. We know, too, that Christianity was carried into the very heart of China by missionaries from the Syrian Church. The Chinese Church has long since perished, but the Indian Church not only survives, but has shown during the twentieth century an increased vitality, and it may well be that, when Indian Christianity becomes a self-conscious whole, the ancient Church will absorb all other types and forms. Whether the Nestorian mission to China carried its Bible with it or not, we cannot say, though we do know that the Syriac language was not wholly forgotten, for the famous Si-an-fu inscription contains a list of names in good Estrangela character. To this day, the official Bible of the Indian Church is the Syriac version known as the Peshitta, and Syriac is used in ecclesiastical circles much as Latin was employed during the Middle Ages in Europe.

But for the irruption of Islam, which cut the Eastern Churches off from the west, and placed their ecclesiastical centres under Moslem control, Syriac might have covered as large a Christian area as did Greek. It is true that the Eastern Church produced no great thinker, and its contribution to Christian theology is almost negligible. But the world which lay before it was much larger than that of the Mediterranean basin, and we are still far from seeing the full results which will issue from the labours of the early Syriac-speaking missionaries.

As the Scripture of this great Church, the Syriac Bible is necessarily of considerable historical importance. But it also has a high value for its witness to the text of the Old and of the New Testaments. In the former case it does not take the same rank as the Septuagint, it is true, but it stands second to the Greek version both in point of time and in importance. The enormous mass of Greek manuscripts of the New Testament has tended to throw the study of the versions into the background. But, as we shall see, the text, especially of the Gospels, which was used in the early Syrian Church is of a type which has very few Greek representatives, though it has striking affinities with that which was current in northern Africa down to the fourth century A.D. As our knowledge of New Testament textual criticism progresses, we may find that the Syriac versions assume a fresh importance, and, indeed, hold a unique place in the history of the text.

## I. *The Old Testament.*

(*a*) *Peshiṭta.* We have no direct information as to the origin of the Syriac Old Testament. No tradition is extant ascribing it to any particular scholar. We do not even know whether it was produced by Jews or by Christians. There was a considerable Jewish community in and about Edessa, the centre of the area to which Syriac belonged, but they may have been content, like their brethren who spoke other Aramaic dialects,

with a *Targum*, delivered orally by some learned scribe. It is
true that the familiar 'proof-texts' appear in a specifically Christian form; in Isa. vii. 14, for example, the word 'virgin' occurs,
though it is a misleading translation of the Hebrew term. But
in this case the error had been made already by the Septuagint,
whose version is certainly free from Christian bias, and in this,
as in other cases, we may be sure that the Church would see to
it that important passages were presented in the form demanded
by the methods of traditional apologetics. It is quite possible
that a translation, originally Jewish, was modified by Christians
on theological grounds.

What we may call the external evidence gives us little help.
It may be remarked at once that the Syriac New Testament
cannot be cited as a witness. There are numerous quotations
from the Old Testament in the New, but the translators of the
New Testament were satisfied to render these directly from the
Greek text which they had before them. This was sometimes
influenced by the Septuagint, but there are cases where even the
Greek Old Testament was not closely followed. In Matt. iv. 15 ff,
for instance, we have the familiar citation from Isa. viii. 23—ix. 1.
Both the Hebrew text and the Septuagint have: 'The people
that *walked* in darkness have seen a great light.' The Greek
text of St. Matthew, however, has: 'The people that *sat* in
darkness . . .,' a reading which is followed in both the older
Syriac versions of the Gospels. As far as the evidence of the
New Testament goes, it would be quite possible to maintain
that the translators were unaware of the Syriac version of the
Old Testament as it is known to us.

Apart from the Bible, the oldest Syriac work we possess is
that known as 'The Doctrine of Addai'. It is a record of
the evangelization of Edessa by Addai, and it includes a brief
account of the activities of the young Church. These involve
the daily reading of Scripture, both in the Old and in the New
Testaments. Obviously this cannot be an exact description of

the facts as they were in the middle of the first century, and the statement must be ascribed to the final writer or compiler of the book, whose date is probably in the early part of the fourth century. Roughly to the same period belong the earliest of the Syrian Fathers whose work has come down to us in any considerable quantity, Aphrahat and Ephrem. Both quote freely from the Old Testament, and, though their citations are sometimes free, they leave us in no doubt of the fact that it was substantially our present text of the Syriac Old Testament which they used. There is, however, no reason to suppose that the Old Testament had to wait till their age for translation, though they are our earliest direct witnesses to it, and there is general belief that it goes back to the first or second century A.D.

When we turn to the evidence which may be derived from the Syriac Old Testament itself, we are confronted with a serious difficulty. Though Syriac ecclesiastical literature had a history of a thousand years, the language underwent very little change. The medieval Fathers write in a dialect which is substantially that of the Bible, allowing for the fact that they often had to express ideas which do not appear in Scripture, and the Indian Church to this day uses the same type for ecclesiastical purposes. The spoken language, it is true, has gone through a process of development, and modern Syriac is very different from the classical language. But we can make no use of philological considerations to help us in determining the date of the Syriac Old Testament.

The fact which does emerge from a study of the text is that the version is not the work of a single translator. It is quite conceivable that a scholar may not always use the same Syriac word to represent the same Hebrew word, but from time to time we find that differences in rendering are consistent. One instance will suffice; the words which appear in the English versions as 'Lord God' are in some books (the prose books, Psalms, Isaiah, Jeremiah, and Daniel) rendered as in English.

But in Ezekiel and the Twelve Prophets the phrase used is 'Lord of Lords'. It is hardly possible that one translator would have been so consistent in his inconsistency. The general habits, too, of the translators vary a good deal. Some are very literal, and keep close to their original, others allow themselves a certain amount of freedom, especially in dealing with obscure passages. In every case the text was substantially that of our Hebrew Bibles, and though there are occasional variations, they are by no means so great as those which the Septuagint presents. It seems clear that the translators (or later revisers of the translation) were familiar with the Greek version, for we sometimes find clear traces of its influence. In Ezek xiii. 19, for example, the Hebrew text speaks of 'souls which should not die', while both the Greek and the Syriac render 'souls which *must* not die'. Dependence of a different kind may be seen in Joel iv. (E.V. iii) 11. The first word of the verse is found nowhere else, and its meaning is quite unknown; it is conjectured plausibly that the text is corrupt and that we should read a similar word meaning 'hasten'. Both the Greek and the Syriac, however, render 'gather together', and there can be little doubt that the Septuagint guessed the meaning and that the Syriac translator followed suit. In most cases, however, where the two versions agree as against the traditional Hebrew text, it may be assumed that the latter has suffered corruption at a comparatively late period. Thus in Nahum. ii. 12 where.the Hebrew now has *lābī'* ( = lion) both translations evidently read *lābō'* ( = come in). Two instances of a conventional rendering may also be mentioned. The Syriac version agrees with the Greek in using the word 'Lord' for the divine name Yahweh; this is possibly due to an ancient tradition familiar to both sets of translators. Again, in the Psalter the Septuagint renders the mysterious word 'Selah' by διάψαλμα, which the Syriac adopts and simply transliterates, without, apparently, understanding either the Greek or the Hebrew. It would be difficult to find clearer evidence of dependence, and it is surprising that the Syriac has so thoroughly maintained its independence in other ways.

(*b*) *Later Versions*. As time passed, the traditional version ceased to appeal to certain sections of the Syrian Church, and new translations were made. The first of these was the work of Philoxenus of Mabbogh, who had the whole Bible revised, in or about the year 508 B.C. The second was due to Paul of Tella (A.D. 616), and was made from Origen's Hexaplar text of the Septuagint. Neither took firm root in the Syrian Church, and of the Philoxenian Old Testament only small portions survive. The later version, however, is represented by a number of manuscripts including different parts of the Old Testament, and is our principal source of information as to the Hexapla itself, since it recorded Origen's critical notes and a number of readings from the later Greek versions.

The version, then, which has been the main Syriac Old Testament for nearly two thousand years is still the oldest. It is written, in spite of the different hands which produced it, in a fairly uniform style, and is generally clear, smooth, and idiomatic. All the contributors allowed themselves some degree of latitude, especially in the omission or insertion of conjunctions, and in the interpretation of obscure passages. Syriac is a beautiful language, deserving of far fuller study than it generally receives. While it lacks the stately dignity and deep music characteristic of Hebrew, its common use to represent Greek thought gave it a flexibility and a delicacy of expression shared by no other form of Semitic speech; it alone, for instance, possesses 'tenses' in the sense in which the word is applied to verbal forms in Indo-European languages, and it alone developed a full supply, not only of adjectives, but also of adverbs. The Old Testament is one of the greatest monuments of the language.

The Canon of the Old Testament followed by the Syrians was practically that of the Septuagint. There was some doubt about Chronicles, Ezra, Nehemiah, and Esther; it is worth noting that the translation of the first named frequently diverges very widely from the Hebrew text, though it has no affinities with the Septuagint. It is rather unfortunate that the best-known printed edition, that of Lee, includes only the books found in the Hebrew Canon, though the Apocryphal books were certainly recognized by the early Church and are still regarded as canonical in India. We have no record of the process through which the Eastern Church reached its conclusions as to the authentic books, but we may suppose that this covered some centuries; the Syriac version of the Apocrypha was the work of a number of different hands.

## II. *The New Testament.*

It seems clear that the Syriac-speaking Church needed the New Testament (or parts of it) at a very early period. There are grounds for suspecting that the Gospels were translated into Syriac during the first half of the second century, and the Acts and Epistles cannot have been neglected much longer. The New Testament underwent several important revisions, and we may distinguish four main versions. These are:

1. The Old Syriac, comprising the Gospels alone (Syr[Vt.]).

2. The Peshitta, dating from the fourth century, and said to have been the work of Rabbula (Syr[P.]).

3. The Philoxenian, of the same date as the Philoxenian Old Testament, i.e. 508 (Syr[Phil.]).

4. The Harkleian, corresponding to the version of the Old Testament made by Paul of Tella, and to be dated at the same time, i.e. A.D. 616 (Syr[Hark.]).

(*a*) *The Diatessaron.* To these may be added the so-called Diatessaron, a harmony of the Gospels made in the second century by Tatian, a disciple of Justin Martyr who appears both as a heretic and as an apologist. No copy of the Diatessaron is known to exist, but it was certainly much used in the early Church; Rabbula alone is said to have destroyed four hundred copies, replacing them with the separate Gospels of the Peshitta. Aphrahat seems to have used it, and Ephrem wrote a commentary on it. This last document survives in an Armenian translation, and we are dependent on it for most of the knowledge we possess concerning the Diatessaron itself (an Arabic Diatessaron, which is still extant, has undergone so much revision as to give us little or no light on the original form). It gives us some indication as to the text, and shows that at times it took a form which is not known from any other source. For example, in Luke viii. 46 we have the words 'For I know that *great* virtue is gone out from me'. But it fails to tell us for certain whether the harmony was made originally in Greek, and then translated into Syriac, or whether it was made from a Syriac text. In the latter case, it may be assumed that the text would have been the Old Syriac. There are few passages in which an accurate comparison is possible, but it is interesting to observe that once or twice the Diatessaron clearly had a reading characteristic of Syr$^{Vt.}$. Perhaps the most striking example is in John iv. 25, where the Diatessaron, as cited by Ephrem, and the Old Syriac alone read 'behold', where all other authorities read 'I (we) know'. This is clearly due to a variant reading in Greek and not in Syriac. On the other hand, there are several places in which the Diatessaron is against the Old Syriac, e.g. in John xi. 25, where the latter (and also some manuscripts of the Old Latin) omitted the words 'and the life' after 'the resurrection'. It is worth observing, however, that some of the divergences between the Old Syriac and the Diatessaron are due to the omission of words from the former; in one case (John v. 12) a whole verse is missing. These may well be idiosyncrasies of the individual manuscript of Syr$^{Vt.}$, and not of the version as a whole. The general impression we get is rather that the Diatessaron was made from a Greek text, not unlike that which underlies the Old Syriac, though it is impossible to speak on this point with any degree of certainty (see Chapter II, p. 79).

(b) *Old Syriac (Syr$^{Vt.}$)*. We are on much safer ground when we come to the Old Syriac version of the Gospels. It is known to us only through two manuscripts, one, a Nitrian manuscript of the fifth century, whose text was published by Cureton in 1858, containing less than half the Gospels, the other a palimpsest found in 1892 by Mrs. Lewis in the monastery of St. Catherine on Mount Sinai, which includes seven-eighths of the whole. From these two, which sometimes differ, it is possible to reconstruct the whole of the Gospels in this version.

We have no clue as to the origin of this translation, but it can hardly be later than the second century A.D. Aphrahat, it is true, apparently used the Diatessaron as a rule, but it seems to have been known to Ephrem, though some of his quotations are more naturally assigned either to the Diatessaron or to the Peshitta. It represents a form of text which is found in none of the great Greek uncials, though there are affinities with the 'Ferrar group'. It seems that Clement of Alexandria used Gospels of the same general type, though the 'Chester Beatty' papyrus exhibits a very different text, and its closest parallels are to be found in the manuscripts of the Old Latin, especially in those of African origin. Its relation to the recognized groups of Greek manuscripts is interesting, since it sometimes exhibits a 'Neutral' reading, sometimes a 'Western' reading, and sometimes one which is entirely independent of both. The facts may be illustrated from a series of 535 passages, grouped as follows:

|  | *With B against D* | *With D against B* | *With neither B nor D* |
|---|---|---|---|
| St. Matthew . | 24 | 40 | 48 |
| St. Mark . | 33 | 24 | 39 |
| St. Luke . | 39 | 62 | 79 |
| St. John . | 16 | 31 | 100 |
|  | 112 | 157 | 266 |

In more than half these instances, Syr$^{Vt.}$ has the support of the Old Latin, and even when it differs from both B and D it often agrees with ℵ, A and later manuscripts. It is sometimes claimed that the great Freer MS. (W) approximates in type to Syr$^{Vt.}$, and the two have many readings in common. But these nearly always have other support, and, of the passages enumerated in the third column above, barely 10 per cent. appear also in W. It should be added that the figures given are based on Burkitt's text, which takes both the Old Syriac manuscripts into account. Had the Sinai palimpsest alone been considered, the contrast with the oldest Greek copies would have been still more marked, for the Curetonian already shows signs of that process of accommodation to the Greek tradition of Caesarea and Antioch which culminated in the revision we know as the Peshitta.

The conclusion is irresistible. The Old Syriac, especially in its Sinaitic form, is our oldest and purest representative of a third line of textual tradition, standing quite apart from both those typified by B and D. It is curious to observe how the degree of independence varies, being least noticeable in St. Mark and strongest in St. John. While no Greek manuscript of this type has survived, its readings were frequently incorporated in the developing Greek text, and it must be taken seriously into account in considering the history of the complex form which ultimately prevailed and has become known as the Textus Receptus. Its influence may be seen both in ℵ and in W—two fourth-century manuscripts—and is still more evident in the conflate form represented by A. Its disappearance, in its pure state, from Greek tradition may seem strange, but we should remember that neither B nor D (especially the latter) has any very near relative among our extant manuscripts. It was natural that the great revisions of the Greek text, both Antiochian and Hesychian, should tend to eliminate all the simpler forms. But the type represented by Syr$^{Vt.}$ was the most widely diffused of all at the end of the second century; a text used by Aphrahat, Clement of Alexandria, and Cyprian can hardly be called local. It has strong claims to be considered as reliable as either of the other main lines of tradition, and there may be passages (e.g. the arrangement of John xviii. 13–24) in which the Sinai palimpsest *alone* has preserved the original reading. It may fairly be said that this copy of the Gospels is the most important single volume known to exist in the world to-day.

The question now arises as to whether there was also an equally distinct Syro-African text of the rest of the New Testament. It goes without saying that the remaining books (apart from the four disputed Epistles, 2 Peter, 2 and 3 John, and Jude, and the Apocalypse) were known in Syriac at an early date. But it is less certain that this text differed widely from that current elsewhere or from the later Peshitta. Some scholars, e.g. the late Professor F. C. Burkitt, have held that it was as distinctive as the Old Syriac Gospels. But in its Syriac form it can be known only through quotations, and even the evidence of the African Latin manuscripts is defective. A fresh study of Aphrahat suggests that Burkitt may have been misled by that author's occasional lax quotations, and the question can be settled only by a comprehensive and discriminating study of the text illustrated in the Syrian and African Fathers, particularly Aphrahat, Ephrem, and Cyprian.

(c) *The Peshitta*. The Syrian Church was always extremely sensitive to Greek influence, and the general spread of the conflate Greek text commonly called 'Syrian' or 'Antiochian' gave the impression that the versions of the Gospels, both the Diatessaron and the Separated Gospels, were inadequate. Accordingly, at the beginning of the fifth century, a complete revision of the New Testament was undertaken by Rabbula, Bishop of Edessa, and this version has maintained its position throughout the history of Syriac-speaking Christianity. The biographer states that the translation was made 'accurately, exactly as (the text) was', and the reason given is the 'modifications' or 'differences' in the existing texts. There was abundant ground for this complaint. Not only were the Gospels extant both in the form of the Diatessaron and in that of the Separated Gospels, but (as our two manuscripts show) there was no standard text of the latter. The result was that this new version, or rather revision, very soon took its place as the Authorized Version of the Syriac-speaking world. It was copied with the greatest care, and even the Massoretic Text of the Old Testament hardly shows more uniformity. Such variations of reading as are found in different manuscripts are invariably matters of slight importance, and it is possible to cite the version as a whole, with only occasional reference to the readings of a particular manuscript.

The text of the Peshiṭṭa itself is clearly of the general mixed type which became current in the fourth century, whose most ancient representative is the Codex Alexandrinus (A), though the great Freer MS. (W) shows tendencies in the direction of its formation. In attempting to establish the original text of the Gospels it has little value as compared with the Old Syriac, but its influence on eastern Christianity was incalculable. Not only did it become the official New Testament of the greater part of Asiatic Christendom, but it was the parent of other versions, notably the Armenian and the Georgian. It was used for some of the earlier Arabic versions, though that which has survived is based on a comparatively late Egyptian text. Its style is beautifully smooth and clear, and it can claim to be one of the great literary achievements of the Eastern Church.

(*d*) *Later Versions.* The Monophysite section of the Eastern Church eventually became dissatisfied with the Peshiṭṭa and attempted new translations, or rather revisions. The best known of these are the so-called Philoxenian and the Harkleian. The former was the work of Philoxenus of Mabbogh (see above on the Old Testament) completed in A.D. 508, the latter, that of Thomas of Harkel (A.D. 616), forming the New Testament part of that Bible to which the Old Testament was contributed by Paul of Tella. The version of Philoxenus has hardly survived; only the five 'disputed' books are known, and this was the first time that they were rendered into Syriac. The Harkleian, however, is complete, and is represented in Syriac Bibles by the Apocalypse. The four small Epistles, on the other hand, are usually printed in the Philoxenian version. Except in these five books the later versions were but seldom used, and had little influence. It is worth noting that, for these books, the two versions seem to have enjoyed almost equal popularity. In his commentary on the Apocalypse the twelfth-century Father, Dionysius Bar-Salibi, showed familiarity with both, though many of his quotations are independent translations from the Greek text of Hippolytus, on whose *De Christo et Antichristo* he drew freely.

(*e*) *Palestinian Syriac*. It is usual to include among the Syriac versions the so-called Palestinian Lectionary, of which portions have survived. Its only claim to be 'Syriac' rests on the script in which it is written. The language is a western dialect of Aramaic, much nearer to the Aramaic of the *Targums* and the Talmud than to that of Edessa. It is comparatively late, probably of the sixth century, and its main interest lies in the fact that it is the only instance known to us of any part of the New Testament in a western Aramaic dialect. While it is not free from the influence of the Peshitta, it is, in the main, an independent translation from the Greek text current in the sixth century in Palestine.

### Note on 'Targums'

The mention of the Palestinian Lectionaries introduces the *Targums*. Their origin and function has been indicated in Chapter I; it is enough to note here that they are not always translations in the strict sense of the term. Since they were used in worship, their character was necessarily exegetical, and they vary from an almost exact transcript of the Hebrew text into Aramaic to a homiletic discourse in which imagination played a large part. In the greater part of *Judges*, for example, the rendering is fairly close to the Massoretic text, but the Song of Deborah is largely allegorized, and presents a picture which recalls a rabbinic school rather than a battle-field. So, too, the *Targum* on Hosea makes no mention of the prophet's domestic tragedy; chaps. i and iii are simply given as denunciation of Israel's sin. Nevertheless, the *Targums* often give us useful light on the Hebrew text as it was about the beginning of the Christian era.

### Note on Other Ancient Versions

It is not possible to do more than enumerate other versions. Some of them are of considerable importance for the history of the Biblical text, though none approach to those which have already been considered. The Bible was translated into two indigenous African languages, Coptic and Ethiopic. In the former three versions are known, the Bohairic, in the dialect of Lower Egypt, that of the Fayyum (New Testament only), and the Sahidic, coming from upper Egypt. In the Old Testament both Bohairic and Sahidic were taken from the Septuagint; the latter has an interesting form of the Book of Job, based on Origen's Hexaplar text, with the asterisked lines omitted. The New Testament versions are interesting for the light they throw on the history of the text; the Sahidic, the earliest, showing affinities with both the 'Neutral' and the 'Western' forms. Its relation to the Syro-African text has not yet been adequately determined. The Bohairic, on the other hand, is much nearer to the 'Neutral' type.

The Ethiopic version was made directly from a Greek text, both in the Old Testament and in the New, though it seems that parts of the Old Testament were revised with the help of Hebrew and other manuscripts. There are traces of an earlier New Testament, whose basis was the Old Syriac, but the surviving manuscripts are comparatively late, and we can seldom use this version as strong evidence for any particular form of text.

The other early version which calls for a note is the Gothic, of which only portions survive. It was made from a Greek text of the type current in Constantinople in the fourth century, and has little value for the textual critic, though it is of great importance to the Teutonic philologist.[1]

It remains only to point out the dominating influence that these translations of the Bible, mainly in the east and south, have exercised on the languages in which they were produced. Just as Tyndale may be called the creator of the English language as we know it, so the Syriac Bible set the standard for all later literature in that tongue, and no Syriac Father or historian offers any serious difficulty to one who can read the Peshitta. In the Egyptian dialects and in Ethiopic we have little literary work beside the Bible, while the Gothic fragments are the sole remains of that language. It is, perhaps, to be regretted that the early missionaries in India and China did not, as far as our knowledge goes, render their Bible into the vernacular. An early Chinese Bible or a Bible in one of the older forms of a Dravidian language, would have been both interesting and important. It may well be that the failure of these two great enterprises completely to conquer the lands they invaded may have been due in part to the fact that they did not give the people the Word of God in their own vernacular. Wherever it has gone, and wherever it has been brought within the reach of the plain man, it has never failed to contribute to that 'great multitude which no man could number, of all nations, and kindreds, and peoples, and tongues', that stands 'before the throne and before the Lamb'.

In conclusion, it may be remarked that the Syriac versions have exercised little or no direct influence on the history of our English Bible. But, as we have seen, in the Old Syriac Gospels we have a type of text which is represented in equal purity by no extant Greek authority. This need not surprise us, nor

[1] For a brief popular account of this Bible, see *The Bible and its Literary Associations* (ed. by M. B. Crook; New York, 1937), Chap. IX. (Ed.)

should it detract from the value of the tradition; both the Codex Vaticanus and the Codex Bezae, the clearest representatives of the other main lines, are unique, and we must regard it as a happy accident that they have been preserved for us in their Greek form. But the Syro-African text did exercise a very great influence on the conflate form on which the Authorized Version is based, best represented among the great uncials by the Codex Alexandrinus. It is, then, of the highest value in offering us clear evidence as to one of the sources from which the main stream grew, and in helping us to understand the process by which the Word of God has been transmitted to us from those to whom it was first committed.

T. H. Robinson.

# IV

# THE LATIN BIBLE

## SYNOPSIS

1. *The Latin Bible before Jerome.* Greek and Latin in the West. The origin of the Latin Bible to be sought among Christians who knew no Greek. Jewish influence on the early translation. The process of translation haphazard and gradual, conditioned by the growth of the Canon and local needs. Manuscript and patristic evidence for the text of the Old-Latin Bible. One version or many? Division of the Old-Latin authorities into families and characteristics of these families. Date and place of origin of the version. Its vocabulary and style.

2. *Jerome and the Latin Bible.* Qualifications of Jerome as a Biblical scholar. Commissioned by Damasus to revise the Old-Latin. Publication of the Gospels and certain Old Testament books translated from the Septuagint. His new translation from the Hebrew. Two points obscure: (i) the extent of his revision of the Greek Old Testament; and (ii) the extent of his revision of the New. Estimate of Jerome's work both as a reviser and as a translator of a new version.

3. *The Latin Bible after Jerome.* Gradual acceptance of Jerome's version. The period of ordering. Prefaces and Chapter-headings. Cassiodorus, the first real editor of the 'Vulgate' Bible. Contents of the Vulgate. Deterioration of the text particularly due to mixture with the Old-Latin. Recensions of Alcuin and Theodulf in the ninth century, and of the University of Paris in the thirteenth century. Early printed editions. Editions of Sixtus V and Clement VIII. Extant manuscripts of the Vulgate and their classification. Modern critical editions of Wordsworth and White, and of the Curia.

4. *The Latin Bible and Theological Study.* The value of the Latin Bible for the textual criticism of (i) The Hebrew Old Testament, (ii) The Septuagint, and (iii) The New Testament. It also throws light on certain associated problems, e.g. the origin of the Diatessaron, the 'shorter' recension of Romans, and the authorship of Hebrews. The Latin Bible as a mirror of the thought, beliefs, and practices of both the Church at large and of individual Christians.

## 1. *The Latin Bible before Jerome*

IN its march of progress 'to the bounds of the West' Christianity carried with it as Scripture, not the Palestinian Hebrew Bible, but the Greek Bible of the Jewish Dispersion. At first this was sufficient to supply all needs. For not only was the education of the upper classes at Rome considered deficient without a knowledge of Greek, but the slaves and freedmen, from among whose number the new religion was particularly successful in gaining converts, were mostly Greek in origin and antecedents, to whom Latin was a foreign and largely unknown tongue. These facts will explain why for more than a century all the linguistic affinities of the Roman community are Greek and not Latin, and further, why the earliest traces of a Latin translation of any part of the Scriptures are very much later than the first impact of Christianity upon the western world. Though the State used two languages, the Church was content with one.

Thus St. Paul naturally wrote to the Romans in Greek in 58, as did also Ignatius more than fifty years later. Greek, too, was the normal medium employed by the Bishops of Rome in communicating with other Churches, as witness the letters to Corinth of Clement as early as 96 (?) and Cornelius as late as 250. And this was no accident of correspondence, for Hermas could still address his Roman fellow Christians in Greek in 140, while Hippolytus published his *Refutation of the Heresies* in Greek about 220.

But Latin was slowly making its way. Pope Victor (*c.* 190) is mentioned by Jerome as the first author who wrote theological treatises in Latin; and he was soon followed by Tertullian (*c.* 160–230) at Carthage and Novatian (*c.* 200–60) at Rome. Henceforward the use of Greek declined, and the decline was in large measure due to the increase in number, size, and importance of those Churches outside Rome, which had no share in the social and cultural traditions of the capital—for we must beware of manufacturing a primitive and consistent 'western use' in this matter out of evidence valid only for Rome itself. It is true that Irenaeus (*c.* 180) in Gaul used Greek as a medium, but he came from Asia Minor and his practice was not necessarily universal. The regions of northern Italy were in all probability evangelized by Latin-speaking missionaries from Rome, while the Acts of the Scillitan Martyrs (180), no less than the writings of Tertullian, suggest that at a much earlier date than in Rome the language of the African Churches was exclusively Latin. Indeed, in so far as in Africa the population was very largely Semitic in extraction and Latin was the only official State language, it is doubtful if it was ever otherwise.

Accordingly, among those Christians who knew little or no Greek, whether in Rome or in the provinces, we must seek the genesis of the Latin Bible.

But were the Christians first in the field? We have seen above that the Christian Bible was initially the Septuagint version of the Jewish Dispersion—i.e. it was a translation into Greek of a Hebrew original. We must reckon therefore with the possibility that the process of translation had been already carried one stage farther, and that the Roman and African Jews possessed a rudimentary Latin version of the Old Testament before ever Christianity came upon the scene, and that this translation was taken over subsequently by the Church. Just as the *Targums* originated in the oral Aramaic paraphrases which accompanied the reading of the Lessons in the services of the Palestinian synagogues, and the Septuagint was the ultimate response to a demand for the Scriptures in a language 'understanded of the people' in the Hellenistic synagogues, so in the synagogues of the West an 'interpretation' must have been necessary for those proselytes and adherents who were ignorant of both Hebrew and Greek. Yet there is no direct evidence that such oral 'interpretation' was ever crystallized in written form by the Jews themselves, or, even if it was, that it was borrowed by Christians. These are interesting possibilities, but no more.

No careful student, however, can fail to recognize certain indications of Jewish influence which pervade all the earliest translation.[1] But especially instructive for our purposes are those reversions in the New Testament to the correct Hebrew forms as against the Greek forms naturally employed by the

[1] Cp. Kaulen, *Geschichte d. Vulgata*, pp. 140 ff., and Ziegler, *Die lateinischen Bibelübersetzungen vor Hieronymus*, &c., p. 126.

apostolic writers,[1] and such other phenomena as the quotation of Isa. vi. 9 ff. at Matt. xiii. 15, which in codices *a* and *k* follows the Hebrew and not the Septuagint paraphrase preferred by the Evangelist. Here are traces of the traditions, scholarship, and translational activity, not of Jews, but of Jewish-Christian converts, of whom the Church in the early period could boast a great number. Jewish influence is no less noteworthy because it was indirect.

It is only from similar fragmentary, and often ambiguous, evidence furnished by the Old-Latin[2] Bible itself, that we can reconstruct its origin and history. 'In the early days', says Augustine, 'whoever chanced upon a Greek codex and thought he had a little aptitude in both Latin and Greek attempted a translation', and we lack more precise information. The process of translation was both haphazard and gradual, conditioned on the one hand by the growth of the Canon, and on the other by local needs and individual preferences. Alongside the Old Testament inherited from Judaism there grew up a Christian New Testament, part of which was accorded 'canonical' authority almost from the first. Obviously those of the new books most widely received had the prior claim to be translated. But there was no universally recognized list of Scriptural books in the West before the Council of Carthage pronounced in 397, and the use varied from province to province and from Church to Church. The books translated will have varied accordingly. Furthermore, however strongly a belief in the inspiration and authority of the Bible as a whole might be held, no one could have seriously maintained that all books were upon the same level in interest or importance, or that some parts were not more valuable in living the Christian life than others.

---

[1] e.g. *Eleazarus* for Λάζαρος in *e* at Luke xvi. 20 ff., and *Mambres* for Ἰαμβρῆς in all manuscripts at 2 Tim. iii. 8.

[2] In common with most modern scholars I use the term 'Old-Latin' to describe the Latin Bible before Jerome rather than 'Itala' or 'Vetus Itala', to avoid ambiguity.

Those parts considered most valuable will have been translated first, the Gospels before the Apocalypse and Isaiah before Leviticus. Nevertheless, we can lay down no hard and fast rules. We can only speculate from the remains that have come down to us.

There is no extant codex of the entire Old-Latin Bible. But this is hardly surprising since Latin pandects (complete Bibles) are not referred to until the seventh century when the *antiqua translatio* had been almost completely supplanted by Jerome's new version. For our knowledge of the Old-Latin text we are dependent upon manuscripts containing single books or groups of books (often fragmentary, particularly in the Old Testament), together with quotations by Latin Fathers which sometimes amount to whole chapters or more. It is only in the form of quotation that much of the evidence for the Old-Latin Old Testament has survived, yet even so, a large part still remains unattested. Among the Old Testament manuscripts may be mentioned the celebrated Lyons Heptateuch (containing about one-third of Genesis, one-half of Exodus, three-quarters of Leviticus, and the whole of Numbers, Deuteronomy, Joshua, and Judges, except the last chapter and a half of Judges), the Würzburg Palimpsest (containing not only fragments of the Pentateuch, but also portions of Hosea, Jonah, Isaiah, Jeremiah, Lamentations, Ezekiel, Daniel, and Bel and the Dragon), and the Codex Sangermanensis of the Psalms. For the New Testament the amount of available material is much greater. To give an approximate estimate, there are between fifteen and twenty manuscripts of the Gospels (mostly either mutilated or incomplete), five or six of the Acts (with which in most cases went the Catholic Epistles and Apocalypse), and four or five of St. Paul. These manuscripts vary in date between the fourth and thirteenth centuries, thus proving that the Old-Latin was still copied long after it had gone out of general use. The oldest is in all probability the Vercelli gospel codex (*a*) said to have been written by the hand of Bishop Eusebius himself, who was martyred in 371. In addition, we may note the pseudo-Augustinian *Speculum*, consisting of verses from Scripture arranged to illustrate special points of conduct, and the *Liber Comicus*, a lectionary of the Church of Toledo corresponding roughly to the Epistles and Gospels of the Anglican Book of Common Prayer, though the field from which the extracts are taken is much wider.

Sabatier's great collection of the Old-Latin manuscript fragments and patristic quotations still remains the prime store-house for the student, though it needs supplementing here and there from material discovered since the editor's day, while in the New Testament it will shortly be rendered obsolete from the manuscript point of view by Jülicher's new edition, the first part of which (St. Matthew) was published in 1938.[1]

But in spite of the fact that the authorities for the text of the Old-Latin Bible are small in number as compared with those for the Greek Bible, the variations between them are very much greater. Sometimes, indeed, they are so great as to raise acutely the question whether we have any right to speak of the Old-Latin version in the singular at all, but ought not rather to speak of a plurality of Old-Latin versions. It is mainly upon these variations that those scholars who support the theory of a plurality of versions base their case. 'It is now certain', wrote Ziegler in 1879 after comparing all the available evidence, 'that the widespread assumption of the existence of a single version cannot stand the test of serious criticism.'[2] We may also observe that in the same authority the translation of a single Greek word will vary from book to book, and vary with perfect consistency:[3] this will argue a diversity in translators. And further, this diversity in

---

[1] It is unfortunate that so far Jülicher has taken no account of the Fathers, who in some cases constitute the only available evidence.

[2] Ziegler, *Die lateinischen Bibelübersetzungen vor Hieronymus*, &c., p. 131.

[3] e.g. in the text of Tyconius ὑψηλός in Isaiah is translated by *altus* (four times out of four), but in Ezekiel by *excelsus* (both times).

translators is indicated by several passages in the Fathers such as Augustine's dictum already quoted.

Yet if there are differences between our authorities, there are also surprising agreements, which suggest an original identity. How is it possible, for instance, to explain the translation of *to hudōr tēs thalassēs* at Exod. xv. 19 by *aquas maris* in all authorities[1], the unanimous insertion of *hunc* in Deut. xxxi. 26 with the support of no Greek manuscript whatever, or the transposition 'no one looking back and putting his hand to the plough' in Luke ix. 62 against all the Greeks[2], except on the hypothesis of a single primitive version? So too *vetus editio, antiqua interpretatio,* and the other similar terms by which the Fathers commonly referred to the Old-Latin Bible, point also in the direction of unity.

This is not to maintain, however, that one man, an unknown Jerome before Jerome, made unaided a translation of both Old and New Testaments. In the early days such a feat would be as unnecessary as it was impossible, for, as explained above, the growth of the version was both haphazard and gradual. We must think of the needs of a community demanding the translation of a particular book or a group of books, and of a local scholar supplying the need. But since the needs of neighbouring communities would be roughly similar, the translation would be borrowed and copied out. Translations of other books would quickly be added, the work of other hands, while the solecisms, crudities, and ambiguities of the first translation would be 'ironed out' and improvements substituted. When a reviser was competent to do so, he would compare his manuscript with the Greek original and introduce emendations accordingly. So 'the edition' was spread abroad and underwent meanwhile perpetual

[1] Save in two bilingual Greek-Latin Psalters where *aquam maris* represents an assimilation to the Greek.
[2] Save in the bilingual Greek-Latin Codex Bezae where the Greek has doubtless been influenced by the Latin.

revision to conform to requirements and standards which varied from place to place and from age to age.

Following upon the pioneer work of Hort and Sanday, modern scholars usually divide the Old-Latin authorities into two main families—African and European. It is here that patristic quotations are especially valuable, since they serve to localize and generally to date the manuscript material. The quotations of Cyprian (*c.* 250), it has been noticed, agree very closely with the distinctive readings of the Bobbio manuscript of the Gospels (*k*), Augustine in the Pauline Epistles is frequently to be found in agreement with the Freising fragments (*r*) against all other authorities, while the manuscript *Gigas* of the Acts, written in Bohemia in the thirteenth century, gives almost exactly the same text as that used by Lucifer of Cagliari (†371). We can thus affirm that *k* preserves substantially the Gospels as read in the regions round Carthage in the middle of the third century, that *r* gives an 'African' text of the Pauline Epistles which was in circulation *c.* 400, and that *gig.*, although written so very much later, yet represents faithfully a mid-fourth-century text of 'European' type.

And characteristic of each family are certain renderings—e.g. as a translation of *phōs* the African family prefers *lumen*, the European *lux*; for *doxazein* the African prefers *clarificare*, the European *glorificare*. Such preferences are obviously useful in determining the territorial affinities of a manuscript when patristic quotations are scanty. In this way we can say that in the Lyons Heptateuch Leviticus and Numbers are more 'African' than Exodus and Deuteronomy, which, in so far as 'the history of the African translation is its Europeanisation'[1], means that, in the tradition which the manuscript represents, Exodus and Deuteronomy have been revised more systematically than the intervening books. Since few, if any, extant authorities are pure (i.e. completely unrevised), this basis of classification enables

---

[1] Hans von Soden, *Das Lateinische N.T. in Afrika zur Zeit Cyprians*, p. 354.

us to 'place' a text with very fair accuracy in the process of revision.

As to the date of the version we can only conjecture—somewhere in the second century. Though Harnack has sought to prove that Tertullian had before him the text of the Marcionite New Testament in Latin, it is in Tertullian himself at the end of the century that the first traces of a version definitely appear. Tertullian was an inexact quoter and no doubt often translated direct from the Greek, but there are several indications, sometimes almost amounting to proof, that he was conversant with an already existing Latin version[1], even if he treated it with scant respect. A little later in the Roman Novatian we can see going on 'that process by which the African version developed into the European'.[2]

The names of the translators are of course completely unknown. For place of origin there are three claimants in the field—Syria, Africa, and Rome. We have seen that the first appearance of a translation that we can check was in Africa, but the beginnings of African Christianity are obscure. One would naturally suppose that Africa was evangelized from Rome, the fountain-head of the Western Church, but there is some evidence that she received the Gospel direct from the East.[3] If this be so, it is quite probable that the missionaries brought with them from some such centre as Antioch a key to the Scriptures for the 'barbarian' Africans.[4] The same may be true of mission-

---

[1] e.g. at Ezek. xxviii. 12. Tertullian (*Marc.* ii. 10) reads *resignaculum* for ἀποσφράγισμα against all other authorities, yet Jerome (*Comm. in Ezek.* ad. loc.) says this was found in some Latin manuscripts. Again, in quoting Gal. iii. 26 Tertullian (*Marc.* v. 3) reads *fidei* for θεοῦ, which is plainly a Latin corruption of *dei*.

[2] Billen, *The Old-Latin Texts of the Heptateuch*, p. 78.

[3] Cp. Aug. *Epp.* xliii. 7, lii. 2.

[4] The points in favour of a Syrian origin are (i) the extraordinary agreements with the Old-Syriac, (ii) the agreements with the Lucianic recension of the Septuagint, which was presumably based on an existing Antiochene text, (iii) the knowledge of Hebrew and Aramaic displayed by the translators, (iv) the translation of ἡγεμόνες by *legati* in Gen. xxxvi. 15, &c., suggesting that the translators hailed from an imperial province.

aries from Rome, where the need for a translation among the uneducated masses may be held to have been pressing from the earliest times. What we have ultimately to decide is whether or not the characteristic style of the version in its most primitive form, when judged in the light of contemporary Latin (both literary, and non-literary), is so distinctively African as to prove it a native production. And the balance is in favour of Africa.

No halo of legend surrounds the rise of the Old-Latin version comparable with those which tell of Ezra's magnificent feat in rewriting the Old Testament from memory, or of the inspiration of the Seventy. In fact, the Latin translation had always to yield to the *Graeca auctoritas* of the original. This lack of inherent authority will explain the incessant revision, for it was essentially a popular version which made its way 'from the bottom upwards'.[1] Indeed, the survival of bilingual codices, whether of the parallel (i.e. with the Greek and Latin in parallel columns) or of the interlinear (i.e. with the Latin equivalent of each Greek word written above it) variety, indicates that the Latin was often little more than an 'aid' for the private reader who was weak in Greek, or for the shaky cleric in his oral paraphrase in public worship.

In these circumstances it is not surprising that a modern Latinist can speak of the version's 'jargon'.[2] Many words are transliterated direct from the Greek (e.g. *agape, baptizo, synagoga*), some of which through the version gained a permanent place in a technical Christian vocabulary. In other cases the Greek words are replaced by Latin equivalents similar in sound (e.g. *audacia* for *authadeia*), a phenomenon already observable in the Septuagint. Yet again new words are coined by formal imitation of the Greek original (e.g. *manicare* for *orthrizein*).[3]

---

[1] Turner, *The Oldest Manuscript of the Vulgate Gospels*, p. xiii.

[2] Wordsworth, *Studia Biblica*, i (1885), p. 136.

[3] Cp. Aug. *Quaestt. in Hept.* vii. 46, 'Manicabis autem Latinum verbum esse mihi non occurrit'.

The early practice seems to have been to translate word for word so as to obtain an exact interlinear version. The result was literal in the extreme—thus at Num. iii. 15, &c., the extraordinary combination of preposition and case in *ab unius mensis* is due to a slavish following of *apo mēniaiou*, while the tautology *filii in quibus non est fides in ipsis* in the Munich manuscript at Deut. xxxii. 20 goes back through the Septuagint to the Hebrew. Sometimes the Greek gender is preserved or its peculiarities gratuitously imported (e.g. at Matt. xxvi. 28 *touto gar esti to haima mou* is rendered in Codex Bezae (*d*) as *hoc est enim sanguis meus* and at Rev. viii. 9 *ktismatōn tōn en tē thalassē* appears in the Fleury Palimpsest (*h*) as *animalium quae erat in mari*). There is thus no denying the early fourth-century verdict that the style was 'commonplace and despicable . . . the work of ignorant and uncultured men'[1], and one can hardly wonder that Augustine in his youth was repelled by its inelegance.

But the stage was already set for the most decisive series of events in the whole history of the Latin Bible.

## 2. *Jerome and the Latin Bible*

Even before the baptism of Augustine Jerome had already started upon the great work which was to earn him the Church's lasting gratitude. Born about 346 at Stridon in Dalmatia he had received a good education and had travelled extensively. As a young man at Rome he had studied grammar, rhetoric, Latin, and Greek. From Rome, accompanied by an ever-increasing library, he had journeyed to Gaul, and from Gaul to Antioch. During a five-years' residence as a hermit in the Syrian desert he had received his first lessons in Hebrew from a converted Jew, and subsequently sat at the feet of the celebrated Gregory of Nazianzum in Constantinople.

[1] Arnobius, *Adv. Gentes*, i. 58.

It was only natural therefore that Pope Damasus should select Jerome on his return from the East in 382 as the scholar best qualified to produce the official revision of the Old-Latin Bible that was so sorely needed. Previous revisers had improved the version, in some cases almost beyond recognition, but the very number of revisions, the fact that they represented purely local and not official efforts, the natural mixture of these local texts which ensued, and the habitual carelessness of the copyists, had all combined to create such a state of confusion that there were 'almost as many types of text as manuscripts'. This state of confusion Jerome was commissioned to rectify. The Four Gospels appeared with commendable promptitude in 383, prefaced by a dedicatory Epistle to Damasus setting forth the occasion and scope of the undertaking. They were followed almost immediately by a revision of the Psalter, which from its use by the Churches of Rome and Italy till the latter half of the sixteenth century is known as the 'Roman' Psalter. This was Jerome's first Psalter revision. The rest of the New Testament may also have been revised at this time. But the work was interrupted by the death of the Pope at the end of 384. Jerome, who for some years had been mentioned as a possible successor, was passed over in favour of Siricius, and finding the atmosphere at Rome no longer congenial, decided to go back to the East. In the autumn of 386 he finally settled at Bethlehem and there devoted the remainder of his life to asceticism and Biblical learning.

The first work at Bethlehem was another revision of the Psalter. The text of the Roman Psalter had been speedily corrupted by the scribes, while Jerome himself was dissatisfied with the Greek text upon which it was based. Accordingly he obtained from the library at Caesarea a copy of Origen's Hexapla and with its aid produced a corrected text and a new translation dedicated to his friends Paula and Eustochium. This 'Gallican' Psalter (so-called because of its widespread popularity in Gaul) is the version of the Psalms included in the modern Vulgate.[1] Next came Job and other books revised in accordance with the same principles. But work with the Hexapla and further studies in Hebrew under a Jewish Rabbi were convincing Jerome of the inadequacy of the principles. The text of the Septuagint he was translating was in the first place far from certain, it was itself a translation and often inaccurate, while the Jews refused to admit its authority in matters of controversy. A satisfactory Latin version of the Old Testament could therefore be made only from the original Hebrew, and to produce such a version was now Jerome's main concern. Not only did he accept the Hebrew text current in his day as above suspicion, but his reverence for the *Hebraica veritas* also led him to set those books which found a place in the Hebrew canon upon a higher level than those that did not.[2] In this way he anticipated the Reformers' distinction between 'canonical' and 'apocryphal'. The books of Samuel and Kings with an explanatory Preface (the famous *Prologus Galeatus*) were ready in the new version in 391, the 'Hebrew' Psalter, the Prophets, and Job shortly afterwards, and the whole undertaking was completed in 405.

Yet although the main course of Jerome's work is clear, two points remain obscure—the extent of his revision of the Greek Old Testament, and the extent of his revision of the New.

Of the Septuagint revision only the two Psalters and Job have come down to us; but it was not confined within these limits since Prefaces to Proverbs, Ecclesiastes, the Song of Songs, and

[1] Vulgate, or 'common edition', is the name by which Jerome's new version is distinguished from the Old-Latin. Though popularized by the Council of Trent the use of *vulgata editio* in this sense cannot be traced farther back than the thirteenth century. Previously it had referred to the Septuagint and it was with this meaning that Jerome himself had employed it. His own version he styles *nostra interpretatio* or *translatio nova* and contrasts it with *antiqua interpretatio* or *vetus editio*, and his practice in this respect was followed by all writers of the early Middle Ages.

[2] e.g. The Book of Wisdom which the Church had received through the Septuagint and had always recognized as Scripture he passed over completely, and Tobit (translated from the 'Chaldee') received but perfunctory attention.

Chronicles are extant, although the translations of the books themselves are not. Did Jerome revise more than these? More than once he implies that his work embraced the whole Old Testament[1], and in a letter to Augustine complains that the greater part had been stolen from him.[2] But the absence of further Prefaces, the fact that there is no mention of his having made a previous translation in the majority of the Prefaces which accompanied the new 'Hebrew' version comparable to the references to such translations in the Prefaces to the Hebrew Job, &c., and the obvious difficulty of accomplishing such a labour in four (or at the most five) years, make it unlikely that the Septuagint revision was ever completed. Rather is it likely that Jerome, realizing its inadequacy, abandoned the project in its earlier stages in favour of the more ambitious scheme of translation direct from the Hebrew.

The situation with regard to the New Testament is more difficult. Three times in his letters Jerome speaks of his 'New Testament' translation, and there can be no doubt that the Vulgate Gospels are his work, being based upon good European Old-Latin manuscripts corrected with the aid of ancient Greek codices of the ℵ B type. The remaining books, however, constitute a problem. Not only are the Acts, Epistles, and Apocalypse provided in all Vulgate manuscripts with Prefaces from scholars other than Jerome, but the quotations from the Epistles in which his works abound are almost always nearer the Old-Latin than the accepted Vulgate version. In the commentaries on the Pauline Epistles, written, so far as we can tell, only a year or two after he is supposed to have revised their text, he seems completely to ignore his own work! Augustine, furthermore, although appreciative of the new Gospels, and to a less degree of the Vulgate Old Testament, shows no signs of acquaintance with revised Epistles. There are thus good grounds for supposing either that Jerome's activities did not extend

[1] *C. Rufin.* ii. 24, iii. 25; *Epp.* lxxi. 5, cxii. 19.     [2] *Ep.* cxxxiv. 2.

beyond the Gospels, or that if they did the results have perished. Some would regard our Vulgate Acts, Epistles, and Apocalypse as pre-Hieronymian and associate their origin with such a name as Novatian,[1] others prefer to think of a later anonymous— perhaps a band of sixth-century scholars who worked to purify the corrupted texts in the interests of Catholic orthodoxy.[2] But as the question is still *sub iudice* we shall do best to maintain the traditional view without tying ourselves down to a definite date.

In estimating the value of Jerome's labours we must distinguish between his work as a reviser and as the translator of a new version. Revisers there had been before, but not scholars of Jerome's calibre, whose interests extended far beyond improvement of style to the minutest details of orthography. Where the Old-Latin vacillated between *d̄n̄s* and *d̄m̄s* as an abbreviation of *dominus* Jerome seems definitely to have decided in favour of *d̄n̄s*; where the Old-Latin had loosely transliterated such words as *azima, Isac, sabachtani, thensaurus,* Jerome consistently corrects from the Greek to *azyma, Isaac, sabachthani, thesaurus*; and in a number of instances his knowledge of Hebrew is drawn upon.[3] However, his general practice is by no means uniform,[4] for the corrections are far more common in the earlier chapters of Matthew than in the later, in Matthew and Mark than in Luke and John, and in the Gospels than in the rest of the New Testament, until in the Apocalypse the differences between the Old-Latin and the Vulgate are reduced to a minimum. It is thus apparent that his zeal was

---

[1] So Diehl discussing the text of the Corpus Paulinum in *Z.N.T.W.* xx (1921), pp. 97–132.

[2] So Dufourcq, *De Manichaeismo apud Latinos quinto sextoque saeculo* (Paris, 1900), pp. 71 ff.

[3] e.g. *Beelzebul* (or something like it) in the Old-Latin is corrected to *Beelzebub* (= בעל/ זבוב), while *iste* at Matt. xxi. 42 becomes *istud* because Jerome realized that αὕτη in the Greek was an over-literal translation of זאת.

[4] He alters finite verbs into participles to correspond with the Greek far more often at the beginning of Matthew than he does later: the Old-Latin *pinnam* has been corrected to *pinnaculum* (Greek πτερύγιον) at Matt. iv. 5, but not at Luke iv. 9.

flagging as the work proceeded, and the little evidence available would seem to justify a similar conclusion about the Septuagint revision as well. But the translation from the Hebrew was a 'new work' such as the Gospels could never claim to be. From the Septuagint Jerome had already taken over the custom of writing lists of names in columns to facilitate reading: and now, in order to exhibit their metrical structure, he arranged the Prophets, and perhaps the Psalms and the other poetical books also, in sense lines (known technically as *cola et commata*). As a translator his aim was to produce an accurate rendering of the original, not in the studied eloquence of Cicero, but in the best idiom of popular speech. Sometimes he is over-literal, as when at Ezek. xiv. 4, 7 he translates *'ish 'ish* by *homo homo*; but such literalness is the exception and his declared purpose is to express the sense rather than to give a word-for-word translation.[1] Proper names are occasionally translated, as *Petram diuidentem* for *Sela'-ham-mahlekoth* at 1 Sam. xxiii. 28; and particularly interesting are the interpretative additions, as that explaining the Ephraimite *sibboleth* at Judges xii. 6. Whatever Jerome's contemporaries may have said to the contrary, there can be no doubt that the *translatio noua* was immeasurably superior to anything that had gone before.

### 3. *The Latin Bible after Jerome*

However, the new version was not accorded an immediate welcome. Only the Psalter and the Gospels could claim to have been put forth with official sanction; the remaining books were a private venture undertaken, for the most part, at the request of the translator's friends. His enemies alleged they were tainted with Judaism. The innate conservatism of the mass of church people, furthermore, resented what were regarded as unnecessary changes, and all were suspicious of a translation which called in question the inspiration of the Seventy. But it was

[1] *Ep.* lvii. 5: 'non verbum e verbo sed sensum exprimere de sensu.'

ultimately a case of the survival of the fittest. From about 400
onwards Augustine regularly used Jerome's Gospels. In Gaul,
Prosper of Aquitaine († *c.* 470) sings the praises of the new
version and Avitus of Vienne († 523) cites the Old-Latin for
some books and the Vulgate for others. Pope Gregory the Great
(† 604) says the Roman Church in his day used both translations
though he himself preferred the new, while in the early seventh
century Isidore of Seville can speak of the 'general use' of the
Vulgate 'by all churches everywhere as being more truthful in
substance and more perspicuous in language'. Yet the Old-
Latin died hard. The surviving manuscripts are evidence that
it was still copied for many years to come; commentators such as
Ælfric and Dunstan in the tenth century employed it as the
basis of their commentaries; and in Bohemia it lingered on till
the close of the Middle Ages.

The fifth and sixth centuries were the period of ordering.
Editors of the Old-Latin had already divided up the books into
chapters and provided headings for each chapter which were
collected and placed at the beginning of the book together with
a Preface explaining the contents of the book or the circumstances of its writing. These Prefaces and Chapter-headings
were now taken over by the editors of the Vulgate, who combined them with Jerome's Prefaces, or material of their own
composition. Usually each book was allotted one Preface and
one set of Chapter-headings, though the number of Prefaces
might be increased; and since the selection was entirely in the
hands of the editors it is not surprising that our extant manuscripts differ widely in their prefatory matter.[1] The traditional
Old-Latin order of the books themselves was approximated more
closely to our modern order, and as the process of unification

[1] Particularly interesting are the Priscillianist New Testament Prefaces, the
Donatist Chapter-headings to the Acts, and the Marcionite Prefaces to the Pauline
Epistles, which, though the work of unorthodox or schismatic pre-Vulgate editors, yet
find a place in a large number of Vulgate codices, doubtless through ignorance of
their origin. Their identification is of course due to modern scholarship.

went on the hitherto separate groups of books were formed into Testaments, and the two Testaments into a complete Bible.

The first real editor of the Vulgate Bible of whom we have definite knowledge is Cassiodorus (†c.565),[1] who after a strenuous political life retired in old age to Scyllacium in southern Italy and founded a monastery. For the instruction of his monks he not only collected all the available scriptural commentaries and himself wrote on the Psalms and Catholic Epistles, but he also composed additional Prefaces and carefully revised the Biblical text. Whereas Jerome had written only a limited number of the poetical books of the Old Testament *per cola et commata*, Cassiodorus extended the method throughout the entire Bible, and it is as a constituent volume of his library that we first hear of a Latin pandect. From now onwards 'the Bible' in western Christendom remained to all intents and purposes constant: it was made up as follows: (i) Jerome's translation of the Jewish canonical books from the Hebrew with the exception of the Psalter; (ii) Jerome's 'Gallican' Psalter translated from the Septuagint; (iii) Jerome's free translations from the 'Chaldee'— i.e. Tobit and Judith; (iv) certain Old-Latin 'ecclesiastical' books—Wisdom, Ecclesiasticus, 1 and 2 Maccabees, and Baruch; (v) Jerome's revision of the Gospels; and (vi) a slightly revised Acts, Epistles, and Apocalypse—perhaps by Jerome.

Yet although the contents of the Bible were settled by the seventh century there were several factors which made for the corruption of the text. The scribes who wrote out the new version were no more perfect than their predecessors; they still miscopied, 'improved', or added marginal comments of their own. With an astonishing lack of critical sense 'Peregrinus' had conflated the Vulgate version of certain Old Testament books with readings from Jerome's Septuagint translation. The use

---

[1] Eugippius, Abbot of Lucullanum (†533), Victor, Bishop of Capua (†554), and the shadowy 'Peregrinus' are little more than names so far as the extent of their work as editors of the Vulgate is concerned.

of Latin-Gothic bilingual manuscripts also was inimical to the preservation of the purity of the Latin, since where the two columns differed it was inevitable that assimilation should take place.[1] But the most potent source of contamination was the persistence of the Old-Latin. Whole sections of some Vulgate manuscripts are pure Old-Latin,[2] and few have escaped a modicum of Old-Latin admixture in isolated passages. Such readings are frequently due to unconscious reminiscence of the *antiqua translatio* in copying, but more often to deliberate correction from an Old-Latin manuscript. Sometimes, however, the process seems to have been reversed, especially in the New Testament, where instead of starting completely *de nouo* it was the primitive practice merely to revise the existing Old-Latin codices by inserting in them the more important of Jerome's corrections. Hence arose such incompletely corrected or 'mixed' texts as that exhibited by the Book of Armagh. For missionary work the exact text was unimportant, and so these mixed texts were spread abroad and became still more confused. England, for example, was the meeting-ground of the ancient Irish text introduced by the mission from Iona, the Roman type introduced by Augustine, and the south-Italian (or Cassiodorian) type brought back by Ceolfrid to Jarrow. A mixture of these three was in turn carried back to the continent by the English missionaries of the eighth century.

The beginning of the ninth century witnessed two major recensions—that of Alcuin, Abbot of Tours, and that of Theodulf, Bishop of Orleans. Alcuin's revision was undertaken at the request of Charlemagne and was soon paramount in Gaul. As might be expected of one born in Northumbria and educated

---

[1] The Gothic version being an independent translation from a Greek text of 'Antiochene' type naturally diverged considerably from the Latin.

[2] e.g. in the Codex Ottobonianus about 200 verses of Genesis and Exodus are Old-Latin, in the Codex Sangermanensis (Par. lat. 11553) Tobit, Judith, and Matthew are Old-Latin, in the Codex Colbertinus, the Four Gospels are Old-Latin, but the rest of the New Testament is Vulgate.

at the school at York, the basis of the text was English. Yet Alcuin made no attempt to restore the readings of Jerome: he aimed rather at the production of a text which should follow a grammatical norm and serve as a standard for monastery and school throughout the king's dominions. The Spaniard Theodulf, on the other hand, used Spanish manuscripts as his basis. In the text he put the reading he preferred and wrote the variants in the margin, attaching to each a critical sign to denote its origin.[1] He was thus quite a modern editor. But his revision was a private undertaking and had far less influence than Alcuin's.

The succeeding revisers must be passed over till we come to the thirteenth century. The scholars of the new University of Paris were now demanding, not only a standard text for quotation, but also a Bible more convenient for reference. So a text was agreed upon, the prefatory matter was considerably curtailed, and the modern division into chapters of approximately equal length was introduced by Stephen Langton. Textually the revision represents no advance upon the manuscripts in use in Paris at the time (Roger Bacon could censure it as 'for the most part horribly corrupt') since it was inspired by practical rather than scientific considerations, yet it met a real need.

The early printed editions are almost entirely dependent upon the first of them—the Bible of Forty-two Lines (1450), and this in turn derived from the Paris revision. However, with the publication of the edition of Castello in 1511 a new period opens. Editors are no longer content with reprinting the uniform Paris text, but endeavour to restore the text of Jerome with the aid of the earliest manuscripts. Pre-eminent in this respect are Ximenes, Stephanus (to whose edition of 1550 we owe our modern verse division), Hentenius, and Plantin.[2] Then in 1546 the

---

[1] *a* denoted an Alcuinian reading, *ſ* a Spanish, *ł* a reading in which both agreed, and *aij* other sources.

[2] In the later editions of this period the prefatory matter has completely disappeared.

Council of Trent decreed the use of the Vulgate exclusively and its printing *quam emendatissime*. A papal commission was entrusted with the revision and sat for more than forty years. At last in 1588 Pope Sixtus V, disturbed at the lengths to which the Commission was going, decided to relieve it of its task and undertake the revision himself. His edition appeared in May 1590, and on August 27 he died. On September 5 the College of Cardinals stopped all further sales, as many copies as possible were bought up and destroyed, and preparations made for another edition which should conform more closely to the commissioners' recommendations. This appeared in 1592, and with the names of both Sixtus V and Clement VIII on the title-page it has remained the official Bible of the Roman Church from that day to this.

Since the publication of the Clementine Bible both critical method and our knowledge of the manuscripts have considerably advanced. Of the Gospels the oldest known manuscript is the Codex Sangallensis ($\Sigma$) *c.* 500; of the whole New Testament the Codex Fuldensis (F), written by Victor of Capua in 546; and of the complete Bible the celebrated Codex Amiatinus (A), which, written at Jarrow at the beginning of the eighth century, was taken by Ceolfrid on his last journey to Rome for presentation to the Holy See. But although the number of extant Vulgate codices runs into several thousands, the vast majority are late and worthless for purposes of criticism. A critical text has to be constructed on the evidence of a select few. In grouping the manuscripts the most important criterion is of course the type of text exhibited, but the script in which a manuscript is written, the style of its art and illumination, the Prefaces and Chapter-headings which it contains, and the order in which the individual books are placed, are all helpful in varying degree. When these tests have been applied and the manuscripts which belong to the recensions from Alcuin to the invention of printing have been separated, it is found that the remainder fall into four fairly well-defined families: (i) the north-Italian; (ii) the south-Italian or Northumbrian; (iii) the Spanish; and (iv) the Irish. Characteristic of the Spanish family are frequent interpolations, marginal notes, and even legendary additions, as well as a number of Old-Latin readings which have survived. The Irish texts are still more mixed. Thus, while occasionally the Spanish or Irish families may preserve the true reading against all other authorities, it is mainly upon the two Italian groups that we must rely. The south-Italian group, through its chief representative A, gives the text of the Cassiodorian recension; and since Cassiodorus was a careful scholar, who, working less than 150 years after the death of Jerome, made use of 'ancient' codices, it is probable that this group, especially when supported by the north-Italian, is the surest guide to Jerome's text.

In 1879 John Wordsworth began work upon a critical edition of the Vulgate New Testament, and, associating with himself a young scholar, H. J. White, published the first part (St. Matthew) at Oxford in 1889. The printed text of the edition (known familiarly as 'Wordsworth and White') is based upon A; and it is furnished with a very full critical apparatus, in which, from St. Luke's Gospel onwards, Old-Latin and Greek readings are cited in addition for purposes of comparison. An *Editio Minor*, consisting of text only with a much abbreviated critical apparatus, was issued in 1911. Meanwhile in 1907 Pope Pius X determined on a revision of the whole Bible and Abbot Gasquet, President of the English Benedictines, was appointed head of the Commission to which the work was entrusted. Elaborate preparations were made, and publication started with Genesis in 1926. Slightly more manuscripts are cited than are used by the Oxford editors, though the apparatus is limited to material necessary 'to determine the text of St. Jerome'. When both editions are finished we shall need only a modern edition of the Old-Latin Old Testament to complete the collection of evidence available for the history of the Latin Bible.

## 4. *The Latin Bible and Theological Study*

For the scholar the Latin Bible is of most value in the sphere of textual criticism. But we must differentiate here between Old Testament and New, between Old-Latin and Vulgate.

The earliest complete Hebrew manuscript of the Old Testament is dated A.D. 1008 (see Chapter I), and most are of the twelfth to sixteenth centuries. Jerome's translation therefore was made from a text at least six hundred years older than our oldest manuscript, and from a text, furthermore, which was anterior to the Massoretic revision. In consequence corruptions of the Hebrew text after the year 400 can frequently be identified and the true readings restored—thus at 2 Kings xx. 13 the Vulgate rendering *laetatus est* implies an original 'And Hezekiah *was glad* (וישמח)' instead of the customary 'And Hezekiah *hearkened* (וישמע)'. But we must not be misled into supposing that wherever the Vulgate differs from our modern Hebrew text the latter is in error. The text of the Vulgate also has suffered since it left its author's hands. Jerome's declared purpose was to express the sense rather than to give a word-for-word translation; he himself introduced a number of interpretative renderings or added explanatory glosses; and he sometimes made mistakes.[1] The fact too that he worked from Hebrew manuscripts which are later than the great recension at the end of the first century A.D., and which therefore differed little from our modern Massoretic text, means that the Vulgate is far inferior to the Septuagint as a witness to the original.[2] Indeed, many of the seemingly 'original' readings which appear in the Vulgate[3] do not represent the Hebrew text of 400 at all but were

[1] The washing of the feet of the *camels* instead of the feet of the servant at Gen. xxiv. 32 (all manuscripts read *pedes camelorum* although the official Vulgate emends to *pedes eius*) is a delightful example!

[2] e.g. for the M.T. 'Syria' (ארם) at 2 Sam. viii. 13 we should almost certainly read 'Edom' (אדם). The Septuagint has rightly Ἰδουμαία, but the Vulgate with *Syria* follows the M.T.

[3] e.g. *strauitque Saul in solario et dormiuit* at 1 Sam. ix. 25.

derived by Jerome either from the Septuagint itself or from the other Greek versions, all of which he used very freely. Thus in reconstructing the primitive Hebrew text the Vulgate is of small importance as an independent authority: its main value is that together with the Syriac and the Targums it can serve to confirm, and to some extent to check, the evidence of the Septuagint.

Though the Old-Latin can still less be claimed as an independent witness to the Hebrew, it is a first-class authority for the Septuagint text from which it was translated. With the exception of a few papyrus fragments our extant manuscripts of the Septuagint are subsequent to the recensions of Origen, Hesychius, and Lucian, and most exhibit a state of confusion due to the influence of these recensions. But the Old-Latin represents the tradition of the late second and early third centuries before even the influence of the Hexapla had made itself felt. It is thus an important witness to the pre-Hexaplaric text. Moreover, the word-for-word literalness which mars it as a translation only enhances its value for purposes of textual criticism. In spite of its many crudities[1] a number of cases might be cited where the Old-Latin supports one group of Septuagint manuscripts against another,[2] and some cases where it has preserved the true reading against all Greek authority.[3] In so far as passages asterisked in Hexaplaric manuscripts of the Septuagint are always absent from the earliest form of the Old-Latin, we are provided with an external proof that the signs introduced by Origen are to be relied upon for the reconstruction of the Septuagint, while the occurrence of certain 'Lucianic' readings in the Old-Latin clearly shows that Lucian incorporated in his text some ancient elements which are unrepresented in our leading uncials. In Ecclus. xxx–xxxvi the Greek order

[1] e.g. ταφὴν ὄνου at Jer. xxii. 19 misread as ταφὴν ὃν οὐ and translated as *sepulturam quam non.*

[2] e.g. at Wisd. of Sol. v. 14 *spuma* supports ἄχνη as against πάχνη and ἀράχνη.

[3] e.g. at Ezek. xxviii. 7 *vulnerabunt* implies an original τρώσουσι rather than the στρώσουσι of all Greek manuscripts.

is strained, but the Latin (supported by the Syriac and the Armenian) transposes xxx. 25—xxxiii. 13*a* and xxxiii. 13*b*—xxxvi. 16*a*, and in so doing vastly improves the sequence. There can be little doubt that the Latin is right and that in the ancestor from which all our Greek manuscripts of Ecclesiasticus derive two leaves had exchanged places.

In the New Testament both Old-Latin and Vulgate may be treated together, though it must be remembered that the Old-Latin is much older and therefore the more valuable. Sometimes the Latin variants imply not a different Greek text from our own but only its misreading—as *momento* in *a* at Mark vii. 3 implies a misreading of πυγμῇ as στιγμῇ, or *evidens* in the Vulgate and most Old-Latins at Philem. 6 implies a misreading of ἐνεργής as ἐναργής. Probably the most striking variant which does imply a different Greek text is the Old-Latin attribution of the Magnificat to Elizabeth. For 'Mary' in the familiar 'And Mary said "My soul doth magnify . . ."' (Luke i. 46) *a b l\**, supported by the Latin translators of Irenaeus and Origen, read 'Elizabeth' against all Greek authorities and all other versions. It seems likely that Luke himself wrote ambiguously 'And she said . . .' intending a reference to Elizabeth, who is speaking immediately before the song and is mentioned as 'her' immediately afterwards, and that while the majority of scribes in supplying 'Mary' have misunderstood him, the Old-Latin alone has correctly interpreted his intention. Examples of the Latins supporting one group of Greek manuscripts against another may be found in the critical apparatus on any page of the Greek Testament, and usually it is a 'Western' reading that is so supported. Especially is this true of the Old-Latin codices which are important witnesses to this type of text. On the homogeneity and value of the 'Western' text opinions are at the moment divided, but in reaching a final verdict the evidence of the Latins will play a decisive role.

If not as valuable in other fields as it is in that of textual study, the Latin Bible nevertheless throws a most interesting light on a number of associated problems. The origin of the Diatessaron, for example, is obscure. We no longer possess the Gospel Harmony which was at one time current in the Syriac-speaking churches, and which Tatian appears to have introduced to his native land on his return from his travels in the West. It survives only in an Arabic translation, while a Greek fragment has recently come to light. But the Codex Fuldensis of the Vulgate has the Gospels arranged harmonistically in substantially, though not identically, the same order as the Arabic Diatessaron. Bishop Victor states in his preface that he found this arrangement with no name attached and supposed that it was the work of Tatian. With the order of F agrees the Dutch Harmony translated from Latin *c.* 1250, and for both we must premise an Old-Latin original. We thus have evidence that the Diatessaron circulated from quite early times in a Western as well as an Eastern form. Whether it was originally compiled in Greek or Latin, or whether Tatian was himself the author (he may possibly have found a Diatessaron already in use in Rome on his arrival), we cannot say. What does seem certain is that it was from the West that he transplanted it and gave it a Syriac dress about the year 170.

The evidence, too, that the Epistle to the Romans circulated during the second century in a 'shorter' recension is almost entirely Latin. Although no manuscript of this recension is known to exist, there can be no doubt that the Chapter-headings found in the Codex Amiatinus and kindred manuscripts were composed for an Old-Latin 'Romans' which lacked the last two chapters and probably the initiatory dedication to Rome as well. Whether Marcion subsequently abbreviated the Epistle, or whether St. Paul himself issued it in both a 'longer' and a 'shorter' form, we shall never certainly know. But the Amiatine Chapter-headings, supported by even less direct testimony, recall an almost forgotten stage in the history of the Epistle.

Again, the authorship of the Epistle to the Hebrews is still an unsolved riddle, and the claims of St. Luke have been canvassed by modern scholars. It is instructive to compare the somewhat similar suggestion found in the fourth-century Preface which accompanies the Epistle in the majority of Vulgate manuscripts:

'Why the Apostle Paul in writing this Epistle has not kept to his usual custom by mentioning either his name or the dignity of his Order requires a special explanation. The reason is this. Since he was writing as the Apostle of the Gentiles, and not as the Apostle of the Hebrews, to those who from the Circumcision had believed, he was unwilling to advance the reward of his office, being alike conscious of the Hebrews' pride and anxious to demonstrate his own humility. For in a similar way also the Apostle John in his Epistle did not obtrude his name for the same reason—namely humility. So it is said that the Apostle sent this Epistle to the Hebrews written in the Hebrew language, but that after the death of the Blessed Apostle, the Evangelist Luke produced a version in Greek, retaining both the sense and the order.'

And last, but not least, the Latin Bible is valuable as a mirror of the contemporary thought, beliefs, and practices, not only of the Church at large, but also of the individuals who translated, revised, and copied it from generation to generation. By the addition of 'for the Spirit is God [and born of God]' at John iii. 6 is evidenced the growing realization of the Divinity of the Spirit;[1] in 'the Three Heavenly Witnesses' interpolated at 1 John v. 8 is reflected a consciousness of the need for a more definite Scriptural basis for the Doctrine of the Trinity; while Jerome's own replacement of the Old-Latin *grex* (flock) at John x. 16 by *ouile* (fold) in defiance of the meaning of the Greek original[2] bears witness to an advancing ecclesiasticism, which would conceive all Christendom as obedient to the Papal sway. Through an interpolation in some manuscripts there is preserved at

[1] Cp. the alteration of *spiritui dei servimus* at Phil. iii. 3 into *spiritui* deo *servimus*.

[2] Note, however, that in his *Comm. in Ezek.* xiv. 46 Jerome implies that his Greek manuscripts read μία αὐλή instead of μία ποίμνη.

Acts viii. 37 a specimen of a primitive Baptismal Creed ('I believe that Jesus Christ is the Son of God').

The fact that the Old-Latin is the stronghold of such major interpolations into the text of the Gospels as the Signs of the Times (Matt. xvi. 2, 3) or the Chief Seats at Feasts (Matt. xx. 28) proves that in the early period a scribe would not scruple to expand if he thought a useful purpose might be served by so doing. He was to some extent an editor as well as a copyist. But as time went on the text was fixed and the copyist's liberty curtailed. Now he contented himself with such minor additions as the information given in most Vulgate manuscripts at Exod. ii. 22 that Moses had also a second son (interpolated from xviii. 4); he might reveal his ignorance and translate Tychichus at Eph. vi. 21 by *Murarius* as if it derived from *teichos* (wall); or he might miscopy the Chapter-heading to 1 Tim. v. 1 *De senioribus non increpandis* as *De* sermonibus *non increpandis*—perhaps not entirely a scribal error! These odd little whimsicalities turn the study of the Latin Bible into a really absorbing pastime. It is indeed a human document in the widest and fullest sense.

H. F. D. SPARKS.

# V

## THE ENGLISH VERSIONS (TO WYCLIF)

### SYNOPSIS

Anglo-Saxon poems on Old Testament subjects. The glossed Psalters and translated Psalms. Translation of detached passages from the Old and New Testaments. The glossed Gospels and the West Saxon version. Ælfric's biblical homilies and translation of the Hexateuch. Middle English biblical works in verse. Psalters of the fourteenth century. Beginnings of New Testament versions. The orthodox character of these. Wyclif's advocacy of a knowledge of the Bible for all. The authorship of the Wyclifite version. Nicholas of Hereford and the unknown continuator. The complete Bible in the earlier version. The production of the later version. The General Prologue to this and problems connected with it. The attribution to Purvey and the possible place of origin. Later history of this version.

### 1. Anglo-Saxon Versions

MORE than a century had elapsed from the introduction of Christianity into England by St. Augustine in 596 before there is mention of the translation of any part of the Bible into the tongue of the Saxons or Angles. The obvious reason for this was the lack of a reading public among the converts to the new faith. Those who were instrumental in spreading this, if they had an interest in the scriptures as well as a missionary zeal, were prepared to acquire a knowledge of Latin in order to read them. Outside of that small number anything but an oral literature was unknown, and such portions of the Bible story as became known to the ordinary man, whatever his rank, did so only in the form of the native poetry. The themes which the unlettered poet Cædmon learned from the scholars at Whitby he retold in alliterative verse, and whether they contain any of his work or not there have been preserved Anglo-Saxon poems which relate part of the story of Genesis and Exodus, together with those of Daniel and Judith. From these, and possibly others which have disappeared, the Anglo-Saxon who had no acquaintance with letters could learn not a little of the contents of the sacred books in a form which he could understand and appreciate. For at least four centuries such poetical renderings took the place of any attempt to produce a native version of the Bible.

During this period, however, there are several anticipations of the effort finally made to provide real translations of certain portions of Scripture. In his letter describing the last days of Bede in 735 Cuthbert gives an account of his translation of the gospel of St. John, the last chapter of which was dictated on the day of his death, and the last verse only a few moments before he expired. Of this version no trace has been preserved, nor is there any record of any other book of Scripture being similarly translated during the next century and a half. An approach towards a translation was, however, clearly felt to be useful in the case of a book so constantly in use as the Psalter, and this was provided by inserting Anglo-Saxon glosses between the lines of the Latin text. The earliest example of this now preserved is found in the Vespasian Psalter (MS. Cotton Vesp. A. 1) dating from about 825. Ten other copies similarly glossed are of later dates down to the second half of the twelfth century. While such glosses give a rendering of every word of the text, they naturally follow the Latin order instead of the Anglo-Saxon, and would therefore require to be rearranged, and frequently made more idiomatic, before they could serve as an independent translation. They were indeed not intended to take the place of the Latin text, but to help towards the understanding of it.

According to William of Malmesbury a real attempt to translate the Psalter was made by King Alfred, who, however, died when he had 'barely finished the first part'. Whether this can be identified with the prose version of the first fifty psalms in the bilingual Paris Psalter is a question on which scholars are not in agreement. The earliest specimen of continuous translation, however, is in the introductory section of the Laws of

Alfred, covering portions of chapters xx–xxiii of Exodus, together with a short passage from the Acts of the Apostles. Alfred's version of Gregory's *Pastoral Care* also contains renderings of a considerable number of biblical citations from both the Old and New Testaments. These, as well as the more numerous passages from Ælfric's homilies, are collected and arranged in Professor A. S. Cook's *Biblical Quotations in Old English Prose Writers*, and considerable additions to them can be made from other sources. Such renderings, however, are purely incidental, and give no indication of any demand for, or desire to produce, independent translations of any part of the Bible.

Next to the Psalter, the Gospels, from their regular use in the Church service, formed the most important portion of the Bible, and with these also an interlinear gloss preceded a real translation. Two manuscripts thus glossed have been preserved. One of these is the famous Lindisfarne Gospels, written in that island about 700, in which the Northumbrian gloss was inserted in the neighbourhood of Durham about 950. This is largely the source of the North Mercian gloss in the Rushworth Gospels, made somewhat later at Harewood in Yorkshire. Both of these are of great value as specimens of the northern dialects of Anglo-Saxon, and of interest as indicating the level of Latin learning in the tenth century, at least in the north of England.

About the same time, however, or not much later, a complete translation of the four gospels into West Saxon was made by one or more scholars who had a sound knowledge of Latin and a good command of the native tongue. Slight differences in style and vocabulary suggest that Matthew is the work of one translator, Mark and Luke of another, and John of a third. However this may be, the translation throughout is correct, with a clear and simple style, and evidently obtained some circulation in the eleventh century, as four copies from that period have been preserved. Two later manuscripts (from the second half of the twelfth century) show a continued interest in the version and are valuable on linguistic grounds, as they exhibit a considerable change in the form of the words—a fact which implies a desire to have the translation in a readable form. These gospels were one of the first Anglo-Saxon books to be printed, an edition by John Foxe appearing as early as 1571 with the title 'The Gospels of the fower Euangelistes, translated in the olde Saxons tyme out of Latin into the vulgare toung of the Saxons'.

The production of this scholarly translation was no doubt one of the results of the revival of learning in the south of England which began under Benedictine influence about 960. In the field of Anglo-Saxon literature this culminated in the work of the Abbot Ælfric, whose extensive writings included translations of considerable portions of the Old Testament. In two series of homilies, completed in 992, he had already translated numerous passages from various parts of the Bible, including the New Testament, and in one homily had given a free version of the narrative portion of the book of Job. In the preface to each of these series, both in Latin and in Anglo-Saxon, he expressly states that his aim was to convey religious instruction in plain and simple English for the benefit of those who knew no Latin. Yet he evidently did this with some misgivings, for in an epilogue to the second series he writes, 'I say now that I never henceforth will turn gospel or gospel-expositions from Latin into English. If any one will turn more, then will I pray him, for the love of God, that he set his book apart from the two books that we have turned, we trust through God's direction.' This reluctance to use the native tongue to an unlimited extent for religious subjects is still more clearly expressed in the preface to a third set of homilies, mainly based on the lives of those saints, 'whom not the vulgar, but the monks, honour by special services. I do not promise, however, to write very many in this tongue, lest peradventure the pearls of Christ be had in disrespect.' To excuse himself he adds, 'Let it not be considered as a fault in me that I turn sacred narrative into our own tongue, since the request of many of the faithful shall clear me in this matter, particularly that of the earl Æthelwerd and of my friend Æthelmer.' From this passage, and that cited below, it is clear that it was in response to a demand from the laity, rather than from a natural impulse, that Ælfric occupies so important a place among the early English translators of the Bible.

In this third series one homily is a free rendering of part of the books of the Kings, mainly relating to the prophet Elijah, while another gives at considerable length the story of the Maccabees. Other homilies by Ælfric, not included in this collection, are based on the books of Judges, Esther, and Judith. In addition to these free renderings, which are in an alliterative and metrical prose peculiar to himself, Ælfric undertook direct translation from the Old Testament at the request of the same Æthelwerd already mentioned, who had asked him to translate the book of Genesis only as far as the account of Isaac, 'seeing that some other person had rendered it for you from that point to the end.' At the end of the preface giving this explanation Ælfric adds: 'Now I protest that I neither dare nor will translate any book hereafter from Latin into English.' This positive declaration was apparently made about 997, but in a short general account of the Old and New Testaments, possibly dating some ten or twelve years later, Ælfric admits or claims having also translated from the remaining four books of the Pentateuch, as well as that of Joshua, which 'I also formerly translated into English for Æthelwerd'. In this treatise he no longer expresses any doubts as to the propriety of translating the Scriptures into English, having probably by this time been convinced that such translations did no harm to those who were anxious to have them in a language they could understand.

Ælfric's translation of the Hexateuch is by no means complete. Even in Genesis, which is most fully rendered, there are considerable omissions, and these are increasingly numerous and extensive in the remaining books. Of Joshua only the first eleven chapters are at all adequately represented. The passages omitted are mainly those which would have had little interest for the Anglo-Saxon reader, especially lists of names of persons and places, the description of the tabernacle and the priestly vestments, and the greater part of the Levitical precepts, but also include those poetical passages which presented difficulties of style and meaning. Such portions as are translated show the mastery of a simple and easy style which is characteristic of all Ælfric's work and gave his writings a wide circulation. How far these biblical versions shared in this it is impossible to say. Of the manuscripts which have been preserved only two contain all the Pentateuch and Joshua; the others are limited both in number and contents. The preservation of these two manuscripts, however, is almost certainly due to their handsome appearance, both being beautifully written and one of them profusely illustrated. Ordinary copies of the whole or of separate books, however numerous, had much less chance of surviving, especially if in the possession of laymen, whose possessions were exposed to so many chances of destruction during the eleventh and following centuries.

In Ælfric's translations from the Hexateuch, together with his homilies on Judges, the Books of Kings, Job, Esther, Judith, and the Maccabees, the Anglo-Saxon reader had access to a very considerable portion of the Old Testament. The Psalms were also available in the prose version of the first fifty and the metrical rendering of the remainder, but it is uncertain whether these were at all well known, as they are preserved only in a single manuscript. From the New Testament only the four gospels had been specially translated, the Acts, Epistles, and Apocalypse being represented only by occasional citations in the homilies. There was also a version, preserved only in part, of the Apocryphal Gospel of Nicodemus.

The possibility that these partial translations might in time have led to an Anglo-Saxon version of the entire Bible was destroyed by the complete breakdown of Anglo-Saxon learning and literature in the period immediately following upon that of Ælfric. All that the succeeding generations could do was to copy the work of their predecessors, to an extent which indicates that for the next century and a half there was a lively interest in such biblical matter as was available in the native tongue.

## 2. *Middle English Versions*

The new literature which begins again in the Middle English period, towards the close of the twelfth century, includes a large proportion of religious works in prose and verse, but presents no effort to provide direct translations of any continuous portion of the Bible. The homilies continue to render short passages, usually from the gospels, and from the middle of the thirteenth century onwards there are metrical versions either of special books, as the *Genesis and Exodus*, or of Jewish and Christian history, as the voluminous *Cursor Mundi*, by which the laity could learn the contents, though not the exact words, of a number of books both of the Old and New Testaments. Collectively, these works could supply inquiring minds with much of the knowledge which was fully accessible only to those who could read the Vulgate. The authors of both the works above mentioned state expressly that their aim in composing them was to instruct those who could read or understand no language but their native English.

The earliest book of the Bible to be represented by a full translation in Middle English was not unnaturally the Psalter, of which a northern metrical version was made about 1300. The language of this is curiously archaic in some respects, and other peculiarities of style must have made many of the verses obscure to those who did not know the Latin original. Somewhat later there are prose versions, one in a midland dialect and another in a northern; the latter, by the hermit Richard Rolle of Hampole, was accompanied by an elaborate commentary and held its place as a standard work for more than a century.

Next to the psalms, the New Testament received attention. There is abundant evidence that this was the result of a growing interest, throughout the latter part of the fourteenth century, in the study of the evangelical scriptures on the part of the laity and the less learned among the clergy and members of the religious orders. To a great extent this interest centred round the teaching of Wyclif and his followers, or of those holding similar views and latterly classed with them under the general name of Lollards, but it was also clearly existent among individuals of a less advanced type, who simply desired to increase their religious knowledge without any idea of straying outside the pale of orthodoxy. In response to this interest various portions of the New Testament were translated, and have been preserved in a few copies, the small number being no doubt an indication that such versions were not widely circulated. All of these are anonymous, their exact date is uncertain, and the place of origin can be inferred only from the dialect in which they appear to have been originally written; on this ground the majority can be with some certainty assigned to the north midland area, although the south is also represented. Some are simple translations of the text; in others the translation is accompanied by a gloss or commentary, also usually translated from a Latin source or sources. The latter method is employed in a version of the gospels of Matthew, Mark, and Luke, the commentary here being mainly taken from Peter Lombard, and in one of the Pauline Epistles with occasional short glosses. Of plain translations there are versions of Matthew, of Acts, and of the Pauline and Catholic Epistles, the latter in two versions, one of which is southern. The older and better of two complete copies of these texts is preceded by a prologue in which the translator presents himself as complying with the request of a 'brother' and 'sister' to teach them the vital truths of religion. This he does with some reluctance, 'since we are now so far fallen away from Christ's law, that if I would answer to thy askings, I must perhaps suffer death'. It has been assumed that this implies a possible penalty for the mere fact of translating, but this is not definitely borne out by the context, and may equally well refer to the danger of expressing strong views on the corruption of the Church. The absence of all comment on the matter of the Epistles would thus be in accordance with a desire to keep within the bounds of safety.

While there is apparently no direct connexion between them, these contributions by various hands evidently represent a movement towards producing an English version of the New Testament which was not intended to have anything but an orthodox character, even although it might be accompanied by outspoken criticism of the state of religion and the Church. Thus in the commentary on the Gospels 'there seems to be nothing of controversial doctrine, and few traces of party feeling. At the same time the writer does not conceal his opinion of the too general corruption and worldliness of the clergy, especially those of the higher orders.' The writer, in fact, is careful to clear himself of any charge against the character of his commentary. 'In the which out-drawing I set not of my head nor of mine own fantasy, but as I found in other expositors. In the which I suppose certainly there is nothing set against the faith, against the heal of soul, or else against the worship of God.'

Sound orthodoxy, however, even if unaccompanied by criticism, was not sufficient in the eyes of many churchmen to justify the practice of making the scriptures accessible to everyone. Vernacular versions of the Bible had never been regarded with favour by the Church, and there was all the more reason to disapprove of them when they might be cited in support of views which were becoming dangerously popular at this time. This attitude explains the tendency of translators to excuse themselves, after the manner of Ælfric, by pleading that they are only complying with the requests or suggestions of others. Thus the same writer cited above explains: 'This work some time I was stirred to begin of one that I suppose verily was God's servant, and oft times prayed me this work to begin, because of the profit to men's souls if they had the rule of the Gospel in English', and adds, 'and greatly in this doing I was comforted of other God's servants divers.' Even among those who did not entirely object to translations, however, opinions were divided with regard to the extent to which they might properly be used. The author of the *Chastising of God's Children*, while approving in general of English versions of the Psalter or Gospels or even of the whole Bible, as aids to devotion, considered it a mistake to use them exclusively and neglect the Latin original. Evidently there were some who would have drawn a clear distinction between those who would use the English only as an aid to the understanding of the Vulgate, and those who were entirely unacquainted with Latin and thus unable to make certain that they were understanding the text correctly. The danger would be all the greater if such readers were inclined to think for themselves, and to reason from the bare wording of the text without knowing the manner in which it was understood by the Church and its doctors. There was also the possibility that such versions might be deliberately made to foster unorthodox views by the choice of words or by actual comment.

### 3. *The Wyclifite Versions*

The divergence of opinion on this point was brought to a clear issue by the openly expressed views of Wyclif on the authority and use of the scriptures. Not only did he maintain that these were a sufficient rule of life without any human additions, but he asserted the right of every man, cleric or lay, to study them for himself, even though he might be deficient in learning. 'No man', he insisted, 'was so rude a scholar but that he might learn the words of the Gospel according to his simplicity.' God had ordained three estates, the clergy, the knights, and the commons, but in each of these 'it helpeth Christian men to study the Gospel in that tongue in which they know best Christ's sentence'. The position thus taken up by Wyclif, and unreservedly adopted by his adherents, inevitably led to two results—a demand for an English version of the Bible, so that its contents might be open to all, and the association of any such version with the unorthodox views of those who produced it or made use of it. That the idea of making a study of the Bible as a whole possible for all classes owed its origin to Wyclif is evident not only from his own writings, but from the charges brought against him by his opponents, who without qualification or associating him with any other person attribute to him not only the devising of a full translation of Scripture but the actual execution of the task. So firmly was this view held by his contemporaries and their immediate successors that no other name is mentioned by them in this connexion.

When the translations which have been attributed to Wyclif are examined, however, obvious difficulties arise in the way of accepting his direct share in any part or form of the work. That his name is not attached to the text in any manuscript of the only version to which he could possibly have contributed is not conclusive, nor even significant, since there would be obvious reasons for omitting it. The real difficulty lies in the absence of any clear point of contact between this version and Wyclif's other writings. If a set of sermons on the Sunday Gospels is correctly ascribed to him, and the English is his own, it is note-worthy that the translation of the passages occurring in these is entirely different from that given in the New Testament. No conclusive argument can, however, be based upon this, there being considerable uncertainty with regard to Wyclif's English works as a whole. In the absence of other evidence, internal or external, the only safe point of departure for a study of the origins

of the two 'Wyclifite' versions which have to be clearly distinguished is the portion of the Old Testament from the
beginning of Genesis to Baruch iii. 20, where it ends with the
first words of that verse.[1] The original manuscript of this
(Bodley 959) was obviously dictated to five different scribes,
each of whom uses different dialectal forms, evidently varying
between what he heard and what he was accustomed to write.
That the manuscript is the original is proved by the fact
that 'in numerous instances the renderings have been changed
during the progress of the sentence; sometimes an erasure has
been made, as soon as the word was written, or even before it
was completed, and another expression has been substituted.'
An immediate copy of this (MS. Douce 369) ends with the
same words, and adds *Explicit translacionem Nicholay de herford.*
There is no reason to doubt the correctness of this attribution,
since Nicholas of Hereford was for a time one of Wyclif's most
zealous adherents, but the suggestion that his work was interrupted by his citation before the Blackfriars synod in May 1382,
and his subsequent absence from the country, can be regarded
only as highly probable, though it has commonly been accepted
as providing a definite date for this portion of the Old Testament.
Whatever the precise date, or the reason (other than scribal) for
stopping at this point, it is clear that Hereford went no farther
in the work, since the remainder of the Old Testament, and the
whole of the New, present a vocabulary and dialect differing
from his. For the personality of the continuator there is no
evidence; the suggestion that Wyclif himself took up the un-
finished work is very improbable when the state of his health
and the extent of his writings during the last two years of his life
are considered. It is possible that the New Testament, on account of its evangelical importance, had already been translated,

---

[1] The reason for breaking off just at this point is clearly that the scribe, having
finished the second column on the recto of a leaf, waited for the ink to dry before
turning it over and beginning to write on the other side.

and that the same hand which did this then filled in the gap left by Hereford. Whatever the precise stages were, the result was the production of a complete version of the Bible, including the apocryphal books, in a form so close to the Latin that it approaches to a word-for-word translation. In all probability this was not due to any lack of skill, or to a defective appreciation of style, on the part of the translators, but was intended to facilitate comparison of the English with the Latin. This method of translation, which also appears in other works of the period, had the disadvantage of producing un-English sentences, frequently rendering the meaning obscure, and it must soon have been evident that a version more in accordance with the genius of the language, and consequently more intelligible, was a real necessity for the ordinary reader.

As to when the work of producing a new version of this kind was begun, and how long it took to complete it, there is no direct evidence. Certain facts can, however, be gleaned from the so-called 'General Prologue', specially written to accompany the text, but usually omitted in copies of this, clearly because of the outspoken Lollardism which runs through it. In one chapter, containing a strong denunciation of the vices prevailing in the University of Oxford, there is mention of 'the last parliament', which can most naturally be explained as referring to that of January 1395. From this it may be inferred that the Prologue, or at least this section of it, was written between that date and the next parliament of February 1397. It does not follow, however, that the whole of the new version was complete, or was allowed to get into circulation, at that time. A somewhat later date is certainly suggested by the lack of any manuscript of the whole work earlier than 1408 (a dated copy); those which can be placed earlier (immediately before or after 1400) contain only certain portions, mainly the gospels or epistles or the entire New Testament. Of the Prologue itself no extant copy is earlier than 1400, the majority being considerably later (1420–40). This absence of early copies increases the difficulty of assigning a definite date to the work as a whole.

The fifteenth and concluding chapter of the Prologue gives valuable information regarding the design and method of the translation. After emphasizing the value of the scriptures and the popular demand for a knowledge of them, since even the unlearned people 'crieth after holy writ, to know it and keep it, with great cost and peril of their life', the translator continues in these words.

'For these reasons and other . . . a simple creature hath translated the bible out of Latin into English. First, this simple creature had much travail, with divers fellows and helpers, to gather many old bibles, and other doctors, and common glosses, and to make one Latin bible some deal true; and then to study it of the new, the text with the gloss, and other doctors, as he might get, and specially Lira on the Old Testament, that helped full much in this work; the third time to counsel with old grammarians, and old divines, of hard words, and hard sentences, how they might best be understood and translated; the fourth time to translate as clearly as he could to the sentence, and to have many good fellows and cunning at the correcting of the translation.'

On this follows an explanation of the principles of translation which he had adopted in order to produce an English version which should be a correct rendering of the Latin, and at the same time as clear as this, or even clearer. If anyone could make corrections, he prays him to do so,

'but look that he examine truly his Latin bible, for no doubt he shall find full many bibles in Latin full false, if he look many, namely new; and the common Latin bibles have more need to be corrected, as many as I have seen in my life, than hath the English bible late translated.'

This incidental reference, strangely enough, is the only indication given by the writer that he was acquainted with the earlier Wyclifite version, although it is clear that this was to a great extent the basis of his own. That he was actually working from it is evident in itself from a comparison of the two texts, and is further proved by the fact that three manuscripts, although of late date, represent an intermediate stage in which the readings of the earlier version are frequently retained instead of being altered as in the usual copies. The reason why no open statement was made of indebtedness to the earlier translation was beyond doubt to avoid drawing attention to the connexion between the new version and one which was definitely associated with noted adherents of Wyclif, if not with the reformer himself.

For the same reason, in all probability, neither in the prologue nor in copies of the text is the name of the translator given, and it can be supplied only by inference. The commonly accepted view that he is to be identified with John Purvey, the close associate of Wyclif in his later years, rests upon a number of correspondences between passages in the Prologue and views known to have been held by Purvey; these are also clearly expressed in similar language in contemporary writings which may with equal probability be assigned to his pen. Down to his recantation in 1401 Purvey was certainly the most steadfast advocate of Lollard views, and was as likely as any other to have continued in this way the work begun by Hereford. At the same time there is no contemporary suggestion that a new and complete translation, more likely to come into general use than its predecessor, was one of the things which could be laid to his charge. If the revision was really his, the fact was either generally unknown, or was judiciously ignored in the face of an obvious demand for an English version. It is distinctly remarkable that of the numerous copies of this version almost all are of later date than the constitutions passed at Oxford by the Council held there in November 1407, the seventh of which prohibited anyone from translating on his own authority any book of Scripture into English, or reading any book, booklet, or treatise of this nature 'composed in the time of the said John Wycliffe or later', unless the translation had been approved by the diocesan or by a provincial council. The number of copies still extant of both the earlier and later versions, and the possession of some of them by priests, nuns, and laymen (including two kings), suggest that such approval was not infrequently given, although other evidence makes it clear that to many of the ecclesiastical authorities the mere fact of owning and reading any part of the Bible in English afforded presumptive evidence of heresy. The probability is that the attitude towards the use of an English bible, and the possibility of possessing one without risk, varied greatly at different times and in different parts of the country, and that in giving permission account was taken of the rank and character of the person.

Apart from the question of Purvey's authorship, some of the particulars already cited from the Prologue are possible indications of the provenance of the work. The translator's first task was, with much trouble and assisted by various 'fellows and helpers', to collect 'many old bibles' and expository works, and by the collation and study of these to form a reliable Latin text. When the translation had been made from this, it was also submitted to 'many good and cunning fellows' in order to be improved by their corrections. It is unlikely that so large a collection of books could have been made, and so many helpers found, anywhere else than in a seat of learning such as the University of Oxford, which was already associated with the work of Wyclif and Hereford. The presumption in favour of this is strengthened by the special mention of Oxford in the twelfth chapter of the Prologue. There is also evidence that the question whether English versions of the scriptures were permissible or not was being discussed at Oxford in the early years of the fifteenth century, and that a doctor of the University was prepared to maintain publicly the affirmative, and to support it by 'many powerful arguments'. The reports (in Latin and in

English) of this formal debate have on internal evidence been attributed to Purvey; if not by him, they are by one who fully shared his views. In view of this academic support of the lawfulness of translation, it is possible that the new version, though originating with one man, had behind it the authority of a number of Oxford scholars who had assisted the translator in his work, without necessarily sharing the opinions on controversial matters which are expressed so freely in the Prologue. A knowledge of this may well have been the factor which exempted the version from ecclesiastical censure and enabled it to come into general use.

The second Wyclifite version maintained its position throughout the fifteenth century, and the first quarter of the sixteenth, as the English Bible most commonly in use. Even a scholar like Reginald Pecock, himself capable of translating from the Vulgate, regularly copied from it when he had occasion to cite any passage of scripture. No better version was available until the appearance of Tyndale's New Testament in 1525, his Pentateuch in 1529, and Coverdale's Bible in 1535, after which it must almost immediately have gone out of use. Not long before the first of these appeared, the tradition of the Wyclifite text came to a close with the copy of the New Testament, in the later version, made by a Scot, Murdoch Nisbet, who at the same time adapted it to his own dialect; unfortunately this remained the only attempt to produce a Scottish version of any portion of the Bible.

Even if the conditions for the production of an English Bible from an early date had been more favourable, the radical changes in the form of the language during the centuries from the tenth to the sixteenth would from time to time have made it necessary to subject it to a complete revision, or replace it by an entirely new translation. The Anglo-Saxon renderings of the Hexateuch, the Psalms, and the New Testament could not have been read by any ordinary person after 1200 without considerable changes, nor could any new version made at that date have remained in use in the fourteenth century. Of the Wyclifite versions even the second would have required much rewriting to adapt it for use in the early part of the sixteenth century, and it was necessarily discarded altogether when the Hebrew and Greek originals became the basis of translation instead of the Latin Vulgate. With this change came a decisive break in the history of the English Bible.

W. A. CRAIGIE.

# VI

# THE SIXTEENTH-CENTURY ENGLISH
# VERSIONS

## SYNOPSIS

The manuscript period and the Wyclifite legacy. John Purvey's system of revision. Objections to the translation of the Bible. Archbishop Arundel's prohibition. The age of printing. Caxton's failure to print a Bible. William Tindale. His life in England. His work in Germany. The Cologne fragment 1525. Work interrupted and flight to Worms. The first complete New Testament 1526. Distribution of the translation. Importation into England. Translation of the Pentateuch from the Hebrew 1530. Translation of Jonah 1531. Martyrdom at Vilvorde 1536. Relation to Luther's Testament. Quality of the translation. Revisions. The Old Testament. Treatment of the Hebrew. Epistles of the Old Testament. Miles Coverdale and his Bible. Matthew's Bible of 1537. Its constitution and importance for later revisions. Tindale's section from Joshua to Chronicles. The Great Bible. Authorization and prohibitions. Taverner's revision. Sir John Cheke's fragment. The Protestant exiles and the Geneva versions. Whittingham's New Testament 1557. The Geneva Bible of 1560. Beza's influence on the Geneva New Testament. Return to the 'Hebrue veritie' in the Old Testament. Influence of the French versions. The Geneva division into verses and its previous history. The Bishops' Bible. Its relation to the Great Bible and Geneva. The Roman Catholic Bible. The Rhemes New Testament and the Douai Old Testament. Latin style of the Rhemes Testament. Influence on the Authorized Version.

> *Q. Elizabeth*:
> An English Bible, thanks my good Lord Maior,
> You of our bodie and our soule have care,
> This is the Iewell that we still love best,
> This was our solace when we were distrest,
> This booke that hath so long conceald it selfe,
> So long shut up, so long hid; now Lords see,
> We here unclaspe, for ever it is free.
> T. Heywood, *If you know not me, You know no bodie*, 1605.

## 1. *The Wyclifite Legacy*

THE Wyclifite translations are the end of an old story. They belong to the manuscript age, to the fourteenth century; they are contemporary with Chaucer's *Troilus and Criseyde* and the *Canterbury Tales*, and share their popularity. The surviving manuscripts of the Bible outnumber those of Chaucer many times. At least 170 were used by the learned editors in 1850. Copies once in royal, ducal, and private possession abound. Prohibition and mockery joined in attack, 'what spiryt makith idiotis hardi to translate now the bible into English, sithen the foure greete doctouris dursten nevere do this?' It was a manuscript age and an age of indirect translation through the Vulgate, yet a triumph of endeavour and completeness. There is a wild barbaric quality about Purvey's *Song of Songs* recalling the grim scenery and the long-haired goats of the Judean hills; there is many an inevitable phrase common to Purvey and Tindale: 'a tinkling cymbal', 'the pinnacle of the temple', and 'not one i or titel'. Tindale, even while working close to the original tongues, must have had the familiar English phrases ringing in his ears, and their fidelity to the Vulgate was no hindrance to fidelity towards the Hebrew and the Greek, for in the main the Vulgate was quite a respectable translation. Moreover, Purvey's revision, while toning down some of the earlier bluntness of physical description, and bringing English smoothness of sentence-construction to the Latinate literalness, was a remarkable and prophetic example of the committee method of the Authorized Version, 'with diverse felawis and helperis' establishing a basic Latin text, conferring with grammarians and commentators, translating with 'manie gode felawis and kunnynge at the correcting of the translacioun'. Purvey also enhanced his version of the Vulgate with valuable assistance from 'Lire', the influential Nicolas of Lyra whose literal translation of Rashi's commentary preserved the Rabbinical traditions of the Middle Ages into modern times. Luther's use of the same guidance was notorious:

> Si Lyra non lyrasset
> Lutherus non saltasset.

Until the work of Tindale superseded them, the Wyclifite versions maintained a tenacious popularity with all classes of

Englishmen. Sacrifices of blood and money testified to the hunger for the Bible in English. The equivalent of £40 was paid for a copy, and according to Foxe 'some gave a load of hay for a few chapters of St. James or of St. Paul in English'. 'In this way', said Knyghton the Chronicler, 'the Gospel pearl is cast abroad, and trodden under foot of swine; that which was before precious both to clergy and laity is rendered as it were the common jest of both. The jewel of the Church is turned into the common sport of the people, and what was hitherto the principal gift of the clergy and divines is made for ever common to the laity.' A fascinating document concerning early translations and their vicissitudes is 'A compendious olde treatyse shewynge howe that we ought to have ye scripture in Englysshe', printed from an early manuscript in 1530, probably at the instance of Tindale himself, since it bears the fictitious imprint of Luther's publisher, Hans Luft, which was used by Tindale for his Pentateuch and his controversial writings. It tells of an attempt in the House of Lords in 1391 'to adnulle yᵉ byble that tyme translated into englyshe', and of its frustration by John of Gaunt. 'The duke of lancaster Jhon answered therto ryght sharply saying this sentence. We wyll not be refuse of all other nacions. For sythe they have godes lawe which is yᵉ lawe of ower belefe in ther owne langage, we wyll have owres in englysshe who so ever saye naye. And this he affermyd with a greate othe.' What Parliament would not sanction was done by the Provincial Council at Oxford in July 1408 at the instigation of Archbishop Arundel, and promulgated at St. Paul's in January 1409. The grim and comprehensive prohibition ordained

'that no one henceforth on his own authority translate any text of Holy Scripture into the English or other language, by way of a book, pamphlet, or tract, and that no book, pamphlet, or tract of this kind be read, either already recently composed in the time of the said John Wyclif, or since then, or that may in future be composed, in part or in whole, publicly or privily, under pain of the greater excommunication, until the translation itself shall have been approved by the diocesan of the place or if need be by a provincial council.'

Yet of the 150 copies of Purvey's revision, the larger portion was written after Arundel's prohibition.

One puzzle emerges. The fifteenth century saw the introduction of printing into England, and Caxton as a good business man followed the public taste closely. He supplied popular poetry, popular fiction, and translations, yet issued no edition of the work which was rivalling and even replacing the romances in popular esteem. His contribution to Bible publication was the selection of *The Golden Legend*. It has been suggested that the expense may have deterred him, as well as the obsolete language, to which it may be answered that expense did not prevent the printing of so bulky a work as Malory's *Morte D'Arthur*, and that neither problems of language nor of cost held up the issue of Chaucer's poetry. Had Caxton printed the Wyclifite version our whole Bible history would have been different, but as Sir Thomas More suggested in 1529, 'I thynk ther wyll no prynter lyghtely be so hote to put eny byble in prent at hys own charge, wherof the losse sholde lye hole in hys owne necke, and than hange uppon a doutfull tryall whyther the fyrst copy of hys translacyon was made before Wyclyffys dayes or synnys. For yf yt were made synnys, yt must be approved byfore the pryntynge.'

## 2. *Tindale*

The story of the printed English Bible begins in the sixteenth century, and it is a crowded history. From Tindale's New Testament of 1525 to the Authorized Version of 1611 is only 86 years, and an unbroken line of revision joins the two great works. William Tindale (alias Hutchins), the Father of the English Bible, was born about 1494 in Gloucestershire, took his B.A. at Oxford in 1512 and his M.A. in 1515, and passed on to Cambridge where he may have studied Greek. Later, by the admission of his enemy, More, he was 'well known, before he went over the sea, for a man of right good living, studious and well learned in scripture, and in divers places in England was very well liked, and did great good with preaching'. For some time he was tutor to the children of Sir John Walsh at Little Sodbury, some fifteen miles from Bristol, where, according to Foxe, he used to preach 'in the common place called Saint Austen's Green' (now College Green, in front of the Cathedral). Foxe also gives circumstantial details of discussion at table concerning Luther and Erasmus, of the routing of certain divines with chapter and verse of scripture, and of the translation of Erasmus's *Enchiridion militis Christiani.* His dangerous views led to an accusation of heresy before the chancellor, 'And, indeed, when I came before the chancellor, he threatened me grievously, and reviled me, and rated me as though I had been a dog.' About 1523 he left the country-side in disgust, 'I was so turmoiled in the country where I was, that I could no longer there dwell . . . because the priests of the country be unlearned . . . and therefore, (because they are thus unlearned thought I,) when they come together to the ale-house, which is their preaching place, they affirm that my sayings are heresy.'

He had conceived the idea of translating the New Testament into English, 'And even in the bishop of London's house I intended to have done it.' He brought as credential 'an oration of Isocrates, which I had translated out of Greek into English'. According to Tindale, Bishop Tunstall was a 'still Saturn that seldom speaketh, but walketh up and down all day musing, a ducking hypocrite, made to dissemble', and by his own confession 'God hath made me evil-favoured in this world and without grace in the sight of men, speechless and rude, dull and slow-witted'. 'God saw that I was beguiled . . . therefore he got me no favour in my lord's sight.' The Bishop fobbed him off, 'My lord answered me, his house was full; he had more than he could well find; and advised me to seek in London, where he said I could not lack a service. And so in London I abode almost a year.' His disillusion with England was complete, and he concluded 'not only that there was no room in my lord of London's palace to translate the new Testament, but also that there was no place to do it in all England'. He found a patron, Humphrey Monmouth, a rich cloth merchant, who had heard him preach,

'I took him into my house half a year; and there he lived like a good priest, as me thought. He studied most part of the day and of the night at his book, and he would eat but sodden meat by his good will, nor drink but small single beer. I never saw him wear linen about him in the space he was with me. I did promise him £10 sterling to pray for my father and mother their souls and all christian souls; I did pay it him when he made his exchange to Hamburg. Afterwards he got of some other men £10 sterling more, the which he left with me; and within a year after, he sent for his £10 to me from Hamburg; and thither I sent it him.'

Later, for fear of compromising Tindale, Monmouth burnt his sermons, and, far greater loss, his letters from Germany.

In 1524 Tindale reached Germany. It is suggested that he matriculated on 27 May, 1524, at Wittenberg, where Melanchthon was Professor of Greek, and Aurogallus Professor of Hebrew. Luther was there part of the time, and contemporaries persistently allege that they met. He continued the translation begun, most probably, in Monmouth's house, while Henry VIII was urging the Dukes of Saxony not to allow Luther's translation of the Bible to be printed, and, because 'I could not do alone without one both to write and to help me to compare the texts together', employed Friar William Roye as amanuensis. By the autumn of 1525 Tindale and Roye had moved to Cologne, and thence we have our first detailed information concerning the difficulty of printing the Bible in translation. There one Johann Dobneck or Cochlaeus, described by Roye as

> A little praty foolish poad
> More venomous than any toad,

while engaged in attacking Luther and Lutheranism, made the acquaintance of Peter Quentel the printer and Arnold Birckman, a bookseller doing a large trade with England, and learned that there were 'two English apostates who had been for some time at Wittenberg . . . learned, skilled in languages . . . whom, however, he could never see nor speak to', who were out to corrupt England to Lutheranism 'by means of the New Testament of Luther which they had translated into English'. He invited the printers to his inn, 'and after he had warmed them with wine' discovered that an edition of six thousand copies had been ordered, that the printers had been afraid to risk so large an edition, 'that there were in the press three thousand copies of the Lutheran New Testament translated into English, and that in the order of the quires they had got as far as letter K', and that the venture was being financed by English merchants. Cochlaeus betrayed them to the authorities, a search was made, and the printers forbidden to go on with the work. 'The two English heretics, hastily taking with them the printed quires, made their escape by boat up the Rhine to Worms, where the people were all mad on Luther, in order that there by another printer they might complete the work.' Henry VIII and Wolsey were warned by letter 'so that they might take diligent precaution at all the English ports to prevent these pernicious wares being imported'. Rumours spread throughout Europe. Edward Lee, afterwards Archbishop of York, wrote to Henry VIII from Bordeaux in December 1525, 'I ame certainlie enformed as I passed in this contree, that an englishman your subject at the sollicitacion and instaunce of Luther, with whome he is, hathe translated the newe testament in to Englishe, and within four

dayes entendethe to arrive with the same emprinted in England.'
A unique fragment of this quarto edition, consisting of signatures
A–H only (Matt. i–xxii), without title-page, but demonstrably
from the press of Peter Quentel, was discovered in 1834, and is
now in the British Museum.

In Worms the printing was completed in the early part of
1526, and a fortunate entry in a diary of that year gives us
valuable testimony concerning Tindale's linguistic equipment.
Spalatinus, secretary to the Elector of Saxony, had dined at
Speyer on 11 August with Buschius, one of the authors of
*Epistolae Obscurorum Virorum*, an alert and not easily fooled
humanist:

'Buschius told us that 6000 copies of the New Testament have been
printed in English. The work has been translated by an Englishman,
staying there with two other Britons, who is so skilful in seven tongues,
Hebrew, Greek, Latin, Italian, Spanish, English, French, that which-
ever he speaks, you would think it his native tongue. For the English
(said Buschius) despite the opposition and unwillingness of the King,
so long after the gospel, that they affirm that they will buy the
New Testament, even if they have to give 100.000 pieces of money
for it.'

Two copies of the Worms octavo survive, one in the Baptist
College at Bristol, perfect except for the title-page, and one
imperfect at beginning and end, in the library of St. Paul's
Cathedral. It can be shown to be from the press of Peter
Schoeffer of Worms. Copies had reached England early in
1526, and despite Wolsey's attempts in 1526 and 1527 to crush
the traffic, a flourishing and organized trade sprang up, with
distributing agencies ready to deal with the supplies brought over
by agents from the Continent. The translation was pirated
several times in Holland, and soon replaced the old Wyclifite
versions in public esteem. A portrait of one of these agents at
work survives in the deposition of John Tyball, who in April
1528 said, 'That at Mychaelmasse last past was twelve monethe',

he went to Friar Robert Barnes, then under detention at Austin Friars, to buy a New Testament in English:

'This respondent shewyd the Friar Barnes of certayne old bookes that they had; as of four Evangelists, and certayne epistles of Peter and Poule in Englishe. Which bookes the sayd Friar did little regard, and made a twyte of it, and sayd, a poynt for them, for they be not to be regarded toward the new printed Testament in Englishe; for it is of more cleaner Englishe. And then the sayd Friar Barnes delyvered to them the sayd New Testament in Englishe; for which they payd three shillings and two pence [nearly £2], and desyred them, that they wold kepe it close. And after the delyvrance of the sayd New Testament to them, the Friar Barnes dyd lyken the New Testament in Latin to a cymball tynnklyng and brasse sowndyng.'

The New Testament translated from the Greek and printed, Tindale turned his attention to the Hebrew of the Old Testament. Rumours of the new venture began to spread. Wolsey's news from his Antwerp agent, Hackett, in May 1527, 'I am informed that there be some Englishmen, Luther his disciples, that begins in Dutchland to translate the bible into English', is the first notice we have of the beginning of the work. In 1528 Tindale, writing from his new experience, said that Greek and Hebrew go more easily into English than into Latin, and the completion of the work is circumstantially and plausibly described by Foxe in his second edition, of 1570, possibly from the information of Coverdale himself, who was in London from 1559 to 1568.

'At what time Tindall had translated the fift booke of Moises called *Deuteronomium*, minding to Printe the same at Hamborough, hee sailed thereward: where by the way upon the coast of Holland, he suffred shipwracke, by the which he loste all his bookes, wrytings and copies, and so was compelled to begin al againe a new, to his hinderance and doubling of his labors. Thus having lost by that ship, both money, his copies and time, he came in an other ship to Hamborough, where at his appoyntment M. Coverdale taried for him, and helped hym in the translating the whole 5 bookes of Moises, from Easter till December, in the house of a worshipfull widowe, Maistres Margaret van Emmerson. Anno 1529. a greate sweating sicknesse being the same time in the Towne. So having dispatched his businesse at Hamborough, he returned afterward to Antwerpe againe.'

The Pentateuch was published, 'Printed by me Hans Lufft, in Marborow in the land of Hesse, [but really by John Hoochstraten in Antwerp] January 17, 1530', and copies were in England by the summer of that year. The 'pestilent glosses' in the margins of the New Testament complained of by Henry VIII in his letter to Luther were multiplied in the margin of the Pentateuch. 'To blesse a man's neyboure is to praye for him, and to wissh him good: and not to wagge ii fingers over him' (Gen. xxiv. 60). In 1531 appeared his version of 'Jonah', rediscovered only in 1861; in 1534 he issued a revised 'Genesis', and a revised New Testament with his name on the title-page for the first time: 'The Newe Testament dylygently corrected and compared with the Greke By Willyam Tindale: and fynesshed in the yere of oure Lord God. A.M.D. & XXXIIII in the moneth of November.' A special copy on vellum, presented to Anne Boleyn, is in the British Museum. A final edition 'The New Testament yet once again corrected by Willyam Tindale' appeared in 1535, was chosen as the text of Matthew's composite Bible, and is the basis of all later revisions, the main source, through many vicissitudes, of the Authorized Version.

After many attempts to entrap him, and to lure him back to England, Tindale was betrayed in May 1535, and imprisoned in the Castle of Vilvorde. A pathetic letter from prison is preserved, written in Latin.

'I suffer greatly from cold in the head, and am afflicted by a perpetual catarrh, which is much increased in this cell . . . My overcoat is worn out; my shirts are also worn out. . . . And I ask to be allowed to have a lamp in the evening; it is indeed wearisome sitting alone in the dark. But most of all I beg and beseech your clemency to be urgent with the commissary, that he will kindly permit me to have my Hebrew Bible,

Hebrew Grammar, and Hebrew Dictionary, that I may pass the time in that study.'

He was degraded and condemned into the hands of the secular power, and in Foxe's words, 'He was brought forth to the place of execution, was there tied to the stake, and then strangled first by the hangman, and afterwards with fire consumed, in the morning at the town of Vilvorde, A.D. 1536; crying thus at the stake with a fervent zeal and a loud voice: Lord, open the King of England's eyes.' He left behind in manuscript a translation of the Old Testament from Joshua to the end of Chronicles.

Tindale's personal history is of vital significance towards the understanding of the historical atmosphere in which our first modern Bible translations emerged. His purpose was clearly expressed: 'which thing only moved me to translate the new Testament. Because I had perceived by experience, how that it was impossible to establish the lay-people in any truth, except the scripture were plainly laid before their eyes in their mother tongue, that they might see the process, order, and meaning of the text.' Of the original texts of the Bible, the Hebrew of the Pentateuch was printed at Bologna in 1482 and the complete Hebrew Bible at Soncino in 1488. The Greek of the New Testament was first published in the epoch-making edition of Erasmus in 1516, which, with its new Latin version, challenged the infallibility of the Vulgate text from which all vernacular translations before Luther and Tindale had been made. Luther's German translation appeared in 1522, Tindale's version in 1525, and it was inevitable that contemporaries should regard the latter as an English rendering of the former. Sir Thomas More in his 'Dialogue' is explicit in condemning 'That boke . . . which who so calleth the new testament calleth it by a wrong name, except, they wyl call yt Tyndals testament or Luther's testament'. Colour is given to the accusation by the fact that, so far as externals go, Tindale, in the Cologne fragment, adopts Luther's order of the books, takes over a substantial part of his prefaces and prologues, uses nearly all his marginal references, errors included, adopts his paragraph division, and incorporates a large number of his marginal comments, 'certayne prefaces, and other pestylent gloses in the margentes', as Henry VIII wrote to Luther, 'for the advauncement and settyng forth of his abhomynable heresyes'. It is only in the outer trappings that Tindale is so closely indebted to Luther. In the translation itself he maintains an independence which is as remarkable as it is successful. He works close to Erasmus's Greek text, using the second edition of 1519 and the third of 1522, he is much indebted to Erasmus's Latin rendering, takes full advantage of Luther's example in three different editions, and is not un-mindful of the Vulgate text. He shows every possible variety of agreement and disagreement with his originals and secondary sources, but there is an overwhelming preponderance of render-ings in which the Greek alone remains his authority against the seductions of Luther and the Vulgate. In Eph. iv. 29 he has 'Let no *filthy communicacion* procede out of your mouthes' preferring Erasmus's *sermo spurcus* against the *sermo malus* of the Vulgate and 'naughtie speache' of the Rhemes version. In Matt. vi. 11 he has 'oure dayly breede' against the Vulgate *superstantialem*, and in Luke ii. 14 'and unto men rejoysynge' instead of the Vulgate *hominibus bonae voluntatis*. On the other hand, he accepts from the Vulgate Matt. iv. 5, 'a pynacle of the temple', John xiv. 2, 'In my fathers housse are many mansions', and 1 Cor. xiii. 1, 'tinckling cymbal'. This not infrequent coincidence with the Vulgate has brought an unjustified accusation of dependence on Wyclif. He is led into error by Luther in translating Col. ii. 23, after *selbsterwählte Geist-lichkeit* as 'chosen holynes and humblenes'. He accepts John xix. 17 from Luther, 'the place of deed mens sculles', and intro-duces 'Shewbread' from Luther's *Schaubrot*. He sins by the constant omission of the Greek connecting particles. He interpolates and paraphrases and fills in ellipses, as Acts x.

'a captayne of the soudiers of Italy', John xiii. 8, 'Thou shalt not wesshe my fete *while the worlde stondeth*'. He has anachronistic and homely renderings: Acts xx. 6, 'we sayled awaye from Philippos after the ester holydayes'; Matt. xxvii. 62, 'The nexte daye that foloweth good frydaye'; 1 Cor. xvi. 8, 'I will tary at Ephesus untyll whitsontyde'; Rev. i. 10, 'on a Sondaye'; Acts xiv. 13, 'brought oxen and garlondes unto the churche porche'; 1 Pet. v. 3, 'lordes over the parisshes' [margin: 'the greke hath lottes']; Heb. xii. 16, 'Esau, which for one breakfast solde his right' ('birthright', 1534); Luke ii. 3, 'his awne shyre toune' (later softened to 'his awne citie'). There is frequently a raciness of expression not permitted to survive in the long process of revision after his day: Matt. iv. 24, 'divers diseases and gripinges'; Matt. vi. 7, 'bable not moche' for 'use not vaine repetitions' (A.V.); Matt. xiv. 20, 'they gadered up of the gobbetes that remayned'; Mark vi. 40, 'And they sate downe here a rowe and there a rowe'; 2 Cor. ii. 17, 'For we are not as many are which choppe and chaunge with the worde of God'. It is a pity, in 2 Thess. i. 3, to have lost 'and every one of you swymmeth in love toward another betwene youre selves' in exchange for the colder 'and the charitie of every one of you al towards each other aboundeth' (A.V.), and in 1 Tim. vi. 4, 'wasteth his braynes aboute questions', for 'doting about questions', in 1 Cor. iv. 9, 'For we are made a gazing stock unto the world' (for 'spectacle'), and in 2 Pet. ii. 13, 'they make a mockyngstoke feastynge togedder in their deceavable wayes'.

Tindale's single-handed struggle and his scrupulous desire to render the original in homeliest clarity are seen in the successive revisions of 1526, 1534, and 1535, 'I had no man to counterfet, nether was holpe with englysshe of eny that had interpreted the same or soche lyke thinge in the Scripture before tyme.' He was aware of its imperfections, 'Count it as a thynge not havynge his full shape . . . even as a thing begunne rather then fynesshed', knew his special fault of long-winded rendering, 'and will enfoarce to brynge to compendeousnes that which is nowe translated at the lengthe'. This bringing to compendiousness is seen in such a revision in Matt. vi. 34, from

'Care not therefore for the daye foloynge. For the daye foloynge shall care ffor yt sylfe. Eche dayes trouble ys sufficient for the same silfe day' (1526)

to

'Care not then for the morow, but let the morow care for it selfe: for the daye present hath ever ynough of his awne trouble' (1534).

Some of the changes between 1526 and 1534 are noteworthy: John xviii. 28, 'that they myght eate Pascha' becomes 'that they myght eate the paschall lambe'; Acts. viii. 34, 'and the gelded man sayde', becomes 'and the chamberlayne (A.V. eunuch) sayde'; Matt. xxvi. 17, 'The fyrst daye of unlevended breed' becomes 'The fyrst daye of swete breed'; Acts xxii. 25, 'an under captayne' becomes 'the centurion'.

Two peculiarities, one of vocabulary, and one of style, remain to be considered. In the rendering of technical terms Tindale wilfully chose tendencious and heretical words obnoxious to such orthodox Catholics as Sir Thomas More: 'congregation' instead of 'church' for *ecclesia*, 'senior' for *presbyter* (changed later to 'elder'), 'repentance' instead of 'penance', 'favour' instead of 'grace', 'love' instead of 'charity', 'image' instead of 'idol'. In a desire for variety of style he translates the same word or phrase in a multitude of ways: for 'it came to pass' he has also 'followed', 'fortuned', 'chanced', 'happened'; he alternates between 'similitude' and 'parable', between 'hypocrites' and 'dissemblers', between 'conquer' and 'overcome', and in an extreme example, Rom. xiii. 7, his very padding has a chameleon quality:

'Geve to every man therfore his *duetie*: Tribute to whom tribute *belongeth*: Custome to whom custome is *due*: feare to whom feare *belongeth*: Honoure to whom honoure *pertayneth*.'

Tindale's honesty, sincerity, and scrupulous integrity, his simple directness, his magical simplicity of phrase, his modest music, have given an authority to his wording that has imposed itself on all later versions. With all the tinkering to which the New Testament has been subject, Tindale's version is still the basis in phrasing, rendering, vocabulary, rhythm, and often in music as well. Nine-tenths of the Authorized New Testament is still Tindale, and the best is still his. It is true that many of the most familiar phrases and rhythms are not his, but to him we owe, Matt. xx. 12, 'The burden and heat of the day'; Luke i. 78, 'tender mercy'; Luke xii. 19, 'eat, drink and be merry'; Rom. xiii. 1, 'The powers that be'; Matt. xxvi. 73, 'thy speech bewrayeth thee'; Acts. xvii. 28, 'in him we live, move and have our being'; Luke xv. 23, 'fatted calf'; Matt. vi. 24, 'Ye cannot serve God and Mammon'; Matt. vi. 28, 'Consider the lilies of the field, how they grow'; and John iv. 44, 'A prophet hath no honour in his own country'.

For the Old Testament the problem is somewhat different. Tindale had the Hebrew original, Luther's German version (his Pentateuch as early as 1523, the Historical books in 1524, a separate publication of Jonah (in 1526) which seems to have attracted him specially), the Vulgate, and a remarkable literal translation by Sanctes Pagninus into Latin in 1528. The first complete Hebrew Bible of 1488 was provided with points and accents, a great aid to the beginner. The first Rabbinic Bible appeared at Venice in 1517, and the edition with full Massoretic equipment by Jacob Ben Chayyim in 1524–5. Hebrew grammars were available, Pellican's in 1503, Reuchlin's, complete with dictionary, in 1506. S. Münster's in 1525 was followed by his Chaldee grammar in 1527. Pagninus issued an important dictionary in 1529. The Complutensian Polyglot of 1520 was equipped with a Latin translation of the *Targum* of Onkelos, with a Hebrew grammar and a dictionary of the Hebrew and Chaldee texts. There were also available by 1520 two editions of the Septuagint Greek translation, though whether he used this is not entirely clear. The study of Hebrew was eagerly pursued in Germany, and even Erasmus felt compelled to learn it.

Insufficient attention has been paid to Tindale's translations from the Old Testament, and his Pentateuch of 1530 has often been passed over in silence, or with bare mention, but as a contribution to English Protestant civilization it is even more significant than the New Testament, and a greater physical achievement. He could have contented himself with the New Testament, and still have earned the gratitude of the Christian world, but his sense of the continuity of the Bible demanded satisfaction in a translation of the text that lay behind the New Testament, and affected it both in substance and idiom. In his preface to his New Testament revision of 1534 he says: 'If ought seme chaunged, or not all to gether agreynge with the Greke, let the fynder of the faute consider the Hebrue Phrase or maner of speche lefte in the greke wordes,' and speaks in detail of the 'comen usage' of Hebrew grammar. One of the most remarkable passages in his New Testament rendering, one which makes us regret that he never gave us a version of the Psalter, is that quotation in Heb. i. 10, from Ps. cii, which is preserved almost verbatim in the Authorized Version:

'And thou Lorde in the begynninge hast layde the foundacion of the erth. And the hevens are the workes of thy handes. They shall perisshe, but thou shalt endure. They all shall wexe olde as doth a garment: and as a vesture shalt thou chaunge them, and they shalbe chaunged. But thou art the same [all wayes, 1534], and thy yeres shall not fayle.'

Coverdale in his Bible of 1535 gave this as his version of the Psalm, syllable by syllable, although the Hebrew original demanded some small adjustments. Tindale's conviction of the suitability of English as a vehicle for translation from the Hebrew

M

is recorded, in the midst of his task, in *The Obedience of a Christian Man* in 1528:

'They say it cannot be translated into our tongue it is so rude. It is not so rude as they are false liars.'

'For the Greek tongue agreeth more with the English than with the Latin. And the properties of the Hebrew tongue agreeth a thousand times more with the English than with the Latin. The manner of speaking is both one; so that in a thousand places thou needest not but to translate it into the English, word for word, when thou must seek a compass in the Latin, and yet shalt have much work to translate it well favouredly, so that it have the same grace and sweetness, sense and pure understanding with it in the Latin, as it hath in the Hebrew. A thousand parts better may it be translated into the English than into the Latin. This threatening and forbidding the lay people to read the scripture is not for the love of your souls ... inasmuch as they permit and suffer you to read Robin Hood, and Bevis of Hampton, Hercules, Hector and Troilus, with a thousand Histories and fables of love and wantonness and of ribaudry as filthy as heart can think, to corrupt the minds of youth.'

This outburst may have been occasioned by reading the newly published word for word translation by Pagninus, whose Latin was rightly accused of speaking with a strong Hebrew accent, but whose literal fidelity was a great help to Tindale and all the translators of the sixteenth century.

How Tindale learnt Hebrew, and exactly when, we do not know. There was a great Jewish community at Worms, one of the oldest in Germany. Hebrew was not difficult to learn. Reuchlin's pioneer work was available. Erasmus wrote to Reuchlin in 1516, 'I was visiting lately a very old Carthusian Monastery at S. Omer. The Prior of that house, by reading your books, without any other instructor, had obtained a very considerable acquaintance with Hebrew'. Wherever he learnt it, there is no question, despite persistent ignorant assertions to the contrary, that Tindale knew Hebrew and translated the Pentateuch as directly from the Hebrew as he had translated the New Testament from the Greek. As early as 1526 Buschius testified to his knowledge of Hebrew. He discusses scores of Hebrew words, is concerned with Hebrew constructions and Hebrew customs, is aware of the special force of the complicated Hebrew conjugations, the intensive forms above all, takes account of subtleties and plays upon words, and very frequently corrects his helpers in these matters.

Tindale's 'Pentateuch' was provocative in a score of ways. He seized the occasion to emphasize the contradiction between Church practice and the laws of God. His glosses to this end were indeed 'pestilent': Num. xxiii. 8, 'How shall I curse whom God curseth not' [margin: The pope can tell howe]; Deut. xxiii. 18, 'Nether brynge the hyre of an whore nor the pryce of a dogge in to the housse of the Lorde thy God' [margin: The pope will take tribute of them yet and bisshopes, and abottes desire no better tenants];[1] Gen. xxiv. 60, 'And they blessed Rebecca' [margin: To blesse a mans neyboure is to praye for him, and to wissh him good: and not to wagge ii fingers over him]; Lev. xxi. 5, 'They shall make them no baldnesse apon their heedes' [margin: Of the hethen preastes therefore toke our prelates the ensample of their balde pates]; Deut. xi. 19, 'Talke of them (my wordes) when thou syttest in thyne housse' [margin: talke of robynhod say our prelates]. Against the *Shema*, the Jewish confession of faith in Deut. vi. 4 ff., 'Heare Israel', &c., he has the passionate protest in the margin, 'It is heresy with us for a laye man to loke of Gods worde or to reade it'. He speakes of 'oure domme God the Pope', and Joye, his sometime helper, follows his example in saying that 'Pharao fygured our blodye Bisshops of Rome'.

It was, however, not for its marginal doctrine, but chiefly as an object lesson in musical rendering, independence, and accuracy, that Tindale's version dominated the course of Bible

---

[1] The tactful 'Matthew' tones this down to 'There be now many that desyre no beter rentes'.

translation for over four centuries. He allowed no version to dictate to him, although he leaned heavily on some. Luther's prestige and Luther's literary power swayed him constantly. Where the Vulgate and Pagninus had *gigantes* in Gen. vi. 4, Tindale leaned towards Luther in 'There were tirantes in the world in thos days'; in Exod. xv. 26, 'I am the Lorde thy surgione' comes from Luther's *der HERR deyn artzt.* He deserted in Gen. iii. 24 the picturesque flaming sword of the Vulgate, and kept, with Luther, 'a naked swerde, movynge in and out'. His independence of Luther, and knowledge of Hebrew shows itself in his marginal note to Exod. xii. 3, 'That I here cal a shepe is in Ebrue a worde indifferent to a shepe and a gotte both', where Luther has no note. He makes his own mistakes. In Exod. xv. 4 Luther, the Vulgate, and Pagninus all have the correct 'chosen captains'. Tindale prefers 'His jolye captaynes'. In Deut. xxxii. 11 he deserts Luther and the Vulgate in favour of the Hebrew, 'As an egle that stereth upp hyr nest and flotereth over hyr yonge'. In Deut. xxxi. 16, 'go a whorynge after straunge goddes' which has survived in popular speech despite later revisions, comes verbally from Luther. He takes over incorrect chapter divisions from Luther as against the Hebrew and Pagninus. He follows Luther in translating from the Vulgate a passage in Exod. ii. 22 not in the Hebrew or in Pagninus, and of course omitted in the Genevan and Authorized Versions later.

An important matter is the rendering of personal and proper names. He is aware of difficulties, and an interesting comment in his notes on certain Hebrew words gives his view:

'Cain; so it is wreten in Hebrue. Not withstondynge whether we call him Cain or Caim it maketh no matter, so we understand the meaninge. Every lande hath his maner, that we call Ihonn the welchemen call Evan: the douch hance. Soch difference is betwene the Ebrue, greke and laten: and that maketh them that translate out of the ebrue varye in names from them that translate out of laten or greke.'

He takes 'Heva' from Luther for 'Eve', but 'Moses' from the
Vulgate *Moyses* as against the Hebrew *moshé* and Luther's
*Mosé*; he has the older English 'Noe' where Luther has the
more phonetic *Noah*; where Luther has *Girgosi* Tindale keeps
'Girgosi', where Luther has *Gergesiter* Tindale has 'Gergesites'.
A fascinating chapter could be made of the varied treatment of
certain place-names:

e.g. Num. xxiii. 7:

| | |
|---|---|
| *Heb. and A.V.* from Aram. | *Tin.* from Mesopotamia. |
| *Vulg. and Pagn.* de Aram. | *Cov.* Syria. |
| *Luther.* aus Sirien. | *Bishops' Bible.* Mesopotamia. |

2 Kings xix. 9:

| | |
|---|---|
| *Tin.* (Matt.). Tirhakah, king of the black mores. | *Luther.* Thirhaka dem konige der Moren. |
| *Hebrew.* King of Cush. | *Cov.* Taracha the kynge of the Morians. |
| *Vulg.* Theráca rege Aethiopiae. | |
| *Pagn.* Tirhacah rege Chus. | *Geneva.* Tirhakah king of Ethiopia (or blackemores). |

and Num. xii. 1:

*Tin.* . . . Moses, because of his wife of Inde which he had taken: for
he had taken to wyfe one of India.
*Vulg. and Pagn.* uxorem Aethiopissam.
*Luther.* der morynnen . . . damit das er eyne morynne zum weybe . . .
*Cov.* because of his wife the Morian which he had taken.
[1]*A.V.* the Ethiopian woman [margin: or Cushite (from the
Hebrew)].

In the light of scholarly wrangles during the centuries it is
of importance to note that Tindale was responsible for the
introduction of the word 'Jehovah' into English. Where he got
it we do not know. Luther knows nothing of the word, which

---

[1] The following parallel may not be without interest to students of Shakespeare.
    Lyly, *Euphues.* A faire pearle in a Murrian's eare.
    Shakes., *Romeo and Juliet.* Like a rich jewel in an Ethiop's ear.

is first heard of in the thirteenth century in Raymond Martin, and was put into circulation by Peter Galatinus in 1518. According to Drusius in his *Tetragrammaton* of 1604, 'Ante illum inauditum fuit nomen Iehova'. Tindale uses the word and suggests an explanation of it in a note.

Tindale also published, as an appendix to his 1534 New Testament, 'The Epistles taken oute of the Old Testament which are red in the church after the use of Salsburye upon certen dayes of the yere', being passages from the Pentateuch, Kings, Esther, Isaiah, Jeremiah, and Ezekiel, certain passages from the Apocrypha, the great passage from Prov. xxxi on the virtuous woman, and a fragment from Chapter II of the Song of Songs which must be quoted for comparison with later versions.

'I am the floure of the felde, and lylyes of the valeyes. As the lylye amonge the thornes so is my love amonge the daughters. As the appletre amonge the trees of the wood so is my beloved amonge the sonnes, in his shadow was my desyer to syt, for his frute was swete to my mouth. He brought me into his wyne seller: and his behaver to mewarde was lovely. Beholde my beloved sayde to me: up and hast my love, my dove, my bewtefull and come, for now is wynter gone and rayne departed and past. The floures apere in oure contre and the tyme is come to cut the vynes. The voyce of the turtle dove is harde in oure lande. The fygge tre hath brought forth hir fygges, and the vyne blossoms geve a savoure. Up hast my love, my dove, in the holes of the rocke and secret places of the walles. Shew me thy face and let me here thy voyce, for thy voyce is swete and thy fassyon bewtifull.'

The special qualities of Tindale's Old Testament renderings are (i) his fidelity to the force of the Hebrew construction, e.g. Gen. iii. 4, 'Then said the serpent unto the woman: *Tush, ye shall not die*'; (ii) his bold invention or adoption of words and compounds which persisted in English vocabulary, as 'scapegoat', 'passover', 'mercy seat',[1] 'wave brest', and 'heve

---

[1] From Luther's *Gnadenstuhl*, through 'mercy stool' in the Cologne prologue, 'seate of grace' in Heb. ix. 5, and 'seat of mercy' in Rom. iii. 25.

shulder'; (iii) his native vigour of phrasing, not always followed in later versions, Lev. xiii. 45, 'the leper . . . shall have his mouth muffled', Deut. xxviii. 50 'a herde favoured nacion', Deut. xviii. 14, 'makers of dysemall dayes and bruterars'; (iv) his sense of poetry which, despite his hatred of the 'poetry' of More and of the filthy Ovid, forced him to accept Luther's example, and, for the first time in English, to print the Hebrew poetry of Miriam's song in Exod. xv, and Moses' song in Deut. xxxii as verse, in separate lines, as previously he had distinguished the Magnificat, the Benedictus, and Nunc Dimittis in Luke; (v) his introduction of Hebraisms into the texture of English prose, as 'to die the death', 'The Lord's anointed', 'the gate of heaven', 'in the sweat of thy face', 'a man after his own heart', 'the living God', 'sick unto death', 'flowing with milk and honey', 'to fall by the sword', 'as the Lord liveth', 'uncircumcised lips', 'a stranger in a strange land', 'to bring the head down to the grave', 'apple of his eye'.

### 3. *Coverdale*

The second of the two great pioneers was Miles Coverdale (1488–1568), a gentler and less intransigent personality. 'I am but a private man, and am obedient unto the higher powers.' In 1526 Tindale's New Testament had been prohibited by the Bishop of London. In 1530 Henry VIII proclaimed it unnecessary for the 'Scripture to be in the englisshe tonge, and in the handes of the commen people', but 'his highnes entendeth to provyde, that the holy scripture shalbe by great lerned and catholyke persones, translated in to the englisshe tonge, if it shall then seeme to his grace convenient so to be'. It was widely believed that the King was really in favour of publishing an authorized translation. Towards the end of the year Latimer reminded him of his promise. In December 1534 Convocation at Canterbury, under the new Archbishop Cranmer, petitioned the King to decree 'that the holy scripture shall be translated into the vulgar English tongue by certain upright and learned men to be named by the said most illustrious King and be meted out and delivered to the people for their instruction'. Emboldened by these indications of tolerance, and encouraged by Thomas Cromwell, Coverdale undertook a complete translation of the Bible, and published it in 1535, without authority, but with a dedication to Henry VIII, in which he took the King at his word, 'Josias commanded straytly (as your grace doth) that the lawe of God shulde be redde and taught unto all the people'.

The general belief is that the volume was printed by Froschover at Zürich. This is the first complete Bible printed in English, and the first complete translation from the pen of one single author. In his dedication Coverdale asserts, 'I have nether wrested nor altered so much as one worde for the mayntenaunce of any maner of secte: but have with a cleare conscience purely and faythfully translated this out of fyve sundry inter-preters, havyng only the manyfest trueth of the scripture before myne eyes'. That this is written with one eye on the fires of Smithfield and Vilvorde is shown by a significant bibliographical fact. The original title-page, printed in the same type as the Bible, reads, 'faithfully and truly translated out of Douche [i.e. German] and Latyn into Englishe'. No more dangerous confession of Lutheran heresy could be devised than this, and later copies on sale in England had in English black-letter merely, 'faythfully translated into Englyshe'. That this omission was not, as so often suggested, due to the exigencies of typography to accommodate two more lines of a quotation from Joshua, is proved by the omission of the compromising Lutheran implication from Coverdale's prologue. In the 1535 edition he has 'to helpe me herein, I have had sondrye translacions, not onely in latyn, but also of the Douche interpreters: whom (because of theyr syngular gyftes and speciall diligence in the Bible) I have ben the more glad to folowe for the most parte, accordynge as I was requyred.' In the 1550 edition this is

altered to 'not only in latyn *but also in other lāguages: whom,* &c.'
He alludes to Tindale's labours, 'the mynistracyon of other that
biganne it afore . . . the adversitie of them, which were not
onely of rype knowledge, but wolde also with all theyr hertes
have perfourmed that they bygganne, yf they had not had
impediment'.

Coverdale's Bible is divided into six parts: Genesis to Deutero-
nomion; Iosua to Hester; Iob to Salomon's Balettes; The
Prophets, from Esay to Malachy; The Apocrypha, i.e. 'The
bokes and treatises which amonge the fathers of olde are not
rekened to be of like authoritie with the other bokes of the
byble, nether are they founde in the Canon of the Hebrue';
the New Testament. The Hebrew order of the Old Testament
is rejected in favour of the Vulgate, and the New Testament
arrangement of Luther is preferred to that of Erasmus. The
order of the Apocrypha is that followed in the Authorized
Version. Baruch is placed among the prophets 'next unto
Jeremy, because he was his scrybe, and in his tyme', Samuel 1
and 2 are called Kings 1 and 2, Nehemiah is called 'The seconde
boke of Esdras', Hebrews and James come between 3 John and
Jude. The Prayer of Manasses, not found in the Zürich
edition, is not included. The translation, in accordance with
the claim on the title-page, is out of 'Douche and Latyn' with the
aid of the 'fyve sundry interpreters', i.e. two Latin (the Vulgate
and Pagninus), two German (Luther and the German-Swiss of
Zwingli and Leo Juda), and his chief English guide, the published Pentateuch, Jonah and the New Testament of Tindale.
For the remainder of the Old Testament and the Apocrypha his
English rendering is his own, guided closely by the Zürich
Bible, which is largely independent of Luther. His knowledge
of German was excellent, he had preached in it in Germany,
and whenever he departs from Tindale's renderings it is nearly
always at the command of Luther and of Zürich. Although, in
a letter to Cromwell from Paris in 1538, referring to the Great

Bible, he seems to claim a knowledge of Hebrew, 'We follow . . . a standing text of the Hebrew, with the interpretation of the Chaldee and the Greek', there is no clear evidence that he translated from it, and every assertion to the contrary can be disproved by comparison with the Zürich version, from which he borrows even such details as parentheses and chapter headings. His merit lies in the felicity of his phrasing, the increasing smoothness and music of the sentence rather than in any new accuracy. He is readable to a degree, and even when he differs markedly from the Authorized Version there is a clarity worth noting. In Isa. iii. 16–24 he has no English forerunner.

'Seinge the doughters of Sion are become so proude, and come in with stretched out neckes, and with vayne wanton eyes: seinge they come in trippinge so nycely with their fete: Therfore shal the LORDE shave the heades of the doughters of Sion, and make their bewtie bare in that daye. In that daye shal the LORDE take awaye the gorgiousnes of their apparel, and spanges, cheynes, partlettes, and colares, bracelettes and hooves, ye goodly floured, wyde and broderd rayment, brusshes and headbandes, rynges and garlandes, holy daye clothes and vales, kerchues and pynnes, glasses and smockes, bonettes and taches.

'And in steade of good smell there shalbe stynck among them. And for their gyrdles there shalbe lowse bondes. And for wellset hayre there shalbe baldnesse. In steade of a stomacher, a sack cloth, and for their bewty wythrednesse and sonneburnynge.'

but in Gen. xxii, where Tindale had gone before him, his version, though more Germanic than Hebrew, is yet more English than Germanic.

'And he sayde: Take thy sonne, this onely sonne of thine, even Isaac whom thou lovest, and go thy waye in to the londe of Moria, & offre him there for a burntofferynge, upon a mountayne that I shal shew the. Then Abraham stode up by tymes in the mornynge, and sadled his Asse, and toke with him two yonge men, and his sonne Isaac, and clove wodd for the brent offerynge, gat him up, and wente on unto the place, wherof the LORDE had sayde unto him.

. . . . . . . . . .

'Then Abraham lift up his eyes, and sawe behynde him a ramme, holden fast by the hornes in the breres, and wente, and toke the ramme, and offred him for a brent sacrifice, in steade of his sonne.'

Coverdale has his share of quaint and distinctive renderings. In the sections of which his is the first modern translation: Jer. viii. 22, 'there is no more *Triacle* at Galaad' (from Pagninus); Ps. xci. 5, 'thou shalt not nede to be afrayed for eny bugges by night'; Isa. xxiv. 9, 'the beer shal be bytter to them that drinke it'; Ps. ix. 20, 'O LORDE, set a scolemaster over them, that the Heathen maye knowe them selves to be but men'. In Job (one of the best of books to compare with later versions) v. 7, he accepts the Vulgate against Pagninus, 'man, that is borne unto mysery, like as the byrde for to fle [A.V. as the sparkes flie upward], and again in xv. 2 'fyll his stomacke with anger' [Geneva and A.V. fill his belly with the east wind]. In the New Testament 2 Cor. ix. 13, for Tindale's 'ministring to the sayntes' he takes over from Luther (1522, revised later) 'Of the handreachinge unto y$^e$ sayntes' (handreychung). How far removed he is from the melody and beauty of the Authorized Version can be seen frequently, in passages which make us sometimes question the traditional view of Coverdale's inevitable stylistic superiority.

Job xxxix. 25. He feareth not the noyse of the trompettes, but as soone as he heareth the shawmes blowe, tush (sayeth he) for he smelleth the batell afarre of, y$^e$ noyse, the captaynes and the shoutinge.

A.V. He saith among the trumpets, Ha, ha: and he smelleth the battaile a farre off, the thunder of the captaines, and the shouting.

Jer. xiii. 23. For like as the man of Inde may chaunge his skynne, and the cat of the mountayne hir spottes.

Geneva. Can the blacke Moore change his skin? or the leopard his spots?

A.V. Can the Ethiopian change his skinne or the leopard his spots?

Prov. xx. 1. Wyne is a voluptuous thinge, and dronckennes causeth sedicion.

A.V. Wine is a mocker, strong drinke is raging.

Prov. xv. 17. Better is a meace of potage with love, then a fat oxe with evell will.

A.V. Better is a dinner of herbes where love is, then a stalled oxe, and hatred therewith.

However much of Coverdale has been accepted or rejected in the final revision, one whole section, the Psalter, remains intact, with all its mistakes and all its beauty, in the Prayer Book version.

### 4. *'Matthew's' Bible*

In 1537 appeared the volume which is the foundation of all later English Bible versions, the so-called 'Matthew's' Bible, printed, in Antwerp presumably, at the expense of two London merchants and printers, R. Grafton and E. Whitchurch. The time was now ripe for Royal approval. In 1535 Cranmer had tried, without success, to get the Bishops to produce an authorized version, and in August 1537 he wrote to Cromwell urging him to 'exhibite the boke unto the Kinges highnes; and to obteign of his Grace, if you can, a license that the same may be sold and redde of every person, withoute danger of any acte, proclamacion, or ordinaunce hertofore graunted to the contrary, untill such tyme that we, the Bishops, shall set forth a better translacion, which I thinke will not be till a day after domesday'. On the title-page appear the words 'Set forth with the kinges most gracyous lycence', and the book is therefore the first English Authorized Version. Meanwhile a folio edition of Coverdale's Bible appeared 'Imprynted in Southwarke for James Nycolson', and is therefore the first English Bible printed in England. The licence given to Matthew's Bible was extended to Coverdale's, and the quarto edition of 1537 bears the king's authority on its title-page, and so clearly was the permission accepted that the back of the title contains a prayer by the Bishop of Salisbury for use 'when thou goest to studye in holy scripture'.

'Matthew's' Bible, edited by John Rogers,[1] is a composite work. It is made up of Tindale's Pentateuch, Tindale's New Testament of 1535, Coverdale's Apocrypha, Coverdale's version of Ezra to Malachi, and a hitherto unknown version of Joshua to 2 Chronicles. Internal and external evidence combine to show that this unknown version was left in manuscript by Tindale at his death. The external evidence is given by Grafton, one of the backers of the work, who published a continuation of Hall's Chronicle in 1548, containing the categorical statement, 'This man translated the New Testament into Englisshe and fyrst put it in Prynt, and likewise he translated the v. bookes of Moses, Iosua, Iudicum, Ruth, the bookes of the Kynges and the bookes of Paralipomena, Nehemias or the fyrst of Esdras, the Prophet Ionas and no more of the holy scripture'. The internal evidence is supplied by a comparison of Tindale's Pentateuch and the later section. The first and most important point is that these books are translated from the Hebrew and not at second-hand. Tindale's peculiarities of translation are found in abundance. His characteristic love of variant phrasing appears again. In the Pentateuch he had moved between 'coat of many colours' and 'gay coat', between 'unleavened bread' and 'sweet bread', between 'free cities', 'cities of franchise',' franchised cities' and 'privileged towns' (for the modern 'cities of refuge'). For 'book of the Chronicles' he has 'book of the

---

[1] Dr. W. T. Whitley, in a series of articles published in *The Essex Review* (vols. xliii and xliv, Jan. 1934 et seq.), has argued that the conventional ascription to John Rogers rests on insufficient evidence, and that 'Thomas Matthew' is a real person, whom he identifies with a prominent citizen of Colchester (traceable between 1516 and 1543). This Matthew was connected with a Bible study circle, and was fined by Tonstall in 1527/8. He was absent from Colchester in 1536, presumably whilst engaged on the production of the Bible which bears his name on its title-page [Ed.].

J. F. Mozley, in Appendix E of his *William Tyndale*, 1937, assembles evidence which disposes of this interesting but untenable suggestion. [J.I.]

Stories', 'book of the histories', 'book of the deeds'. Character-istic renderings are continued from the Pentateuch: 'bonde', 'covenant', 'testament', 'appointment' persist, and are varied by 'league' and 'confederation'; Tindale consistently uses 'timbrel' where Coverdale renders 'tabret', and 'ephod' where Coverdale reads 'overbody cote'; Tindale has 'Lebanon' where Coverdale borrows 'Libanus'. The difference in quality and music between Coverdale and Matthew (Tindale) can be seen in the following passages from Solomon's judgement concerning the two harlots, 1 Kings iii. 26, where the Authorized Version goes back almost completely to Matthew.

*Cov.* 'Then sayde the woman whose sonne lyved, unto y$^e$ kinge: (for hir motherly hert was kyndled with pite over hir sonne) Oh my lorde, geve hir the childe alyve, and kyll it not. But the other sayde: Let it nether be myne ner thine, but let it be parted.

*Matt.* 'Then spake the woman whose the lyvyng chylde was/unto y$^e$ kyng (for her* bowelles yerned upon her sonne) and sayde: I besche the my Lorde/geve her the lyvynge chylde/and in no wyse sley it: And the other sayde: it shalbe nether myne nor thyne/ but devyde it.'

* By her bowelles are understand the movynge and shrynckyng of her hart.

Rogers was a careful editor. He preserved Tindale's offending prologue to Romans, he added the Prayer of Manasses in the Apocrypha, which Coverdale, following the Zürich Bible, had omitted, but translated it from the French Bible of John Calvin's relative Olivetan, from which he also included an attack on the authority of the Apocrypha. He borrows largely from Olivetan, and takes over from him a remarkable concordance. 'In the whych also we may fynde (that which helpeth greatly the studye of the readers) the openynge of certayne Hebrewe tropes, trans-laceyons and similitudes, and manner of speakynges (whych we call phrases) conteyned in the Byble'. There is some evidence of scholarship, both Greek and Hebrew. He quotes Rabbinic authority. He rejects intrusive additions admitted by Coverdale in the Psalms and elsewhere. He corrects the numbering of the Psalms to agree with the original Hebrew numbering. He translates Hallelujah as 'Praise the everlasting' (Olivetan), has an interesting note on Selah (Olivetan), different from Coverdale's. He takes the trouble to give the Hebrew form of some of the Prophets, e.g. Iehezekiell as well as Ezekiel, and in some of the alphabetical Psalms gives the actual characters of the Hebrew alphabet before each section and verse where Coverdale had Englished them as Aleph, Beth, Gimel, Daleth, &c. An interesting feature is the treatment of the Song of Songs, which is presented as a drama with various speakers distinguished as 'the voyce of the Churche', 'Christ to the Synagogue', 'the spousesse to her companions', 'the voyce of the Churche in persecution'. Similar divisions (or marginal notes) had been used in the early Wyclifite rendering, but deleted in Purvey's version. The chapter heading of Gen. xxv reads 'Esau selleth his byrthright for a messe of potage'.

Of the two rival authorized editions of 1537, neither was satisfactory. Coverdale's, though pleasant in phrasing and decoratively easy, was notoriously far from the original texts. Matthew's was too closely associated with Tindale, and too provocative in its theological apparatus. The obliging Coverdale, 'I am always willing and ready to do my best in one translation as in another', was entrusted by Cromwell with the task of cleaning up and revising Matthew. The printing was begun in France, was interrupted by diplomatic troubles, and finally the types and sheets were transferred to England, and the first of the 'Great' Bibles, Cromwell's Bible, was published in 1539. This was followed in April 1540 by Cranmer's Bible, and in November 1540 by yet a further revision.

## 5. *The Great Bible*

The first Great Bible claimed to be 'truly translated after the veryte of the Hebrue and Greke textes, by the dylygent studye

of dyverse excellent learned men, expert in the forsayde tonges.'
This might be taken to imply the co-operation of a committee of
experts, but there is no evidence for this. The experts are merely
scholars, translators, and editors whose works Coverdale had
consulted and compared. In the New Testament the Latin of
Erasmus was constantly consulted, and in the Old Testament
the literal translation by Pagninus, and the new literal translation
published in 1534–5 by the learned Sebastian Münster, pupil of
Reuchlin, and Professor of Hebrew at Heidelberg and at Basel.
Most of the changes are due to the use of these several versions.

Ps. xxiii. 2 and 4:

*Cov.* He fedeth me in a grene pasture; and ledeth me to a fresh water.
*1539.* He shall fede me in a grene pasture, & leade me forthe
        besyde the waters of comforte.
*Cov.* thy staffe & thy shepehoke comforte me.
*1539.* thy rodde & thy staffe comforte me.

Coverdale, having promised 'to avoid any private opinion or
contentious words', had intended to add marks indicating
'diversity of reading, among the Hebrews, Chaldees, and Greeks,
and Latinists', showing where 'the sentence, written in small
letters, is not in the Hebrew or Chaldee, but in the Latin, and
seldom in the Greek', and 'some notable annotations, which we
have written without any private opinion, only after the best
interpreters of the Hebrews, for the mere clearness of the text'.
In the published Great Bible the margins are bare of annotation,
and the pointing hands and other signs, reprinted in later issues,
make the omission more apparent. Henry VIII, speaking of 'the
free and lyberall use of the Bible in oure oune maternall English
tonge', granted Cromwell exclusive rights over bible printing
for five years. A last attempt was made by the Bishops to hold
up an English version, 'being demanded by the king what was
their judgement of the translation, they answered that there
was many faults therein. "Well", said the king, "but are there
any heresies maintained thereby?' They answered, there were

no heresies they could find maintained thereby. "If there be no heresies", said the king, "then, in God's name, let it go abroad among our people!" ' In connexion with Cromwell's Great Bible, injunctions had been issued for 'one boke of the whole Bible in the largest volume in Englyshe' to be set up in all churches. In April 1540 appeared the further revision with an important preface by Cranmer, and a clear statement on the title-page: 'This is the Byble apoynted to the use of the churches,' and in the words of a contemporary,

'Englishmen have now in hand in every church and place, and almost every man, the Holy Bible and New Testament in their mother tongue, instead of the old fabulous and fantastical books of the Table Round, Lancelot du Lake, Huon de Boardeux, Bevis of Hampton, Guy of Warwick, &c., and such other, whose impure filth and vain fabulosity the light of God has abolished utterly.'

Cranmer's Great Bible of 1540 is an extensive revision by Coverdale of his ruthless revision of Matthew in 1539, above all in those portions which he himself had translated at second-hand. In the crucial fifty-third chapter of Isaiah he has made forty alterations in 1539 from his own 1535 rendering, and in 1540, another twenty.

e.g. *Cov.* He shalbe the most symple and despysed of all, which yet
     hath good experience of sorowes and infirmities.
   *1539.* He is despysed & abhorred of men, he is soch a man as hath
     good experience of sorowes and infirmyties.
   *1540.* He is despysed & abhorred of men, he is soch a man as is
     full of sorowe & as hath good experience of infirmyties.

For the New Testament Erasmus was again heavily used, particularly in Revelation. Certain passages printed in smaller type are taken over from his fourth edition, of 1527, in which he had introduced some ninety readings obtained from the Complutensian Polyglot, which was belatedly put into circulation after his third edition, of 1522, had been prepared for press.

For the Old Testament further reliance was placed on Pagninus, and still further on Münster, while Luther and the Zürich version were pushed further and further away. Sometimes the translation is radically and not merely verbally altered.

e.g. in Prov. xviii. 1, 1535 and 1539 follow Zürich closely:

'Whoso hath pleasure to sowe dyscorde, pycketh a quarrell in every thinge'

whereas 1540 changes over to Münster in

'He accompanieth hym selfe with all steadfast and helthsome doctryne, that hath a fervent desyre to it, and is sequestrate from companye.'

and in a more familiar passage, Eccles xi. 1,

*1539.* Sende thy vitayles over the waters, and so shalt thou fynde them after many dayes. [yeares, 1535].

*1540.* Lay thy brede upon weate faces, and so shalt thou fynde after many dayes.

A.V. Cast thy bread upon the waters: for thou shalt find it after many dayes.

The chief fault of the Great Bible is that it is still far from being a direct translation of the Hebrew and Greek, that it is a patchwork of revision, and still relies too much on the authority of the Vulgate. Scores of passages not in the original texts are translated from the Vulgate, including about seventy in the Psalms alone. These latter, which are printed in special type in the Great Bible and the 1662 Prayer Book, are not distinguished in modern copies, and consequently give an unfair picture of Coverdale's efforts.

Seven editions of the Great Bible were printed, one in 1539 (Cromwell's), three of Cranmer's in April, July, and November 1540, and three in May, November, and December 1541. The remainder of Henry VIII's reign was a period of retrogression. The Bishops made another determined attempt to down the Protestant version in the interest of the Vulgate. Convocation in 1542 decided, on the King's instructions, to revise the Great Bible 'according to that Bible [the Vulgate] which is usually read in the English Church'. At the sixth meeting Gardiner, Bishop of Winchester, proposed a list of ninety-nine Latin words to be retained in their original form 'for their genuine and native meaning, and for the majesty of the matter in them contained', or 'be fitly Englished with the least alteration'. The list was carefully chosen, including 'Ecclesia, Poenitentia, Pontifex, Baptizare, Sacramentum, Mysterium, Communio, Presbyter, Senior, Episcopus, Gratia, Charitas, Impositio manuum', with a camouflage of less disputed terms. Cranmer, by obtaining the King's authority to have the translation checked by the Universities, foiled the conspiracy, and nothing more was heard of the attempt. An alarming new practice indicated the extent to which, as Cranmer said, 'the word of God hath got the upper hand of them all'. In order to show the pre-eminence of the true Bible text over the Church service, there grew up a habit of reciting the Bible aloud during the service, and people were prosecuted 'for disturbing the service of the church, with brabbling of the New Testament'. It was decreed by Bonner that 'it be not read with noise in time of divine service'. So dangerous to the Church was the unrestricted reading of the Bible in English, that Parliament in 1543 issued restrictions on a clearly marked class and property basis.

'The Chanceller of England, Captaines of the Wars, the King's Justices, the Recorders of any city, borough, or town, and the Speaker of Parliament may use any part of the Holy Scripture as they have been wont . . . Every nobleman and noblewoman, being a householder, may read or cause to be read, by any of his family, servants in his house, orchard, or garden, to his own family, any text of the Bible; and also every merchantman, being a householder, and any other persons, other than women, apprentices, &c., might read to themselves privately the Bible. But no woman, except noblewomen and gentlewomen, might read to themselves alone, and no artificers, apprentices, journeymen, servingmen of the degrees of yeomen, husbandmen or labourers, were to read the New Testament to themselves or to any other, privately or openly, on pain of one month's imprisonment.'

In July 1546 a Royal decree declared that 'No man or woman, of what estate, condition, or degree, was after the last day of August, to receive, have, take, or keep, Tyndale's or Coverdale's New Testament'. Henry VIII, with tears in his eyes, addressing a weeping Parliament, complained that 'the book was disputed, rhymed, sung and jangled in every alehouse and tavern', and the most pathetic testimony to this denial of the free Bible to the whole people of England is seen in a human note written in 1546 on the flyleaf of a copy of Polydore Vergil's *History of Inventions*,

'When I kepe Mr Letymers shepe I bout thys boke when the Testament was oberragated, that shepeherdys myght not rede hit. I pray God amende that blindness. Wryt by Robert Wyllyams, keppyng shepe upon Seynbury hill. 1546.'

In the short reign of Edward VI the open Bible came once again into favour, and some fourteen Bibles and thirty-five New Testaments were printed. Only one attempt at an English Bible was made, but this is so very English as to call for special mention. The Vulgate, as we have seen, exercised a very strong pull. In 1538 Coverdale put forth a Diglott New Testament, with the Vulgate Latin, and an English translation as close to the Latin as possible. In 1539 Richard Taverner, the only layman to issue a complete Bible, published a revision of 'Matthew's' Bible in which the New Testament was improved by his unusually fine Greek scholarship and careful attention to the Greek article, and the Old Testament revised with close attention to the Vulgate. His stylistic qualities were excellent, he tried to keep the renderings as accurate as possible, and as English as possible. In 2 Sam. xii. 5, the Hebrew idiom 'the child of death' is Englished to 'worthye of deathe' (and the

A.V. keeps this in the margin, as the Geneva version had previously kept the Hebrew). For 'advocate' in 1 John ii. 1, Taverner has the more English 'spokesman', and in 1 John ii. 2, where the Authorized Version now has 'propitiation', he has 'a mercystocke for our synnes'. In Matt. xxii. 12 he is collo-quial, 'had never a word to say'. Sir John Cheke, professor of Greek at Cambridge, tutor to Edward VI, spelling reformer and Saxonist, carried the patriotic, anti-Vulgate tendency still further in a fragment, consisting of Matthew and a portion of Mark, perhaps not intended for publication, and in any case not published until 1843. Gardiner's attempt to retain the Vulgate ecclesiastical terms is countered by such renderings as *uprising* (resurrection), *gainbirth* (regeneration), *biword* (parable), *fresh-men* (proselytes), *frosent* (apostle), *crossed* (crucified), *mooned* (lunatic), *hundreder* (centurion), *wizards* (wise men). His rendering is sometimes quaint, as

Matt. i. 17, 'from Abraham unto David there wer fourteen degrees; and from David unto the out-peopling to Babylon, fourteen degrees:'

and sometimes beautifully simple, as

Matt. xi. 27–30. And no man knoweth the Son but the Father, and he to whom the Son will disclose it. Come to me all that labour and be burdened and I will ease you. Take my yoke on you and learn of me, for I am mild and of a lowly heart. And ye shall find quietness for your selves. For my yoke is profitable and my burden light.

Coverdale's Diglott had some influence on the Rhemes New Testament, there are traces of Taverner in the Authorized Version, but Cheke left no mark anywhere.

## 6. *Geneva and Bishops' Bibles*

In the reign of Mary, whose toll of religious martyrs seems strangely amateurish alongside that of present-day experts, no

Bibles were printed in England, the English Bible was no longer used in Church services, and Bibles set up in the churches were burnt. In 1554 even the painting of Scriptural quotations on church walls was forbidden. Of those associated with the translation of the Bible, Rogers was the first martyr, Cranmer followed, but Bishop Coverdale, as he now was, by good luck escaped, and alone of the early translators died in bed. Some eight hundred persons became refugees on the Continent, and in Geneva the more extreme non-conformists continued the task of revising the English Bible. The first fruits appeared on 10 June 1557, when William Whittingham, sometime Fellow of All Souls, and husband of John Calvin's sister or sister-in-law (his tomb in Durham Cathedral reads 'maritus sororis Johannes Calvini theologi'), issued an English New Testament in a completely new form, i.e. in Roman type, and with the text divided into verses. Some copies were introduced into England before Mary's death. In 1559 appeared a translation of the Psalms, as earnest of a complete revised Bible, and in April 1560, with a dedication to Queen Elizabeth, was published at Geneva the 'Bible and Holy Scriptures conteyned in the Olde and Newe Testament, translated according to the Ebrue and Greeke, and conferred with the best translations in divers language', the whole being the work of the exiles 'for the space of two yeres and more day and night'. It became the people's Bible, was Shakespeare's Bible, and is usually known as the Breeches Bible, from the rendering of Gen. iii. 7 'and they sewed figge tree leaves together, and made themselves breeches' (margin: Ebr. things to gird about them to hide their privities). The word, however, had occurred previously in Wyclif, in Coverdale, and in Caxton's *Golden Legend.*

The translation of the New Testament is under the shadow of Calvin and of Beza. Calvin had already helped in the French Bible translated by his kinsman Olivetan in 1535. He contributed an Epistle to Whittingham's New Testament, and the

Congregation of exiles at Geneva, to ensure the accuracy of the rendering, were moved 'with one assent to requeste 2 off there brethren, to witt, Calvin and Beza, eftsonnes to peruse the same notwithstandinge their former travells'. Whittingham's Testament of 1557 is substantially Tindale's of 1534 as in Matthew, with certain changes from the Great Bible, and many new renderings based on Beza. He speaks of the 'Churches of Galatia' and the 'church of God' after Beza 1556, instead of 'congregations' after Tindale, and this use of the disputed term, introduced in the Protestant version, was kept in the Bishops' Bible and the Authorized Version. The Testament of 1560 was a much more thorough revision in the light of Beza's translation and interpretations.

The Old Testament made a deliberate attempt to return to 'the Hebrue veritie'. In the New Testament they followed Tindale in his concern for the Hebrew idiom perceptible through the Greek text, 'the Apostle who spake and wrote to the Gentiles in the Greeke tongue, rather constrained them to the lively phrase of the Ebrewe, then enterprised farre by mollifying their language to speake as the Gentiles. And for this & other causes we have in many places reserved the Ebrew phrases, notwithstanding that they may seeme somewhat hard in their eares that are not well practised.' Where the Hebrew idiom seemed un-English the literal rendering was placed in the margin. A special point was made in certain instances of spelling proper names and accenting them in accordance with the original Hebrew, e.g. Izhák, Iaakób, Iphtáh, Nebuchadnezzar, Ahashverosh, Methushelah. It is often forgotten that fundamental distortion has frequently been produced by changes in English pronunciation, as in Canaan and Aaron, or by the simple change in printing from I to J, as in Joseph and Jerusalem.

The importance of Luther and the Zürich translation to the earlier translations up to Matthew is matched by the often overlooked contribution of the French versions to the translations from Matthew onward, through the Great Bible to the Geneva version. Lefèvre's French Bible of 1534, translated from the Vulgate, supplied part of the preliminary matter, the chapter headings, and many of the marginal notes and references in Matthew's Bible. Olivetan's French Bible of 1535 rendered from Pagninus in the Old Testament, and Lefèvre in the New Testament, gave Matthew the 'Names of all the Books', the 'Table of pryncipall matters', the address 'To the Christian Readers', the Preface to the Apocrypha, the translation of the Prayer of Manasses, certain transliterations of proper names, and certain passages omitted in Coverdale. The Geneva Bible is indebted to Olivetan for the model of the two tables 'the one serving for the interpretation of the Ebrewe names: & the other containing all the chiefe & principal matters of the whole Bible'.

Some special points in the material get-up of the Geneva Bible may be worth tracing to their origin. The first is the matter of division into numbered verses, introduced into English in Whittingham's 1557 Testament, and followed in the whole Bible in 1560. 'As touching the division of the verses, we have folowed the Ebrew examples which have so even from the beginning distinguished them.' Hebrew scrolls of the Law have no verse divisions. Hebrew manuscripts in book form are divided into verses. Modern chapter division is of Christian origin, the Hebrew Massoretic division into sections or paragraphs being indicated in the Rabbinic Bibles, and observed for the first time in English in the Revised Version. The first to divide up the Bible into chapters was Hugo de Sancto Caro, who compiled a concordance to the Vulgate in 1244. He was followed by Isaac Nathan b. Kalonymos in 1437–45, whose concordance is the first Jewish work in which the original text of the books of the Bible is divided into chapters, numbered according to the Vulgate. He also followed the Vulgate order of books. Both these concordances were for convenience of reference in controversial writing, and for more exact reference the chapters were divided into sections marked A, B, C, D, &c. The first edition of the Hebrew text by Christian scholars, in the Complutensian Polyglott, was the first to discard the Massoretic sections and introduce the Christian chapter division to fit in with the parallel Greek and Latin texts, placing Roman numerals in the margin. The Rabbinical Bible of Felix Pratensis 1517–18 at the same time also indicated these divisions, placing Hebrew numerals in the margin. The first printed Bible to indicate the verse divisions was Sanctes Pagninus' literal translation into Latin, Lyons 1528. The text is printed in paragraphs, but the verses are numbered in the margin. In the Old Testament the verses are, within one or two, substantially the same as the Authorized Version, though there are slight variations in chapter division. The New Testament chapter divisions are the same as the Authorized Version, but the verse numbering is quite different, e.g. Luke xi has 18 verses against 54 in the Authorized Version. In the Apocrypha the divisions are quite arbitrary, e.g. in 1 Macc. i where the Authorized Version has 64 verses Pagninus has only 15. The source of the Geneva verse division is usually said to be Robert Etienne's (Stephanus) Geneva New Testament of 1550 or 1551 and his Bible of 1555. The Etienne family seems to have been specially interested in verse numbering, Henri Etienne, in his Latin Quincuplex Psalter, numbered the verses in 1509, and in the Stephanus Vulgate of 1528, the Psalms alone appear in numbered separate verses. The immediate source of the Geneva treatment of the verses, however, is not the earlier Stephanus prints, in which the verses, though numbered, are not set out but run on in paragraphs, but the edition of 1556/7 containing the Old Testament of Pagninus, the Apocrypha of Baduellus, and the first edition of Beza's translation of the New Testament. Here the text is set out in separate verses numbered in the margin. The Geneva also takes over from this edition the use of italics for additions to the text, as the Great Bible had already adopted from Olivetan's 1535 Bible the use of smaller type for interpolations. Münster's Bible had used brackets, without change of type, for the same purpose in 1534.

The significance of the Genevan version in the evolution of the modern Bible is very great indeed. It forms a turning-point in rendering, and the older tradition is broken. Where the Great Bible relies on Matthew, and Matthew largely on Tindale, the Geneva version starts afresh, and a large part of its innovations are included in the Authorized Version. Time and time again the Authorized Version agrees verbally with Geneva, and wholly departs from the older line of Tindale–Matthew's– Great Bible–Bishops': John iii. 3, 'Except a man be born again'; Judges xv. 8, 'smote them hip and thigh' (Cov. 'both upon the shulders & loynes); Eccles. xii. 8, 'Vanity of vanities, sayeth the Preacher'; Eccles. xii. 1, 'Remember now thy Creator in the days of thy youth'; Matt. vi. 29, 'Solomon in all his glory'; Matt. iii. 17, 'My beloved son in whom I am well pleased'; 1 Cor. v. 6, 'A little leaven leaveneth the whole lump' (Great. 'a lyttle leven sowreth the whole lompe of dowe'); Heb. xii. 1, 'cloud of witnesses'; 2 Cor. v. 18, 'the ministerie of reconciliation'.

The popularity of the Geneva Bible, and above all of its controversial notes from the extreme Protestant point of view, was distasteful to the Bishops. Moreover, the marked excellence of the Geneva renderings had drawn attention to the notorious defects of the Great Bible, which was almost completely ousted in popular esteem. Archbishop Parker, about 1566, revived the earlier project of an authorized revision by the English Bishops. He wanted Sir William Cecil to approve of it, and even to take a hand in the revision; the books were apportioned among the Bishops, and rules issued to the revisers. The basis was to be 'the Commune Englishe Translacion used in the Churches' (i.e. the Great Bible), with no departure 'except wher eyther the verytie of the hebrue & greke moved alteracion'. The popular form of the Geneva Bible was followed, but the immediate Protestant source of the verse division was ignored by giving the credit to 'such sections and divisions in the Textes as Pagnine in his Translacion useth'. The Old Testament was to rely on the literal Latin versions of Pagninus and Münster, dull and unedifying passages were to be marked for avoidance in public reading, and a cleaning-up process was adopted whereby 'all such wordes as soundeth in the Old Translacion to any offence of lightnes or obscenitie be expressed with more convenient termes and phrases'. In opposition to the Geneva version it was agreed 'To make no bitter notes upon any text'. The work was published in 1568, and in an improved and revised edition in 1572. The dignity of the episcopal revisers has caused the Bishops' Bible to be more highly regarded than it deserves. It was a backward-looking version, usually ignoring the improvements in music and accuracy of the Geneva version, in favour of the traditional readings of the Great Bible. It was an uneven revision, without any general supervision of the separate revisers. Some portions keep close to the Great Bible, others take as much as possible from Geneva. There is a general desire for accuracy, shown in closer attention to the Hebrew of the Old Testament through Münster's rendering, and numerous marginal notes give the literal meaning of the Hebrew original. Following, and even going beyond the example of Geneva, certain Hebrew proper names are given special phonetic treatment, e.g. Isahac, Putiphar, Habel. The Geneva italics used for interpolations are replaced by square brackets, with round brackets for parentheses.

The Bishops rejected Eccles. xi. 1, 'Cast thy bread upon the waters' in favour of the Great Bible's 'Lay thy bread upon wet faces', and Matt. vi. 7, 'when ye pray, use no vaine repetitions as the Heathen' in favour of Great Bible and Tindale's 'babble not much, as the heathen do', and James iv. 11, 'Speak not evil one of another, brethren' in favour of 'Backbite not one another, brethren'. They kept many a colloquial expression from the earlier versions embedded in the Great Bible: Acts i. 13, 'they went up into a parlour' (Tindale); Acts. xix. 23, 'There arose no little ado' (Tindale); Acts. xix. 29, 'And all the city was on a rore' (Tindale); Job. xvii. 1, 'I am hard at death's doore' (Coverdale); Ps. xxxviii. 6, 'and am exceedingly pulled down' (Great); Jer. xxvi. 20, 'a prophet that preached stiffly' (Coverdale); Nahum ii. 10, 'and their faces black as a pot' (Coverdale). On the other hand they often indulged in fresh rotundity of expression, as Prov. xxv. 27, 'Curiously to search the glory of heavenly things is not commendable'. They used picturesque and original renderings which did not find favour later, as Gen. xxxii. 25, 'he smote hym upon the hucklebone of his thigh, and the hucklebone of Jacob's thigh loosed oute of joynt, as he wrasteled with hym'. Though they cut out most of the interpolations from the Vulgate found in the Great Bible in smaller type within brackets, they are fond of adding explanatory phrases in amplification and clarification of the text: James i. 14, 'enticed *with the baite* of her owne concupiscence'; Job. ix. 24, 'where is he, or who is he *that can shewe the contrarie*'; Rom. xi. 4, 'have not bowed the knee to *the image of* Baal'; Isa. i. 7, 'the destruction of enemies *in the time of war*'. Although in Ps. cxxxvii. 5, Coverdale, Matthew, and the Great Bible of 1539 all read correctly[1] 'If I forget thee, O Ierusalem, let my right hand be forgotten', the Bishops preferred to take over the 1540 alteration 'let my right hand forget [her cunning]' partly encouraged by the Geneva 'forget *to play*'.[2] Although the marginal notes of the Geneva Bible were attacked by Parker as 'prejudicial', the Bishops' Bible incorporated a very large proportion of them, although one original comment is worth noting. Against Ps. xlv. 9, 'upon thy ryght hande standeth the queene in a vesture of golde of Ophir', the 1569 quarto has

---

[1] i.e. according to the LXX and Vulgate, but not the Masoretic Hebrew [Ed.].

[2] Vulg. oblivioni detur. Luth. so werde meiner Rechten vergessen. Münster. obliviscatur dextera mea (operis sui).

'Ophir is thought to be the Ilande in the West coast, of late founde by Christopher Columbo: from whence at this day is brought most fine golde'. This has an earlier parallel in the local patriotism of the *Psalterium Octuplex* published at Geneva in 1516. A prefatory letter is dated 1506, Columbus died in 1506, and against Ps. xix. 4 *Et in fines orbis* there is one of the earliest accounts of the work of *Christophori Columbi genuensis . . . novi orbis inventor.*

In accordance with plan the plain-speaking of 1 Cor. vi. 9 in Wyclif's and Matthew's Bibles was softened, and the awkward term in 2 Kings x. 27 rendered in Wyclif as 'waardropis', in Purvey as 'privies', in Coverdale as 'prevy house' and in the Geneva Bible as plain Elizabethan 'jakes' is presented in the Bishops' Bible as 'draught-house' and so persists in the Authorized Version. A Genealogical Table placed before the New Testament gave occasion for severe comment by the learned Hugh Broughton. 'The cockles of the Seashores, and the leaves of a Forest, and the granes of the Popy may as well be numbered as the grosse errours of this table . . . our Bishops' Bible might well give place to the Alkoran, pestred with lyes.'

In spite of the unevenness and shortcomings, the Bishops' Bible is important in the chain of revision, since the 1572 edition was used as the official basis of the Authorized Version. Much that was offered by the Bishops was not accepted in the Authorized Version, but much was taken. To the Bishops' Bible we owe many a phrase and many a final wording: Matt. iii. 3, 'The voyce of one crying in the wyldernesse'; Eph. iii. 8, 'less than the least of all Saints;' Eph. ii. 19, 'fellow-citizens with the Saints'; Matt. ix. 15, 'children of the bridechamber'; Joel ii. 13, 'Rend your heart and not your garments'; Nahum iii. 2, 'The rattling of wheels, the pransing of horses, and the jumping of chariots'.[1]

---

[1] The quality of the Bishops' Bible may be judged in a famous passage from Eccles. xii [1584 Edition]:

Remember thy maker the sooner in thy youth, or ever the daies of adversitie

### 7. Rhemes and Douai Bible

The last of the revisions before the King James's version is the reply of the Catholic Church to the popular and tendencious Protestant versions. The Council of Trent in 1546 had declared the Vulgate 'onely of al other latin translations to be authentical', although no authentic text was available before that of Sextus V in 1590 and Clement VIII in 1592. In 1582 the English College of Rhemes issued 'The New Testament of Jesus Christ, translated faithfully into English, out of the authentical Latin . . . with Annotations and other necessarie helpes, for the better understanding of the text, and specially, for the discoverie of the corruptions of divers late translations, and for cleering the controversies in religion'. This was not an authorized and official translation, since 'the holy scriptures, though truly and Catholikely translated into vulgar tonges, yet may not be indifferently readde of al men, nor of any other then such as have expresse licence'. So far from being a people's bible like the other English versions, 'we must not imagin that . . . the translated Bibles into the vulgar tonges were in the hands of every husband-man, artificer, prentice, boies, girles, mistresse, maide, man: that they

come, and or the yeres drawe nygh when thou shalt say, I have no pleasure in them:

Before the Sunne, the Light, the Moone, and Starres be darkened, and or the cloudes turne againe after the rayne:

When the keepers of the house shall tremble, and when the strong men shal bow themselves, when the milners stande still because they be so fewe, and when the sight of the windowes shall waxe dimme:

When the doores of the streetes shalbe shut, and when the voyce of the milners shalbe laid downe, when men shall rise up at the voyce of the birde, and when all the daughters of musike shalbe brought lowe:

When men shall feare in high places, and be afraide in the streetes, when the Almond tree shall florish and be laden with the Grashopper, and when all lust shall passe: because man goeth to his long home, and the mourners goe about the streetes:

Or ever the silver lace be taken away, and or the golden well be broken: Or the pot be broken at the well, and the wheele broken upon the cesterne.

·   ·   ·   ·   ·   ·   ·   ·   ·

All is but vanitie (sayth the preacher) all is but playne vanitie.

were sung, plaied, alleaged, of every tinker, taverner, rimer, minstrel: that they were for table talke, for alebenches, for boates and barges, and for every prophane person and companie'. The work was begun in 1578 at the instigation of William Allen, afterwards Cardinal, 'with the object of healthfully counteracting the corruptions whereby the heretics have so long lamentably deluded almost the whole of our countrymen'. Gregory Martin was the chief translator, and his daily stint of two chapters was revised by Allen and by Richard Bristow. The preface was a long and controversial document, highly instructive in its statements of purpose and of method.

'We translate the old Vulgar Latin text, not the common Greek text . . . We are very precise and religious in folowing our copie, the old vulgar approved Latin: not only in sense, which we hope we alwaies doe, but sometimes in the very words also and phrases, which may seeme to the vulgar reader and to common English eares not yet acquainted therewith, rudenesse or ignorance . . . Moreover we presume not in hard places to mollifie the speches or phrases, but religiously keepe them word for word, and point for point, for fear of missing, or restraining the sense of the holy Ghost to our phantasie, as Eph. vi. 12 'Against the spirituals of wickedness in the celestials' . . . We adde the Latin word sometime in the margent, when either we can not fully expresse it, or when the reader might thenke, it can not be as we translate.'

The Rhemes Testament is distinguished by its strongly latinate style, and by its deliberate retention of technical terms in their original form. 'If *Hosanna*, *Raca*, and *Belial* and such like be yet untranslated in the English Bibles, why may not we say *Corbana* and *Parasceve*, especially when they Englishing this latter thus "the preparation of the Sabbath" put three words more into the text than the Greeke word doth signifie.' They have *pasche*, *Azymes*, *Areopagus*, *neophyte*, *Python*, *prepuce*, *Paraclete*, *depositum*, *sancta sanctorum*, *archysynagogue*, *anathema*. They read 'proposition of loaves' for 'shew-bread', 'scenopegia' for 'feast of tabernacles', 'sindon' for 'leven', 'chalice' for 'cup'. A special point is made of rendering ecclesiastical terms in an ecclesiastical manner. Gregory Martin complains of 'the absurd translation of the English bibles . . . namely when they translate "congregation" for "church", "elder" for "priest", "image" for "idol", "dissension" for "schism", "general" for "catholic", "secret" for "sacrament", "overseer" for "bishop", "messenger" for "angel", "ambassador" for "apostle", "minister" for "deacon", and such like, to what other end be these deceitful translations, but to conceal and obscure the name of the Church and dignities thereof, mentioned in the holy scriptures.' In this spirit the translation reads Heb. xiii. 7 'remember your *Prelates*', and 2 Cor. v. 20, '*legates* for Christ'. So closely is the Vulgate followed that hosts of Latin words appear with only the slightest attempt at disguise: *inquination, potestates, longanimity, correption.* Many passages of so-called English need translating into English by the light of the Latin: Matt. vi. 11, 'supersubstantial bread'; Rom. i. 30, 'odible to God'; Rom. ii. 25, 'if thou be a prevaricator of the law, thy circumcision is become prepuce'; Gal. v. 21, 'ebrieties, commessations'; Eph. iii. 6, 'concorporat and comparticipant'; Philipp. ii. 7, 'exinanited himself'; 2 Pet. ii. 13, 'coinquination and spottes, flowing in delicacies'; Rev. x. 7, 'shall be consummate, as he hath evangelized'. The gibe of the King James Preface 'that since they must needs translate the Bible, yet by the language thereof, it may be kept from being understood', is almost justified by these specimens. The rendering of Eph. iii. 8–10 clearly illustrates the method.

'To me the least of al the sainctes is given this grace, among the Gentiles to evangelise the unsearchable riches of Christ, and to illuminate al men what is the dispensation of the sacrament hidden from worlds in God, who created al things: that the manifold wisedom of God may be notified to the Princes and Potestats in the celestials by the Church, according to the prefinition of worlds, which he made in Christ Jesus our Lord.'

It is, however, unfair to dwell on this negative though real side of the Rhemes version. There is also a positive side. In addition to the Vulgate the Greek text was closely consulted and produced improved renderings of the article, not without effect on the Authorized and Revised Versions. Gregory Martin was a careful student of the earlier English versions, and of the Bishops' Bible and the Geneva Bible, and through them the earlier translations from Tindale onwards contributed much to the Catholic New Testament. From the Geneva come Matt. xii. 45, 'this wicked generation', xiv. 14, 'a great multitude', xxiii. 27, 'whited tombs'; Mark ix. 49, 'salted with salt', xii. 17, 'the things that are Caesar's'; Luke ix. 12, 'a desert place'; John iv. 22, 'salvation is of the Jews'; Acts xxi. 32, 'Centurions'; 1 Cor. viii. 1, 'Knowledge puffeth up'; 1 Cor. x. 25, 'in the shambles'; 1 Cor. xvi. 8, 'Pentecost'; 2 Cor. v. 19, 'the word of reconciliation'; 2 Cor. xii. 19, 'before God in Christ'; Eph. vi. 5, 'according to the flesh'. In all these passages the Authorized Version has accepted the reading. One important source of the Rhemes, and sometimes of the Geneva Bible (as in several of the coincidences above) is the Diglott version of Coverdale in 1538, made presumably to satisfy Cranmer's injunction to the clergy to study the Bible or New Testament, 'conferring the Latin and English together'. This was a deliberate attempt on Coverdale's part to bring his English version closer to the Vulgate text, and was rewarded by the plentiful use which the Rhemes translators made of it. From Coverdale's Diglott, through the Rhemes New Testament, the Authorized Version received such renderings as Matt. viii. 20, 'The Son of Man hath not *where to lay his head*'; Mark viii. 24, 'I see men as it were *trees walking*'; Acts xvii. 16, 'given to idolatry'; Acts xvii. 19, 'brought him *unto Areopagus*'; 1 Cor. xiii. 2, 'and understand all *mysteries*'; 1 Cor. xv. 33, 'evil communications'.

To counterbalance the inflated and Latinate diction there are many pieces of plain colloquial speaking, and clear rendering:

Matt. ix. 2 'have a good heart'; Matt. xviii. 28, 'throttled him'; Matt. xxv. 27, 'bankers' (for 'exchangers'); Mark v. 39, 'why make you this a doe? the wench is not dead'; Luke ii. 3, 'all went to be enrolled'; John viii. 44, 'a mankiller from the beginning'; Mark ii. 12, 'We never saw the like'; and two renderings with a prophetic tinge: Gal. v. 4, *'evacuated* from Christ'; and Rom. vi. 23, 'the *stipends* of sin is death'.

The Rhemes New Testament was extensively used by the King James's revisers; the Douai Old Testament, published in 1609–10, came too late, but it is full of curious interest. It was translated before the appearance of the Sixtine and Clementine Vulgates, but was revised before publication 'and conformed to the most perfect Latin edition'. The Vulgate was justified as the basis of translation because 'both the Hebrew and Greeke editions are fouly corrupted by Iewes, and Heretikes, since the Latin was truly translated out of them, whiles they were more pure'. The rendering of the Psalms is more startling than most other books, since Jerome's direct translation from the Hebrew is rejected in favour of the Vulgate Psalter, which is merely his revision of the old Latin translation from the Septuagint. Where Coverdale had translated Ps. xci. 5 as 'thou shalt not nede to be afrayed for eny bugges by night, nor for arowe that flyeth by daye', Douai has 'of business walking in darkness, of invasion and the midday devil', which can only be understood in the light of 'a negotio perambulante in tenebris, ab incursu et daemonio meridiano'. Ps. xxiii. 5, reads 'Thou hast fatted my head with oil; and my chalice inebriating, how goodlie it is'. Christology has run wild here, since chalice is said to mean 'the blessed Sacrament and Sacrifice of Christ's bodie and bloud', and also in such passages as 1 Sam. ii. 10, 'shall exalt the horne of his Christ' (A.V. Anointed). Ecclesiastical terms, some of them anachronistic, are found: Ps. cix. 8, 'Let another take his bishopric'. Hebrew words embedded in the Vulgate are retained as Deut. xxiii. 2 *mamzer* for 'bastard'. The latinate flavouring of the

New Testament is continued everywhere, and the same contrast of plain English is also to be found, as Amos ii. 13, 'Behold I will screake under you, as a wayne screaketh loden with hay'; Gen. xxix. 17, 'Lia was bleare-eyed' (from Geneva margin); Prov. vii. 13, 'Taking the young man she kisseth him, and with malapert countenance speaketh fayre'; Jer. viii. 22, 'Is there noe rosen in Galaad'. Prov. xxiii. 31 for 'Look not thou upon the wine when it is red' (A.V.), reads 'Behold not wine when it waxeth yellow'. The choice of a different original has produced some strange differences; in Joshua xv. 18 the Authorized Version has 'she lighted off her asse', Douai has 'she sighed as she sate on her asse'; in Amos iv. 2 the Authorized Version has 'he will take you away with hookes, and your posterity with fish hookes', Douai reads, 'They shall lift you upon poles, and your remnant in pots boyling hot'. The Douai Old Testament is a forgotten book, and had no influence on the Authorized or any later Protestant version, but it is the last of the translations made in the sixteenth century, and so must come into our survey.

There is no parallel in literary or religious history to the seventy-five years of endeavour from Tindale's Testament of 1525 to the end of the century, nothing like this concentrated history of pioneer endeavour and patient scholarship. With all their limitations of scholarly equipment, 'there were Giants in the earth in those daies', and greatest of these giants was Tindale. Of him must be said, as Sir Philip Sidney said of Chaucer, 'I know not, whether to mervaile more, either that he in that mistie time, could see so clearely, or that wee in this cleare age, walke so stumblingly after him.'

J. Isaacs

# VII
# THE AUTHORIZED VERSION AND AFTER
## SYNOPSIS

King James and the Hampton Court Conference 1604. Inception of the Authorized Version. Selection of the translators. Disposition and constitution of the Committees. Distribution of the revision. Rules to be observed. Report to the Synod of Dort. Dr. John Bois at work. Disappearance of the manuscript. Payment for the revision. The Preface of the translators. Methods and principles of translation. Sources and aids. Marginal notes of the Authorized Version, Geneva, and Bishops' Bibles. Chapter summaries and headings. Quality of the translation. Treatment of Hebraisms. Hebrew idioms in English. Variety of rendering in the New Testament. Proper names. Music of the revision. Treatment of the Psalter, of the Song of Songs, of Revelation. History and treatment of the Apocrypha in English. Evolution of some famous passages. Struggle between the Authorized Version and the Geneva Bible for popular favour. Origin of the present text of the Authorized Version. Dr. Paris's and Dr. Blayney's changes. Puritan translations and proposals for revision. New texts of the Greek Testament. Eighteenth-century translations. Colloquial versions, dignified versions, and paraphrases. Specimens of Mace, Franklin, Wesley, Purver, and Harwood. Other notable versions. The first Jewish translations. Bishop Lowth and the rehabilitation of Bible poetry.

'It happens very luckily, that the Hebrew idioms run into the English tongue with a particular grace and beauty. Our language has received innumerable elegancies and improvements, from that infusion of Hebraism, which are derived to it out of the poetical passages in Holy Writ. They give a force and energy to our expressions, warm and animate our language, and convey our thoughts in more ardent and intense phrases, than any that are to be met with in our own tongue. There is something so pathetick in this kind of diction, that it often sets the mind in a flame, and makes our hearts burn within us. How cold and dead does a prayer appear, that is composed in the most elegant and polite forms of speech, which are natural to our tongue, when it is not heightned by that solemnity of phrase, which may be drawn from the Sacred Writings.'

Addison, *Spectator*, No. 405, June 14, 1712.

## 1. *Inception and Execution*

The Authorized Version of the Bible arose from a chance suggestion by Dr. John Reynolds, the Puritan President of Corpus Christi, at the Hampton Court Conference on Monday 16 January 1604. 'He moved his Majestie, that there might bee a newe translation of the Bible, because those which were allowed in the raignes of Henrie the eight, and Edward the sixt, were corrupt and not aunswerable to the truth of the Originall.' King James, who loved scriptural quotation and disputation, who had written a 'Paraphrase upon the Revelation of St. John', and had translated the Psalms into metre, was flattered by the suggestion, took it up gladly, and ordained on 10 February 1604 'that a translation be made of the whole Bible, as consonant as can be to the original Hebrew and Greek, . . . and only to be used in all Churches of England in time of Divine Service'. Bancroft, Bishop of London, scoffed, but made a fortunate suggestion, and the King 'gave this caveat (upon a word cast out by my Lord of London) that no marginall notes should be added, having found in them which are annexed to the Geneva translation (which he sawe in a Bible given him by an English lady) some notes very partiall, untrue, seditious, and savouring too much of dangerous and trayterous conceits'. This attack on the Geneva version is inexplicable, since it was the first Bible ever published in Scotland, and dedicated to himself in 1579, was the version he was brought up on, and the version he quoted from in his own writings. However, his enthusiasm for the project continued, and within six months he had approved the list of translators and was urging the work on. The Bishop of London wrote on 30th June to the Cambridge translators, 'for as much as his Highness is very anxious that the same so religious a work should admit of no delay, he has commanded me to signify unto you in his name that his pleasure is, you should with all possible speed meet together in your University and begin the same'. On 22 July 1604 the King wrote to Bancroft, then acting Archbishop of Canterbury,

'we require you to move all our bishops to inform themselves of all such learned men within their several dioceses, as having especiall skill in the Hebrew and Greek tongues, have taken pains, in their private studies of the scriptures, for the clearing of any obscurities either in the

Hebrew or in the Greek, or touching any difficulties or mistakings in the former English translation, which we have now commanded to be thoroughly viewed and amended, and thereupon to write unto them, earnestly charging them, and signifying our pleasure therein, that they send such their observations either to Mr. Lively, our Hebrew reader in Cambridge, or to Dr. Harding, our Hebrew reader in Oxford, or to Dr. Andrews, dean of Westminster, to be imparted to the rest of their several companies; so that our said intended translation may have the help and furtherance of all our principal learned men within this our kingdom'.

The King had appointed 'certain learned men, to the number of four and fifty for the translation of the Bible', but only about fifty of these can be identified. Two committees met at Oxford, two at Cambridge, and two at Westminster. The Oxford group was headed by Dr. John Hardinge, Regius Professor of Hebrew, and included Dr. John Reynolds, the originator of the project, 'his memory and reading were near to a miracle', Dr. Miles Smith, who 'had Hebrew at his fingers' ends', Dr. Richard Brett, 'skilled and versed to a criticism in the Latin, Greek, Chaldee, Arabic and Ethiopic tongues', Sir Henry Saville, editor of the works of Chrysostom, and Dr. John Harmer, · Professor of Greek, 'a most noted Latinist, Grecian and divine'. The Cambridge committee was at first presided over by Edward Lively, Regius Professor of Hebrew, who died in 1605 before the work was really begun, and included Dr. Lawrence Chaderton, 'familiar with the Greek and Hebrew tongues, and the numerous writings of the Rabbis', Thomas Harrison, 'noted for his exquisite skill in Hebrew and Greek idioms', Dr. Robert Spalding, successor to Lively as Professor of Hebrew, Andrew Downes, 'one composed of Greek and industry', and John Bois, 'a precocious Greek and Hebrew scholar'. The Westminster group was headed by Lancelot Andrewes, Dean of Westminster, afterwards Bishop of Chichester, of Ely, and finally of Winchester, 'who might have been interpreter general at Babel . . . the world wanted learning to know how learned he was', and included the Hebraist Hadrian Saravia, and William Bedwell, the greatest living Arabic scholar. Pointedly omitted from the great task was the cantankerous Dr. Hugh Broughton, reputed to be the greatest of living Hebraists, who had offered some valuable suggestions in 1597 'touching translating the Bible' and had been invited, unofficially, to give the King his views on methods of procedure for the new version. His reputation was such, however, that Bancroft thought it wise to remind Lively, an old enemy, of Broughton's suggestions.

## 2. *Methods and Principles*

Westminster was entrusted with the translation of the Pentateuch and the historical books from Joshua to the Second Book of Kings, with the 'Epistles of St. Paule, and the Canonical Epistles'. Cambridge had 'From the first of Chronicles, with the rest of the Story, and the Hagiographi, viz, Job, Psalmes, Proverbs, Cantica, Ecclesiastes' and the Apocrypha with the prayer of Manasses. Oxford was allotted 'The former greate Prophets, with the Lamentations, and the twelve lesser prophets', as well as 'The Four Gospels, Acts of the Apostles, Apocalips'. Fortunately a very full list has survived of 'the Rules to be observed in the Translation of the Bible'.

1. The ordinary Bible read in the Church, commonly called the *Bishops Bible*, to be followed, and as little altered as the truth of the original will permit.

2. The Names of the Prophets, and the Holy Writers, with the other Names of the Text, to be retained, as nigh as may be, accordingly as they were vulgarly used.

3. The old Ecclesiastical Words to be kept, viz. the Word *Church* not to be translated *Congregation* &c.

4. When a Word hath divers Significations, that to be kept which hath been most commonly used by the most of the Ancient Fathers, being agreeable to the Propriety of the Place and the Analogy of the Faith.

5. The Division of the Chapters to be altered, either not at all, or as little as may be, if Necessity so require.

6. No Marginal Notes at all to be affixed, but only for the Explanation of the *Hebrew* or *Greek* Words, which cannot without some circumlocution, so briefly and fitly be express'd in the Text.

7. Such Quotations of Places to be marginally set down as shall serve for the fit Reference of one Scripture to another.

8. Every particular Man of each Company, to take the same Chapter, or Chapters, and having translated or amended them severally by himself, where he thinketh good, all to meet together, confer what they have done, and agree for their Parts what shall stand.

9. As any one Company hath dispatched any one Book in this Manner they shall send it to the rest, to be consider'd of seriously and judiciously, for his Majesty is very careful in this Point.

10. If any Company, upon the Review of the Book so sent, doubt or differ upon any Place, to send them Word thereof; note the Place, and withal send the Reasons, to which if they consent not, the Difference to be compounded at the General Meeting, which is to be of the chief Persons of each Company, at the end of the Work.

11. When any Place of special Obscurity is doubted of Letters to be directed, by Authority, to send to any Learned Man in the Land, for his Judgement of such a Place.

12. Letters to be sent from every Bishop to the rest of his Clergy, admonishing them of this Translation in hand; and to move and charge as many as being skilful in the Tongues; and having taken pains in that kind, to send his particular Observations to the Company, either at *Westminster, Cambridge* or *Oxford*.

13. The Directors in each Company, to be the Deans of *Westminster* and *Chester* for that Place; and the King's Professors in the *Hebrew* or *Greek* in either University.

14. These translations to be used when they agree better with the Text than the Bishops Bible.
$$\left\{ \begin{array}{l} \textit{Tindall's} \\ \textit{Matthews} \\ \textit{Coverdale's} \\ \textit{Whitchurch's} \\ \textit{Geneva.} \end{array} \right.$$

15. Besides the said Directors before mentioned, three or four of the most Ancient and Grave Divines, in either of the Universities, not

employed in Translating, to be assigned by the Vice-Chancellor, upon Conference with the rest of the Heads, to be Overseers of the Translations as well *Hebrew* as *Greek*, for the better Observation of the 4th Rule above specified.

These would appear to be the original instructions according to which the undertaking was to proceed, and some time in 1607 the whole machine was set in motion. In November 1618 the English delegates to the Synod of Dort, including Dr. Samuel Ward, of the Cambridge company, reporting on 'the very accurate English version', gave an interesting summary of the work, which adds some important details:

After each section had finished its task twelve delegates, chosen from them all, met together and reviewed and revised the whole work.

Lastly the very Reverend the Bishop of Winchester, Bilson, together with Dr. Smith, now Bishop of Gloucester, a distinguished man, who had been deeply occupied in the whole work from the beginning, after all things had been maturely weighed and examined, put the finishing touch to this version.

The rules laid down for the translators were of this kind:

In the first place caution was given that an entirely new version was not to be furnished, but an old version, long received by the Church, to be purged from all blemishes and faults; to this end there was to be no departure from the ancient translation, unless the truth of the original text or emphasis demanded.

Secondly, no notes were to be placed in the margin, but only parallel passages to be noted.

Thirdly, where a Hebrew or Greek word admits two meanings of a suitable kind, the one was to be expressed in the text, the other in the margin. The same to be done where a different reading was found in good copies.

Fourthly, the more difficult Hebraisms and Graecisms were consigned to the margin.

Fifthly, in the translation of Tobit and Judith, when any great discrepancy is found between the Greek text and the old Vulgate Latin they followed the Greek text by preference.

Sixthly, that words which it was anywhere necessary to insert into the text to complete the meaning were to be distinguished by another type, small roman.

Seventhly, that new arguments should be prefixed to every book, and new headings to every chapter.

Lastly, that a very perfect Genealogy and map of the Holy Land should be joined to the work.

Unfortunately almost nothing is known of the actual procedure of translation, and only a very little more about the final revision. John Selden, speaking of the committee of revisers, said, 'The translators in King James's time took an excellent way. That part of the Bible was given to him who was most excellent in such a tongue (as the Apocrypha to Andrew Downes) and then they met together, and one read the Translation, the rest holding in their hands some Bible, either of the learned Tongues, or French, Spanish, Italian, etc: if they found any fault they spake, if not he read on.' Our only glimpse of one of the revisers at work is given in Dr. Anthony Walker's life of Dr. John Bois.

'When the translators were to be chosen for Cambridge, he was sent for thither by those herein employed, & was chosen one . . . Sure I am, that part of the Apocrypha was alotted to him (for he hath shewed me the very copy he translated by), but to my grief I know not which part.

'All the time he was about his own part, his commons were given him at St. John's; where he abode all the week, till Saturday night; & then went home to discharge his cure: returning thence on Monday morning. . . .

'Four years were spent in this first service; at the end whereof the whole work being finished, & three copies of the whole Bible sent from Cambridge, Oxford & Westminster, to London; a new choice was to be made of six in all, two out of every company, to review the whole work; & extract one out of all three, to be committed to the presse.

'For the despatch of which business Mr. Downes & Mr. Bois were sent for up to London. Where meeting (though Mr. Downes would not go till he was either fetcht or threatened with a pursivant) their four fellow labourers, they went dayly to Stationers Hall, & in three quarters of a year, finished their task. All which time they had from the Company of Stationers xxx$^s$ [each] per week, duly paid them: tho' they had nothing before but the self-rewarding, ingenious industry. Whilst they were imployed in this last businesse, he & he only, took notes of their proceedings: which notes he kept till his dying day.'

These notes, alas, no longer survive; nor does the manuscript from which the work was printed in 1611. It was last heard of in 1660, when a pamphlet entitled 'The London Printers Lamentacion' complains of certain wicked printers, John Feild and Henry Hills, 'Have they not obtained, (and now keep in their actuall possession) the Manuscript Copy of the last Translation of the *Holy Bible* in English (attested with the hands of the Venerable and learned Translators in King James his time) ever since 6 March 1655', and probably perished in the Great Fire.

Dr. Walker's note of the payment for revision brings up the larger question of the cost of the work. King James provided only enthusiasm. He had no cash, but he suggested to the Bishops that they should reserve Ecclesiastical preferment for the workers, promising to do the same for prebends and benefices in his gift, and it is true that seven of the revisers were made Bishops, and ten more received substantial preferment, though whether this was solely on account of their contribution to the translation cannot be established. The payment to the revisers was probably only a small part of the cost of printing and publication. The copyright was claimed in 1651 for 'Matthew Barker, citizen and stationer of London, in regard that his father paid for the amended or corrected translation of the Bible, £3,500, by reason whereof the translated copy did of right belong to himself and his assigns'.

The 'Preface of the Translators', written by Dr. Miles Smith, gives important information concerning the translators' intentions. They intended a revision, and not a completely new work: 'Wee never thought from the beginning, that we should neede to make a new Translation, nor yet to make of a bad one a good one . . . but to make a good one better, or out of many good ones, one principall good one, not justly to be excepted against; that hath bene our indeavour, that our marke.' They translated with the original tongues before them: 'If you aske what they had before them, truely it was the Hebrew text of the Olde Testament, the Greeke of the New. . . If trueth be to be tried by these Tongues, then whence should a translation be made, but out of them.' They indulged in no undue haste: 'the worke hath not bene hudled up in 72 dayes, but hath cost the workemen, as light as it seemeth, the paines of twise seven times seventie two dayes and more'. They sought aid wherever it presented itself, at home or abroad: 'Neither did wee thinke much to consult the Translators or Commentators, Chaldee, Hebrewe, Syrian, Greeke, or Latine, no nor the Spanish, French, Italian or Dutch.' They steered a mid course between the Puritan and Papist versions: 'wee have on the one side avoided the scrupulositie of the Puritanes, who leave the olde Ecclesiasticall words, and betake them to other, as when they put *washing* for *Baptisme*, and *Congregation* in stead of *Church*: as also on the other side we have shunned the obscuritie of the Papists, in their *Azimes, Tunike, Rational, Holocausts, Praepuce, Pasche*, and a number of such like, whereof their late translation is full'. This same Preface, by a strange irony, shows the power of the condemned Geneva version, for the author quotes, not from the version he had himself revised, or even from the Bishops' Bible, but from the Genevan, and when he urges 'neither yet with Esau sell your birthright for a messe of potage', although the margin refers to Heb. xii. 16, the wording is taken from the Geneva chapter heading.

### 3. *Quality*

The Authorized Version is a miracle and a landmark. Its felicities are manifold, its music has entered into the very blood

and marrow of English thought and speech, it has given countless
proverbs and proverbial phrases even to the unlearned and the
irreligious. There is no corner of English life, no conversation
ribald or reverent it has not adorned. Embedded in its tercentenary wording is the language of a century earlier. It has both
broadened and retarded the stream of English Speech. It is
more archaic in places than its forerunners, and it is impossible
for us to disentangle from our ordinary talk the phrases of Judea,
whether Hebrew or Greek, whether of the Patriarchs, the
Prophets, the Poets, or the Apostles. Only the closest scrutiny
can give precision to the rhapsodical vagueness with which the
Authorized Version is worshipped at a distance.

The official basis of the revision was the Bishops' Bible, and
the text used was that of 1602. Every earlier English translation
was consulted, not only those laid down in the formal instructions, Tindale, Matthew, Coverdale, the Great Bible, and the
Geneva, but also the unmentioned Rhemes New Testament.
Every possible foreign aid was utilized, those available to the
earlier translators, Luther, Leo Juda, and Zwingli in German,
Olivetan in French, Pagninus, Sebastian Munster and Castalio's
Latin, as well as the Vulgate and Erasmus, and those which had
come into being since the Bishops' revision. An important
revision of the French Bible appeared at Geneva in 1587–8
with the help of Bertram and Beza, a new Spanish translation
had appeared in 1602, an Italian translation by J. Diodati in
1607. A new work of the highest importance for Old Testament study was the Plantin Polyglott of 1572 in which Arias
Montanus gave an interlinear translation of the Hebrew on the
basis of Pagninus' Latin, providing a crib which drew forcible
attention to the Hebrew idiom, and accounting for much of the
improved Hebrew scholarship of the Authorized Version. In
1579 Tremellius, a converted Jew, who had been King's Reader
of Hebrew at Cambridge, published yet another Latin translation of the Old Testament, with the addition of a version of the

Apocrypha by his son-in-law Junius. The Chaldaic Targum was specially studied, and its readings recorded. The Syriac New Testament in Tremellius's version was consulted, and Beza's New Testament text was heavily leaned upon.

The seriousness of the revision can be gauged from the profusion of marginal notes. Controversial notes were excluded, and textual scholarship emphasized. In the Old Testament, according to Scrivener, there are 6,637 marginal notes, of which 4,034 give the literal meaning of the Hebrew and 77 of the Chaldee, 2,156 offer alternative readings, 63 give the meaning of proper names, and 31 give the Massoretic differences of *Keri* and *Ketib*. In the New Testament there are 765 notes, of which 35 give variant readings, 582 alternative renderings, and 112 literal translations. It has been asserted that the best scholarship, as in the Revised Version later, remained as a minority report in the margin. Hugh Broughton indignantly asked, 'who bade them put the errour in the text and right in the margent?' and Robert Gell, perhaps preserving a tradition of the translators' method, said 'many mis-translated words and phrases, by *plurality of voices*, were carried into the *context*, and the better translation most what, was cast into the *Margent*'. The enormous number of marginal notes in the Old Testament, approached only by that in the Genevan Bible, is proof of the new feeling of responsibility towards the original Hebrew text, and a comparative study of the notes in the Authorized Version, the Genevan Bible, and the Bishops' version is highly instructive. In hundreds of places the Authorized Version is the first to indicate the Hebrew reading in the margin, sometimes giving an idiomatic English rendering, sometimes ignoring the implication and teaching, but always leaving the literal form of the original lest something might be lost. Sometimes the Geneva text and the Geneva margin are taken over intact, sometimes the text becomes the margin and the margin the text. Sometimes the margin becomes the text and no alternative is offered. Very often the Genevan margin becomes the Authorized Version text with or without verbal change. Occasionally the Bishops' text, too literally rendered, as Gen. ii. 16 'eating thou shalt eate', is relegated to the Authorized Version margin. Sometimes when the Bishops' . . . had taken the margin from the Geneva into its text the Authorized Version rejects both for a new rendering and has no marginal note at all. Sometimes the Geneva margin offers a more idiomatic English than the text, as Gen. xiv. 22, 'I have lift up my hand' . . . (text) and 'I have sworn' (margin), but the Authorized Version does not take up the suggestion, and keeps the literalism in the text; or as in Gen. xv. 12 preserves the Hebrew phrase of the margin while making a slight alteration in the wording, 'A verie fearful darkenesse' (margin: a feare of great darkenesse) becomes 'an horrour of great darkenesse'. The immense advance, in the matter of notes, of the Authorized Version over the Geneva, and the Geneva over the Great Bible, may be gauged from a statement in the Great Bible concerning the proposed notes of 'the difference of readyng bytwene the Hebrues and the Chaldees':

'But for so moche as they are verye longe and tedyous, and this volume is very great and houge alreadye, we have therfore lefte them out.'

The chapter summaries and page headings, supplied by the final revisers Bilson and Smith, are of considerable interest. Coverdale is the first to introduce chapter summaries, and Matthew follows. The Great Bible pays much attention to the matter, revising considerably in successive editions. The Geneva headings are important and influential, and the Authorized Version pays very great respect to them. An example of the Great Bible revision, in Gen. xxvi, illustrates certain points in the spelling of proper names, in Christological tendency, and in plainness of speech.

*1540*. Isaac is rebuked of Abimelech, for callynge Rebeca his syster. Chryst is promysed. The chydynge of the shepherdes for the

welles. Isaac is conforted. The atonement betwene Abimelech and Isaac. The bigamie of Esau.
*1541.* The iorneye of Isahac toward Abimelech. The promes made unto Isahac and hys seede. Isahac is rebuked of Abimelech for callyng hyse wyfe his syster. The chydyng of the shepherdes for the welles. Isahac is conforted. The atonement betwene Abimelech and Isahac.

Coverdale's phrasing is concise: Gen. xix, Loths wyfe is turned to a pyler of salt; Exod. xii, The use of the Easterlambe; Gen. xxv, Esau selleth his byrth righte  Lev. xiii, Of Leprosy or Mezell; Lev. xxiii, Sabbath, Easter, Whyt sondaye (otherwise called the feast of wekes); 1 Sam. xviii, Jonathas and David are sworne lovers; 2 Sam. iii, Ioab stycketh Abner; 2 Sam. xx, Ioab stycketh Amasa; Isa. liii, testifieth clearly of Christ; Ezek. xl, the mystery of the Church of Christ.

The relation between the headings of the Geneva, Bishops', and Authorized Version may be seen in some examples. Jer. x, 'Their pastours are become bruite beastes' (Geneva), 'Of evill curates' (Bishops'), 'foolish pastours' (A.V.) Gen. xviii, 'Christ is promised to all nations' (Bishops'), but Geneva and Authorized Version reject this. Gen. xxxvi, 'Of the petigree of Esau' (Bishops'), 'The genealogie of Esau' (Geneva), 'The Dukes that descended of Esau' (A.V.). In one instance, Gen. l, 'He [Joseph] dieth and is *chested*', the word is taken from the Bishops' and Geneva text. Certain page headings may be singled out for comparison as bold pointers:

*A.V.* The first Sabbath. Marriage instituted. The fall of man. The first Monarch. Babel builded. Lot's incest. Mandrakes. A cup put in Beniamin's sacke. Pharaohs crueltie. The rod a serpent. Bloody waters. Pharaoh obstinate. Moses is angry. The eating of blood is forbidden. Meates cleane and uncleane.
*Geneva.* The woman created and seduced. The serpent cursed. Christ promised. Abraham justified by fayth. Abraham goeth to offer Izhak. Dinah is ravished by Shechem. Iaakob cleanseth

his house of idoles. The Dukes and Kings of Edom. The butlers and bakers dreames. The Passeover instituted. Israel chosen above all people. Reverence due to magistrates. Moses face shineth. What beastes, fishes, or birdes be cleane or uncleane.

In Mark vi the Bishops' heading runs 'The inconvenience of dauncing'. In general the Authorized Version provides a completely fresh set of chapter summaries. Taken as a running comment they have something of the same relation to the text as Coleridge's prose summary to his *Ancient Mariner*, and as exercises in allegorical fiction it is pleasant to compare the summaries of The Song of Songs in the Authorized and Genevan versions.

Magnificent as the translation itself is, it is uneven, and has many faults. These were duly pointed out by critics and would-be improvers. Hugh Broughton took revenge for his exclusion from the task by saying firmly, 'The late Bible . . . was sent me to sensure, which bred in me a sadnesse that will grieve me while I breath. It is so ill done. Tell his Majesty that I had rather be rent in pieces with wild horses, than any such translation by my consent should be urged upon poor churches'. John Selden complained that 'the Bible is rather translated into English words than into English phrases. The Hebraisms are kept and the phrase of that language is kept'. Dr. Robert Gell in his 'Essay towards the amendment of the last English Translation of the Bible', complained in 1659 that 'The further we proceed in survey of the Scripture, the Translation is the more faulty, as the Hagiographa more than the Historical Scripture, and the Prophets more than the Hagiographa, and the Apocrypha most of all; and generally the New more than the Old Testament'. These complaints must be dealt with in their place.

First, it is necessary to answer Selden's reproach, and to make clear when we are dealing with Hebrew idioms, and when we are confronted with age-old English phrases. Certain expressions regarded as Biblical and supposedly Hebrew are survivals of ancient English practice. 'Abraham *gave up the ghost*' (Gen.

P

xxv. 8) is a thousand years old. Wyclif, who knew no Hebrew or Greek, has, for Matt. xxvii. 50, 'Ihesus eftsoone criede with a greet voyce and *gaf up the goost*'. 'Well stricken in age' (Gen. xviii. 11) has no warrant in the Hebrew which reads literally 'coming on in days'. 'And Jacob *held his peace*' (Gen. xxxiv. 5) again is pure English, where the Hebrew has 'caused to be silent' or 'was silent'. Certainly the Marriage Service of 1552 intended no Hebraism in 'or els hereafter for ever *holde hys peace*', and the Clown in *Twelfth Night* singing 'Hold thy peace thou knave' intended no Biblical allusion. It is perhaps by contagion with the noble Hebrew salutation 'Peace be unto you' that this phrase has lost its English birthright. The universally known phrase, 'Three score years and ten' in Ps. xc. 10, is an English expression, introduced here by Coverdale, where the Hebrew, and even Wyclif, has plain 'seventy'. Even 'to know' in the sense of carnal knowledge is older English than the translations of the Bible.

'It is in other phrases and categories of phrase that the Hebrew idiom has left its mark: superlatives, such as 'Holy of Holies', 'Song of Songs', 'King of Kings', and 'Vanity of Vanities'; striking idioms such as 'and his countenance fell' where a long chain of revision finally fixed the Hebrew form in popular speech. Tindale has pure English in Gen iv. 5, 'and Cain was wroth exceedingly *and loured*'. Coverdale is not much nearer with 'and his countenance *changed*'. The Great Bible of 1539 comes half-way towards the literal idea with 'and his countenance *abated*', and the Geneva with its customary bluntness has 'and his countenance *fell doune*', while the Bishops remain conservative with '*abated*'. Similar idioms are 'in the eyes of the Lord', 'the face of Pharaoh'. Many a popular inversion owes its origin to Bible English: 'throne of ivory', 'altar of stone', 'helmet of brass' for 'ivory throne' and 'stone altar' and 'brass helmet', and such phrases as 'man of war', 'children of wickedness', 'man of truth', 'wine of astonishment', 'prisoners of hope', 'ways of pleasantness', 'oil of gladness', 'man of sorrows', 'Son of Man', are purely Hebrew in origin. A curious instance of the power of this particular Hebraism is found in Isa. xxvi. 4, where the Authorized Version text has 'everlasting strength' preferred to the Geneva 'strength for evermore', and the Authorized Version margin has the literal 'rocke of ages'. A specimen of close Hebrew phrasing is found in Gen. vi. 4:

> There were Giants in the earth in those daies: and also after that, when the sonnes of God came in unto the daughters of men, & they bare *children* to them; the same became mightie men, which *were* of old, men of renowme.

The translators were specially skilful in their treatment of those 'rehearsals of words' for intensive purposes so beloved of Hebrew idiom, and showed great ingenuity in their variety of rendering, as Gen. ii. 16, 'thou mayest *freely* eate [margin: eating thou shalt eate]; Gen. ii. 17, 'thou shalt *surely* die' [margin: dying thou shalt die]; Gen. xx. 7, 'thou shalt *surely* die [Geneva: 'thou shalt *die the death*]; Isa. xxiv. 20, 'the earth shall reele *to and fro*'. Other typical repetitions are rendered with felicity and variety, as Ps. xii, 2, 'with a double heart do they speake' [margin: an heart, and an heart]; Isa. xxvi. 3, 'in perfect peace' [margin: peace, peace]. These felicities are not always original to the Authorized Version, since many of the difficulties had been solved in the Geneva and even earlier versions. Both the examples given here are found in the Geneva version.

The problem of variety or uniformity of rendering had been much in the minds of the translators, and one of the most important sections of the preface is devoted to its discussion.

> 'An other thing we thinke good to admonish thee of (gentle Reader) that wee have not tyed our selves to an uniformitie of phrasing, or to an identitie of words, as some peradventure would wish that we had done, because they observe, that some learned men some where, have beene as exact as they could that way. Truly, that we might not varie

from the sense of that which we had translated before, if the word signified the same thing in both places (for there bee some wordes that bee not of the same sense every where) we were especially carefull, and made a conscience, according to our duetie. But, that we should expresse the same notion in the same particular word; as for example, if we translate the *Hebrew* or *Greeke* word once by *Purpose*, never to call it *Intent*; if one where *Journeying*, never *Traveiling*; if one where *Thinke*, never *Suppose*; if one where *Paine*, never *Ache*; if one where *Joy*, never *Gladnesse*, &c. Thus to minse the matter, wee thought to savour more of curiositie then wisedome.'

In this matter they were following the right instinct of Tindale, and deliberately rejecting Broughton's advice which had been drawn to their notice by Bancroft:

'Now the last point is to remember to translate with uniformity, all that is a like, though it be often repeated. The Reader will be greatly confounded, when he hath divers words in a translation, where the original hath the same unaltered . . . Tremellius herein deserved high commendation, he was very careful to be uniform in his translation. And if many translate, each a part, when they have brought a good English style, and a true sense, a new labour should others take to make a uniformitie, and that will be a very tedious pain; but many hands will make light work.'

Much of the musical variety which beautifies the Authorized Version is due to this practice, but equally much confusion and obscuring of important relationship has resulted therefrom, especially in the New Testament. An extreme example is *katargeo* and *katargeomai*, occurring twenty-seven times in the New Testament, and rendered in seventeen different ways, as Rom. vi. 6, ' to destroy '; Rom. iii. 31, 'to make void'; Rom. iv. 14, 'to make of none effect'; 1 Cor. i. 28, 'to bring to nought'; 2 Cor. iii. 13, 'to abolish'. This is balanced, if not justified, by making one word 'trouble' serve for a dozen different Greek words.

One important aspect of this stylistic variety is that many

significant relationships between the gospels are obscured. Matt. xxvi. 41 and Mark xiv. 38 are identical in the Greek, but the Authorized Version renders the two passages 'Watch and pray, *that* yee enter not into temptation: the spirit *indeed* is willing, but the flesh is weake', and 'Watch *ye* and pray, *lest* yee enter into temptation: the spirit *truly* is *ready*, but the flesh is weake.' This difference, while fitting in with the general policy of the translators, is here the result of a close adherence to Tindale's renderings, although Coverdale and Geneva had preserved the identity. Again Luke vii. 50 and Luke xvii. 19 contain identical words in the original, but are represented by 'Thy faith hath *saved thee*' and 'thy faith hath *made thee whole*', also after Tindale, who preserved the identity in 1526, but changed the wording in 1534. In Matt. xix. 20, and Mark x. 20, the Authorized Version makes a difference not found in Tindale or Geneva. Many instances of rhetorical points made in the original are obscured by translating identical or related words differently, as 1 Cor. iii. 17, 'If any man *defile* [margin: destroy] the temple of God, him shall God *destroy*. This follows Tindale, but Geneva preserves the point. In 2 Cor. iii. 5, 6 the Authorized Version is led by Geneva into abandoning an echo in 'our *sufficiencie* is of God: Who also hath made us able ministers' where Tindale has 'our *ableness* commeth of God, which hath made us *able* to minister'.

An interesting case is the thrice repeated quotation of Gen. xv. 6 which appears in the Old Testament as 'and hee *counted* it to him for righteousnesse', and in the New Testament, Rom. iv. 3, as 'and it was *counted* unto him for righteousnes', Gal. iii. 6, 'and it was *accounted* [margin and Geneva: *imputed*. Tindale: *ascribed*] to him for righteousnesse', and James ii. 23, 'and it was *imputed unto* [Tindale: *reputed*] him for righteousnes'. Or again the quotation from Deut. xxxii. 35, 'To me belongeth vengeance, and recompence' is given as 'Vengeance is mine, I will repay' in Rom. xii. 19, and 'Vengeance belongeth unto

me, I wil recompence' in Heb. x. 30, again substantially
following Tindale's example. It is not uninteresting to see how
the Bishops dealt with the problem: Deut. xxxii. 35 has 'Vengeance is mine, and I will rewarde', Rom. xii. 19 has 'Vengeance
is mine, I will repay, and Heb. x. 30, 'Vengeance [belongeth]
unto me, I will render'. Sometimes the variations may be
attributed to the practice of the different revisers, especially in
the treatment of proper names, which appear variously in different parts of the Bible, sometimes following the Hebrew form,
sometimes the Greek, and sometimes even the Latin, as Jeremiah,
Jeremias, and Jeremie, Tyrus and Tyre, Elijah and Elias,
Noah and Noe, Elisha and Eliseus, Hosea and Osee, Isaiah,
Esaias, and Esay, Hezekiah and Ezekias, Marcus and Mark,
Lucas and Luke, Joshua and Jesus.

Too close a scrutiny of the English text can obscure the main
truth, that however much the Latin or the earlier English
translations may have influenced the rendering, or even the
choice of phrases, the final wording is the English wording of
the revisers, and the final music is the result of sure instinct
working subtly on the vast and various material offered. An
excellent instance of this subtlety is Prov. iii. 17, where Coverdale, the Great Bible and the Bishops' agree in reading

Her wayes are pleasant wayes and all her paths are peaceable.

Geneva has:

Her wayes are wayes of pleasure and all her paths prosperitie.

The Authorized Version takes these, turns back to the Hebrew
text more accurately than the others, adds a music of allitera-
tion and tactful balance which gives the final version a perfect
melody in

Her wayes are wayes of plesantnesse, and all her pathes *are* peace.

It is in the Psalter, with its special problem of poetical
parallelism, that the triumph is most clearly seen, and a glance

at the evolution of certain famous passages will illustrate the point.

Ps. cxiv. 4:

> *Cov. & 1539.* The mountaynes skipped lyke rammes, and the lytle hilles lyke yonge shepe.
>
> *Geneva.* The mountaines leaped like rams, & the hilles as lambes.
>
> *Bish.* The mountaynes skypped lyke rammes; and the litle hilles like young lambes.
>
> *A.V.* The mountaines skipped like rammes: and the little hilles like lambes.

Ps. ciii. 15:

> *Cov.* That a man in his tyme is but as is grasse, & florisheth as a floure of the felde.
>
> *1539.* The dayes of man are but as grasse, for he florysheth as a floure of the felde.
>
> *Geneva.* The dayes of man are as grasse: as a flower of the field, so florisheth he.
>
> *Bish.* The dayes of man are as [the dayes] of an hearbe: he florisheth as a floure in the fielde.
>
> *A.V.* As for man, his dayes *are* as grasse: as a flower of the field, so he flourisheth.

In these the brilliance of the music is equalled only by the fidelity to the Hebrew original.

In Ps. viii. 4–6, however, the fact that we find the passage quoted in Heb. ii. 6–8 has dominated the translation from Tindale downward. In 1525 Tindale had 'What is man, that thou art myndefull of him? other the sonne of man, that thou visitest hym', but though Geneva had correctly rendered 'For thou hast made him a little lower than God', where the Bishops' reads 'Thou hast made hym somethyng inferiour to angels', the Authorized Version keeps the 'angels' of Tindale's New Testament and Coverdale's Psalter in the memorable 'For thou hast made him a little lower than the angels' and despite the Revised Version correction the musical error is likely to persist.

This rejection of the Genevan reading is characteristic of the whole treatment of the Psalms in this respect. A fundamental revision and often a completely new translation was made, there are enormous differences from the Geneva, though the reading of the Geneva is often transferred to the margin. There are very many marginal notes from the Hebrew, as though a serious attempt was made to supply the materials for a correct rendering in accordance with the original, although the pull of the older versions and the avowed policy of making 'out of many good ones, one principall good one', prevented a completely new and accurate translation without deference to traditional error. On the other hand, the revision of the *Song of Songs* owes very much to Geneva. It owes, among other things, 'stay me with flagons' as against the Bishops' 'set about mee cuppes of wine', and 'terrible as an army with banners' against the Bishops' 'feare full as an armie of men with their banners', but adds of its own the 'Rose of Sharon' and 'many waters cannot quench love'.

In the New Testament the treatment of Revelation is particularly noteworthy. Special use was made of the version based on Junius which appeared in the later Geneva Testaments alongside of Tomson's revision of the earlier Geneva translations. Sometimes the traditional wording which had persisted unchanged from Tindale is deserted in favour of Junius, e.g. i. 1, 'sent and *shewed*' becomes 'sent and signified'; sometimes the authority of Junius is accepted for a return to Tindale against Geneva and Tomson as in i. 5, 'his *oune* bloud', though occasionally a return is made to a forceful and idiomatic rendering in Tindale on the authority of the Bishops', e.g. ii. 27, 'as the vessels of a potter shall they be broken to shivers' from Tindale's 'shall he breake them to shevers', where Geneva has merely 'be broken'. In general Revelation is very close indeed to Tomson, with verbal rearrangements and many tiny verbal changes from Junius. To Junius, also, is due the reshaping of clumsy and complicated sentences.

The treatment of the Apocrypha should rightly need a

chapter to itself. The Apocrypha is the Cinderella of Bible
translation. Luther insulted it, Coverdale, following Zürich,
apologized for it. The Prayer of Manasses appears for the first
time in Matthew's Bible, and even there only in a literal
rendering from Olivetan's French. Sometimes even its title is
mistakenly given as 'The Bokes of Hagiographa', as in the Great
Bible of 1539 and later. An interesting edition is Becke's
*Taverner* printed in 1551, where 3 Esdras, Tobit, and
Judith are entirely retranslated from Greek and Latin, and
3 Maccabees, with its delightful and topical stories of Divine
Providence foiling the plots of dictators against the Jews by
means of paper shortage and trampling elephants, appears in
English for the first time. The Puritans rejected the Apocrypha
as an addition to the inspired text. Scotland had very little use
for it, and very frequently Bibles were issued without it. Or-
dinances were issued to compel the inclusion of the Apocrypha,
as in 1615 when Archbishop Abbot forbade any printer to issue
a Bible without the Apocrypha on pain of a year's imprisonment.
The Bible printed in America in 1782–3 had no Apocrypha,
and, according to Sir H. Howarth,[1] the offer of the Bible Society
to supply a Bible for the Coronation of Edward VII was rejected
by Archbishop Temple, on the grounds that, wanting the
Apocrypha, it was an imperfect and mutilated Bible.

When we compare the Authorized Version Apocrypha with
earlier renderings we find some important differences. Coverdale's 'Boke of Tobias' is a narrative in the third person, the
Authorized Version and Geneva follow an entirely different
text written in the first person, and the Bishops' Bible follows
Coverdale. Judith in Coverdale and the Bishops' Bible is based on
a different text from that followed in Geneva and the Authorized
Version. For the 'rest of the Chapters of Esther' which Coverdale says 'are not to be founde in the text of the Hebrue, but in
the Greke and Latyn', the Bishops' version has 'which are

[1] *Journal of Theological Studies*, Oct. 1906.

neither found in the Hebrew nor in the Chalde. The XI Chapter after the Latine', Geneva has 'which are found in some Greek and Latin translations', the Authorized Version has 'neither in the Hebrew nor in the Calde. Part of the tenth chapter after the Greeke'. Ecclesiasticus has two prologues, the first wanting in Coverdale and the Bishops', but present in Geneva ('this argument was found in a certaine Greeke copie') and in the Authorized Version. Certain passages in square brackets in Geneva are 'read in the Latine copies and not in yᵉ Greeke'. The Authorized Version translation of the Apocrypha is on the whole a complete revision. I and II Esdras wavers among the older versions in arbitrary fashion, rejecting in I. i. 1, 'the feast of Easter' from Coverdale and Bishops', but keeps in I. i. 19, 'the feast of sweet bread' with Coverdale and Bishops' against Geneva's 'unleavened bread', or as in II Esdras xii. 3, rounds out a phrase like 'the trouble and traunce of my minde' with Geneva and the Bishops' against the simpler Coverdale, or arbitrates between Geneva and the Bishops' in II. xiii. 30, where Geneva rejects Coverdale's 'in a traunce of mynde shall he come upon them' in favour of 'And hee shall astonish the hearts of them that dwell upon the earth', where the Bishops go back to Coverdale in the text and borrow the Genevan rendering for their margin, and overgoes them both in the fine 'And he shall come to the astonishment of them that dwell on the earth'. 'Tobit' is a perfunctory revision closely indebted to Geneva, even to the marginal notes. 'Judith' relies on Geneva, but is considerably revised in detail, choosing a memorable phrase such as 'Her beautie tooke his minde prisoner' from Geneva in xvi. 9 against the older 'captivated his minde'. In 'the chapters of Esther', the Authorized Version is mainly guided by Geneva against the Bishops', when not original. 'Susanna' is very close indeed to Geneva.

e.g. *Cov. and Bish.* They burned for lust to her, yee they were allmost out of their wittes.

*Gen. and A.V.* So that their lust was inflamed toward her.

The evolution of certain famous or significant passages will indicate more clearly the relation of the Authorized Version to its forerunners in various triumphs of smoothness, of dignity, felicity, force, and music.

Isaiah ii. 4:

*Cov. and Matt.* So that they shal breake their swerdes and speares, to make sythes, sycles & sawes thereof. From that tyme forth shal not one people lift up wapen agaynst another, nether shal they lerne to fight from thensforth.

*Gen.* they shall breake their swords also into mattocks, and their speares into sithes: nation shall not lift up a sworde against nation, neither shall they learne to fight any more.

*Bish.* they shall breake their swords into Mattockes, and their speares to make sithes: And one people shall not lift up a weapon against another, neither shall they learne to fyght from thenceforth.

*A.V.* they shall beate their swords into plow-shares, and their speares into pruning hookes [Or, sythes]: nation shall not lift up sword against nation, neither shall they learne warre any more.

Job. xxxviii. 7:

*Cov.* When the mornynge starres gave me prayse, and when all the angels of God rejoysed.

*Matt. and Bish.* When the morning starres praysed mee together, and all the Children of God rejoyced triumphantly.

*Gen.* When the starres of the morning praysed *me* together, and all the children of God rejoyced.

*A.V.* When the morning starres sang together, and all the sonnes of God shouted for joy.

Job. iii. 17:

*Cov.* There must the wicked ceasse from their tyranny, there soch as are overlaboured, be at rest.

*Gen.* The wicked have there ceased from their tyrannie, and there they that laboured valiantly, are at rest.

*A.V.* There the wicked cease *from* troubling: and there the wearie[1] be at rest.

---

[1] Heb. wearied in strength.

Isa. iii. 15:

> *Cov. Matt. and Tav.* Wherefore do ye oppresse my people, and marre y^e faces of the innocentes.
>
> *Gen.* What have ye to do, that ye beat my people to peeces, and grinde the faces of the poore.
>
> *Bish.* What meane ye that ye bray (as in a mortar) my people, and grinde the faces of the poore.
>
> *A.V.* What meane yee *that* yee beat my people to pieces, and grinde the faces of the poore.

2 Sam. i. 26–7:

> *Cov.* I am sory for the my brother Ionathas: thou hast bene very lovely unto me: Thy love hath bene more speciall unto me then the love of wemen. How are the Worthies fallen, and y^e weapens destroyed.
>
> *Matt.* Woo is me for the my brother Ionathas: delectable to me wast thou excedyng. Thy love to me was wonderfull, passing y^e love of wemen. How were thy mightie overthrowen, & how were the wepons of warre forloren.
>
> *Gen. and Bish.* Woe is me for thee, my brother Ionathan: very kinde hast thou bene unto me: thy love to me was wonderful, passing the love of women: how are the mighty overthrowen, and the weapons of warre destroyed.
>
> *A.V.* I am distressed for thee, my brother Ionathan, very pleasant hast thou beene unto mee: thy love to mee was wonderfull, passing the love of women. How are the mightie fallen, and the weapons of warre perished!

Isa. i. 18:

> *Cov. and Matt.* Though youre synnes be as read as scarlet shal they not be whyter then snowe: And though they were like purple shall they not be like white wolle.
>
> *Bish.* Though your sinnes be as red as scarlet, they shalbe as whyte as snow: and though they were lyke purple, they shalbe as whyte as wooll.
>
> *Gen.* Thogh your sinnes were as crimsin, they shalbe made white as snowe: thogh they were red like skarlet, they shal be as woll.

*A.V.* Though your sinnes be as scarlet, they shall be as white as snow; though they be red like crimsin, they shall be as wooll.

Matt. xxiii. 27:

*Tin.* Paynted tombes, which appere beautyfull outwarde (marginal summary 1534: Paynted sepulchres).

*Cov.* Paynted Sepulchres, that appeare beutyfull outwarde.

*Cran. and Bish.* paynted sepulchres, which indeed appear beautiful outward.

*Gen.* whited tombes which appeare beautifull outward (margin: or painted).

*A.V.* whited sepulchres, which indeed appeare beautifull outward.

1 Cor. xiii:

*Tin.* And though I coulde prophesy, and understode all secretes, and all knowledge: yee, yf I had all fayth so that I coulde move mountayns oute of ther places, and yet had no love, I were nothynge.

. . . . . . . .

Love suffreth longe, and is corteous. Love envieth not. Love doth not frowardly, swelleth not dealeth not dishonestly, seketh not her awne, is not provoked to anger, thynketh not evyll, reioyseth not in iniquite: but reioyseth in the trueth, suffreth all thynge, beleveth all thynges, hopeth all thynges, endureth in all thynges.

. . . . . . .

When I was a chylde, I spake as a chylde, I understode as a childe, I ymagened as a chylde. But assone as I was a man, I put awaye childesshnes. Now we se in a glasse even in a darke speakynge: but then shall we se face to face.

*Gen.* And though I had the *gift* of prophecie, and knew all secretes and all knowledge, yea, if I had all faith, so that I coulde remoove mountaines, and had not love, I were nothing.

. . . . . . . .

Love suffereth long: it is bountifull: love envieth not: lov doeth not boast it selfe: it is not puffed up:

It disdaineth not: it seeketh not her owne thinges: it is no provoked to anger: it thinketh not evill:

It reioyceth not in iniquitie, but reioyceth in the trueth:

It suffereth all things: it beleeveth all things: it hopeth all things: it endureth all things.

.   .   .   .   .   .   .   .

When I was a childe, I spake as a childe, I understode as a childe: I thought as a childe: but when I became a man, I put away childish things.

For nowe we see through a glasse darkely: but then *shall we see* face to face.

*Bish.* And though I have prophecie, and understande all secretes, and all knowledge: yea if I have all faith, so that I can remoove mountaines, and have not charitie, I am nothing.

.   .   .   .   .   .   .   .

Charitie suffereth long, and it is courteous: charitie envieth not, charitie doeth not frowardly, swelleth not, [Or, is not puft up].

Dealeth not dishonestly, seeketh not her owne, is not bitter, thinketh not evill.

Reioyceth not in iniquitie, but reioyceth in the trueth:

Suffereth all things, beleeveth all things, hopeth all things, endureth all things.

.   .   .   .   .   .   .   .

When I was a childe, I spake as a child, I understood as a child, I imagined as a child: but as sone as I was a man, I put away childishnesse.

Nowe we see in a glasse, even in a darke speaking: but then [shall we see] face to face.

*A.V.* And though I have the gift of prophesie, and understand all mysteries and all knowledge: and though I have all faith, so that I could remoove mountaines, and have no charitie, I am nothing.

.   .   .   .   .   .   .   .

Charitie suffereth long, and is kinde: charitie envieth not: charitie vaunteth not it selfe [Or, is not rash], is not puffed up,

Doeth not behave it selfe unseemly, seeketh not her owne, is not easily provoked, thinketh no evill,

Rejoyceth not in iniquitie, but reioyceth in the trueth: [Or, with the trueth].

Beareth all things, beleeveth all things, hopeth all things, endureth all things.

.    .    .    .    .    .    .

When I was a childe, I spake as a childe, I understood as a childe, I thought [Or, reasoned] as a childe: but when I became a man, I put away childish things. For now we see through a glasse darkely: [Gr. in a riddle] but then face to face.

### 4. *Subsequent History*

The King James Bible was published in a Black Letter folio in 1611, and a second issue appeared in the same year. The New Testament was printed separately in Black Letter 12mo in 1611. The first edition of the Bible in Roman type, in quarto, was in 1612, and the first folio in Roman type in 1616. The next third of a century saw a struggle between the Geneva and the Authorized Version for popular favour. The older struggle was between the Geneva and the Bishops' version. Between 1560 and the beginning of King James's reign some ninety editions of the Geneva Bible were printed, but in the years between 1568 and the date of its last issue in 1606 only about thirty editions of the Bishops' Bible appeared, though the Bishops' New Testament persisted in five editions until 1618. The supremacy of the Geneva version in the early years of the seventeenth century is shown by the appearance before 1611 of thirty editions as against a single edition of the Bishops'. By 1640 Barker, the King's Printer, and his followers had issued fifty editions of the King James Version, but only about ten editions of the Geneva Bible appeared in those years. The Geneva, however, was the favourite of many distinguished men. It is used after 1611 even by members of the translation committee, and the Preface to the 1611 Bible itself, as we have seen, quotes from the Geneva text. One reason for the continued popularity of the Geneva Bible was the guidance and interpretation provided by the voluminous commentary. In 1642 a Dutch publisher reprinted the Authorized Version with the Geneva notes, and in 1649 there was an English edition, reissued in 1679, 1708, and 1715. In calculating the number of editions account must always be taken of surreptitious and pirated issues from the Continent. A pamphlet entitled 'Scintilla' 1641, reprinted in Arber's transcript of the *Stationers' Register*, gives a valuable glimpse of the import trade in bootleg Bibles, and the attempt to break the monopoly of the King's Printers.

During the Commonwealth the desire for notes bore fruit in a petition by the printers and stationers of London in 1644 for licence to print annotations. This resulted in a huge collection popularly known as 'The Assembly's Annotations', wherein the marginal notes of a distinguished body of scholars were magnified into 'an entire commentary on the Sacred Scriptures, the like never before published in English'. A chance surviving letter from the Rev. John Allen in London to a friend at Rye in 1664 gives a glimpse of one customer at least. 'I cannot yet get a Bible for the old woman, but one printed 1661, 12s price, and 6d if claspet; but I count that too deare, and not of the edition she desires, with Bezas annotations.' Cromwell's pocket 'Soldier's Bible' in 1643 consisted of extracts, mainly from the Geneva Bible, and with the last issue of the Geneva in 1644 the Authorized Version had become the general Bible of the English people. In 1714 the first Bible was printed in Ireland. The first New Testament in America is dated 1742 with a London imprint, though printed at Boston, and a Bible was issued in the same manner in 1752. The first acknowledged American Bible is the Philadelphia edition of 1782.

The Authorized Version as generally printed to-day differs widely from the original edition of 1611, as a comparison with Dr. A. W. Pollard's tercentenary reprint will show. Almost every edition, from the very beginning, introduced corrections and unauthorized changes and additions, often adding new errors in the process. The edition of 1613 shows over three hundred differences from 1611. The Cambridge edition of 1629 was carefully revised by an anonymous editor, but it was the edition of 1638, a folio by Buck and Daniel, which first seriously attempted to supply an 'authentique corrected Bible', in a revision by some of the survivors of the original body of translators. Special attention was paid to the treatment of words in italics. It was in the eighteenth century, however, that the main changes were made. In 1762 Dr. Paris at Cambridge made the first attempt at an extensive revision of the text, and Dr. Blayney at Oxford in 1769 put in an enormous amount of work lasting nearly four years. The marginal references were checked and verified, over 30,000 new marginal references were added, the chapter summaries and running headnotes were thoroughly revised, the punctuation was altered and made uniform in accordance with modern practice, textual errors were removed, the use of capitals was considerably modified and reduced, and a thorough revision made in the form of certain kinds of words: 'fetched' was substituted for 'fet', 'burned' for 'burnt', 'lifted' for 'lift', 'since' for 'sith', in 35 instances 'more' was written for 'moe', and in 364 'ye' for 'you'. Dr. Paris had already altered 'neesed' to 'sneezed', 'cruddled' to 'curdled', and 'glistering' to 'glittering'.

The issue of the King James's Version in 1611 did not put an end to translation of the Bible. New translations and proposals for translation began to arise in the seventeenth century and filled the eighteenth century. The Puritan translators were actuated by a desire to keep as close to the original text as possible, and there are some important translations in 'The Five Books of Moses, the Psalms, and the Canticles' published in 1639 by Henry Ainsworth, the Brownist leader and a remarkably fine Hebrew scholar. His faithful renderings, however, are not accompanied by felicity or music of style, and retain an over strict Hebrew order contradicting the English idiom. From Scotland in 1655 came an important proposal by

John Row for a revision of the Authorized Bible, suggesting, among other things

    I. That all useles additions be lop't off, y$^t$ debase the wisdom of y$^e$ spirit;—to instance

        All y$^e$ Apocryphall writings; being meerly humane.

    II. Many evil changes are to be amended, as these 9 in particular.

        1. When words, or sentences, are mistaken.

        2. When y$^e$ margin is righter than y$^e$ line, as in 800 places (and more) it is.

        3. When particles are confounded.

        4. When a word plurall is translated as singular.

        5. When the active is rendered as if a passive.

        6. When the genders are confounded: as mostly y$^e$ cantic bee.

        7. When Hebrismes are omitted, in silence, or amisse.

        8. When participium paül is rendered as if it were nyphall.

        9. When conjugatio pyël is Inglish't as if kal.

    III. Good changes are to be warily endeavour'd, viz.

        1. Put more in Inglish (even *propria nomina*:) less in Heb., Gr., and Latin terms.

        2. That Ingl. words (not understood in Scotland) be idiomatiz'd.

        3. Something equivocal to Keri, and Kethib, be noticed.

Ainsworth's and Row's activities were but symptomatic of much that was being done, and in April 1653 a bill was brought before the Long Parliament

'It being now above forty years since our new translation was finished . . . And forasmuch as the translation by Mr. H. Ainsworth of Moses and the Psalms, and Song of Solomon, is greatly commended by many of the learned as far more agreeable to the Hebrew than ours; and it is said that there are MSS. of his translations of some other Scriptures both of the Old and New Testament. And also in other parts of the Holy Scriptures, some have translated verses and some chapters; and we hear that some have translated the New Testament, if not the Old also, and would have them printed and published in our nation. Which if it should be done on their own heads, without due care for the supervising thereof by learned persons sound in the fundamentals of the Christian religion, might be a precedent of dangerous consequence, emboldening other to do the like.'

A committee was appointed, including Dr. John Owen, Dr. Ralph Cudworth, and Mr. John Row, Hebrew professor in Aberdeen, without whose authority no new translation should be permitted to appear. In 1657 a further committee, including Brian Walton, editor of a handsome Polyglott Bible, was appointed to consider Ainsworth's and other translations, to examine and if necessary promote the 1611 and other marginal readings to be 'in the line', and to print a revised translation for public use. This project fell through on the dissolution of Parliament.

## 5. *Eighteenth-century Versions*

The seventeenth century was, in the main, too much under the domination of the 1611 version for much alternative to be offered, but the eighteenth century burgeoned. Immense advances in Biblical scholarship had caused dissatisfaction with the older renderings. The presentation of the Codex Alexandrinus to Charles I in 1628 and the issue of Walton's Polyglott in 1654–7 with its appendix of 'various readings' had shaken the belief in a divinely inspired and unalterable text of the Greek New Testament. The publication of Dr. John Mill's new folio edition of the Greek Testament in 1707, with its 30,000 readings, was an even greater shock, and the controversy between the deist Anthony Collins and the great scholar Richard Bentley brought even more publicity to the matter. Professional and amateur scholarship during the eighteenth century resulted in a flood of translation, both in prose and in verse, which strikingly parallels the growth of English literature during the period. Three main trends may be distinguished: (1) that which illustrates the use of colloquial style; (2) that which illustrates the dignified style of the age of Dr. Johnson; and (3) that which illustrates the change towards the new romantic conception of poetry.

The course of English prose had moved away from the glories of the Renaissance. Andrewes, Donne, Hooker, Browne, Burton, and Jeremy Taylor had been replaced by the calmer, clearer, more scientific prose of the Royal Society, of Cowley and Sprat, Dryden, Defoe, and Swift, and Bible translation endeavoured to reflect this change. Music became clarity, and clarity became pertness. A new colloquial style, headed by Roger L'Estrange and Jeremy Collier, and culminating in the low journalese of Ned Ward and Tom Brown, had inaugurated a new fashion of retranslating the older classics 'in the humour of the age'. In 1729 one Mace published anonymously *The New Testament in Greek and English . . . corrected from the Authority of the most Authentic Manuscripts* in which not only a new Greek text, of some importance historically, was provided, but an entirely new English translation was added, in free-running paragraphs, using the language of the day, and breaking sharply away from traditional dignity and traditional phrasing:

Matt. vi. 16. When ye fast, don't put on a dismal air, as the hypocrites do.

1 Cor. vii. 36. if any man thinks it would be a reflexion upon his manhood to be a stale batchelor.

Mark xiv. 65. and the domestics slapt him on the cheeks.

Luke xvii. 27. eating and drinking, marriages and matches, was the business.

James ii. 3. if you should respectfully say to the suit of fine cloths, sit you there, that's for quality.

James iii. 5, 6. the tongue is but a small part of the body, yet how grand are its pretensions! a spark of fire! what quantities of timber will it blow into a flame? the tongue is a brand that sets the world in a combustion: it is but one of the numerous organs of the body, yet it can blast whole assemblies: tipp'd with infernal sulphur it sets the whole train of life in a blaze.

1 Cor. xiii. 4. Social affection is patient, is kind;

There is also an interesting double rendering of the nautical chapter, Acts xxvii, in plain English and in sea terms. 'we had a hard gale at northeast', 'were forced to lye a-try (i.e. to drive under a reef mainsail)'. In America, Benjamin Franklin, whether wholly seriously we cannot say, offered a specimen of 'Part of the First Chapter of Job modernized':

6. And it being *levee* day in heaven, all God's nobility came to court to present themselves before him; and Satan also appeared in the circle, as one of the ministry.

7. And God said to Satan: You have been a long time absent; where were you? And Satan answered: I have been at my country seat, and in different places visiting my friends.

8. And God said: Well, what think you of Lord Job? You see he is my best friend, a perfectly honest man, full of respect for me, and avoiding every thing that might offend me.

9. And Satan answered; does your Majesty imagine that his [Job's] good conduct is the effect of mere personal attachment and affection?

10. Have you not protected him, and heaped your benefits upon him, till he is grown enormously rich.

11. Try him; only withdraw your favor, turn him out of his places, and withhold his pensions, and you will find him in the opposition.

An important but neglected revision midway between familiarity and stiffness, was John Wesley's New Testament published in 1755 with notes 'for plain, unlettered men who understand only their Mother Tongue'. This was a careful, humble work, based on minute study of the Greek text. 'I have never, so much as in one place, altered it, for altering sake: But there, and there only, where, First, The Sense was made better, stronger, clearer, or more consistent with the Context: Secondly, Where the Sense being equally good, the Phrase was better or nearer the Original . . . there is, to my Apprehension, I know not what peculiarly solemn and venerable in the Old Language of our Translation'. An interesting feature was the return to the pre-Geneva practice of paragraphing. 'Though the old division of chapters is retained for the more easy finding of any text: yet the whole is likewise divided, according to the sense, into distinct Sections: a little circumstance which makes many passages more intelligible to the Reader.' There are some 12,000 alterations from the 1611 text, partly due to the use of a different text, and partly to a free use of the Authorized Version margins. 1 Cor. xiii reads as follows, the italics marking the differences are mine:

*Love* suffereth long and is kind; *love* envieth not; *love acteth not rashly*, is not puffed up: Doth not behave *indecently*, seeketh not her own, is not provoked, thinketh no evil.

When I was a child, *I talked* as a child, I understood as a child, *I reasoned* as a child; but when I became a man, I put away childish things. *And* now we see *by means of* a glass *obscurely*.

A *New and Literal Translation* by the Quaker Anthony Purver in 1764 is also on the whole a good and much under-rated specimen of the middle style, and may be judged from the following specimens of varying quality:

Judges v. 26. She put forth her Hand to the Nail, and her right Hand to the working Hammer; so struck Sisera, she struck into his Head, and continuing the Strokes, pierced through his Temples.

27. Between her Feet he bended, he fell, he lay along: between her Feet bending, falling; where he bended, there he fell down bereaved of all.

Eccles. xii. 8. Every Thing is Vanity, says the Preacher, very vain.

Song. ii. 5. Support me with Cordials, strew Choice of Apples for me; because I am sick with Love.

12. Earth's Lap displays her infant Flowers, the warbling Spring is welcomed in, and hark how the Turtle-dove cooes in our Clime.

Matt. v. 40. And let him that will sue thee, and take thy Coat, have also the Waistcoat.

vi. 9. Thus therefore do you pray: Our Father who art in Heaven, sacredly reverenced be thy Name; Let thy Kingdom come; may thy Will be done, even on the Earth according as in Heaven; Give us our daily Bread to Day; And forgive us our Trespasses, as we also forgive those that trespass against us; And do not bring us into trial, but deliver us from Wickedness; since the Kingdom, Power, and Glory is thine for ever: so let it be.

It is difficult, as we see from one or two of the above passages, to keep the accent of an age out of its writings, and one of the most discussed and insulted of all eighteenth-century renderings, that of Dr. Edward Harwood in 1768, is a mirror of the later century. It has often been regarded unfairly as a literal translation, but was published as *A Liberal Translation of the New Testament; Being an Attempt to translate the Sacred Writings with the same Freedom, Spirit, and Elegance, with which other English Translations from the Greek Classics have lately been executed.* 'This is not a *verbal* translation, but a *liberal* and *diffusive* version of the sacred classics, and is calculated to answer the purpose of an explanatory paraphrase as well as a free and elegant translation.' This should remove much of the reproach hurled against it, and the author would be rewarded 'if men of cultivated and improved minds, especially YOUTH, could be allured by the innocent stratagem of a *modern style*, to read a book, which is now, alas! too generally neglected and disregarded by the young and gay'. The work is a monument, and asks to be measured by the language, of 'Hume, Robertson, Lowth, Lyttelton, Hurd, Melmoth, Johnson and Hawkesworth'.

Matt. v. 17. Do not think that the design of my coming into the world is to abrogate the law of Moses, and the prophets—I am only come to supply their deficiencies, and to give mankind a more complete and perfect system of morals.

v. 18. For I tell you that the precepts of morality are of eternal and immutable obligation, and their power and efficacy shall never be relaxed or annulled, while the world endures.

vi. 7. Think not the design of prayer is by the dint of importunity to teaze the Deity into a compliance with our requests—Carefully avoid therefore the errour of the heathens who think that the supreme Being can be prevailed upon by enthusiastic clamours, and a constant unvaried repetition of noisy expressions.

The Lord's Prayer becomes a remarkable document of the eighteenth century.

> In order to guard you from mistakes in this important concern I will propose the following as a model for your devotions—O Thou great governour and parent of universal nature—who manifestest thy glory to the blessed inhabitants of heaven—may all thy rational creatures in all the parts of thy boundless dominion be happy in the knowledge of thy existence and providence, and celebrate thy perfections in a manner most worthy thy nature and perfective of their own!
>
> May the glory of thy moral government be advanced, and the great laws of it be more generally obeyed—May the inhabitants of this world pay as cheerful a submission and as constant an obedience to thy will, as the happy spirits do in the regions of immortality—
>
> As thou hast hitherto most mercifully supplied our wants, deny us not the necessaries and conveniences of life, while thou art pleased to continue us in it—
>
> Pardon the numerous errours and sins, which we have been guilty of towards thee; as we freely forgive and erase from our hearts the injuries that our fellow creatures have done to us—
>
> Suffer no temptation to assault us too powerful for the frailty of our natures and the imperfection of our virtue—but in all our trials may thine almighty aid interpose and rescue us from vice and ruin—
>
> These requests we address unto thee, for thou art possessed of power which enables thee to succour, and of goodness, which disposes thee to befriend all thy creatures—and these thy glorious perfections will continue immutable, and be the subjects of praise and adoration throughout all the ages of eternity! amen!

The Unitarian version of Gilbert Wakefield in 1791, the Universalist rendering of Nathaniel Scarlett 'assisted by Men of

Piety and Literature' in 1798 with its assignment of *Dramatis Personae*, the *New Testament* of Philip Doddridge, 1765, the *Four Gospels*, by George Campbell, 1790, the *New Testament* of Archbishop Newcome 1809 (printed 1796) and the *Epistles* of James Macknight, 1795, are all worthy of special attention, as are Bishop Lowth's *New Translation of Isaiah* 1778, Benjamin Blayney's *Jeremiah and Lamentations* 1784, and *A Revised Translation and Interpretation of the Sacred Scriptures after the Eastern manner* by David Macrae 1799. Two works of considerable importance, not for any great intrinsic merit, but as the first English translations by Jewish scholars, are Isaac Delgado's 'Pentateuch' of 1785, and David Levi's 'Pentateuch' of 1787. These are the first of a long line of independent translations culminating in the 'The Holy Scriptures according to the Masoretic Text: A new Translation, with the aid of previous Versions and with constant consultation of Jewish authorities . . .', issued by a Committee of Jewish scholars in America in 1917. This preserves the traditional order and grouping of the books, as well as the paragraphing of the Rabbinical Bible.

The eighteenth century has one last merit to be considered. It is the century which saw the final rehabilitation of Hebrew poetry. There was never a period when the poetry of the Bible was not held in esteem by poets and scholars. It was a constant theme of the Renaissance, and Spenser's poetical version of the Song of Songs is one of the lost glories of English literature. Milton exalted the literature of the Bible, and Addison elegantly praised it. It remained for a new current of European poetical feeling to bring the poetry of the Bible into its proper place. The cry in poetry was for the pure, the primitive, and the passionate. The pre-romantic searchers sought lyric passion in the North, the South, the West, and finally in the East, adding to Icelandic, Indian, Gothic, Celtic, and Eskimo poetry the familiar but overlooked Hebrew. Bishop Lowth's Oxford lectures in Latin on 'The Sacred Poetry of the Hebrews', published in 1753 and translated later into English, opened up a new world of poetical wonder. He spoke of poetical imagery, of mystical allegory, of sublimity of expression, sentiment, and passion, and in the nineteenth lecture dealt seriously for the first time with the 'parallelism' of Hebrew poetic structure. His discussion of the Psalms, of Job, and of the Song of Songs marked an epoch in the literary study of the Bible. In the light of new scholarship and new interpretation the poetical books of the Bible were printed in scores of new prose and verse renderings. The story is a long and complicated one, and is told in a remarkable M.A. Thesis on 'Some Aspects of the treatment of the Psalms and the Song of Solomon in English Eighteenth-Century Literature' written for me in 1937 by Mr. B. Simmons. He tells the story of the dissolution of the Augustan conception of poetry with the aid of the reaffirmation of the poetic value of the Bible in the years from 1740, and picks out Bishop Percy's *Song of Solomon* 1764 as an important landmark. 'From Percy's version onwards, all literary renderings aimed not only at bringing out the beauty of the "Song" as a secular love lyric, but strove also to make it appear an Eastern love song.'

The versions of the Bible, in whole or in part, are manifold, and their history can be traced. A giant work, still to be done, perhaps in the old manner by committees of committees, is to trace the permeation of English religious and secular life by the substance and idiom of the English Bible. The prayers of Bishop Lancelot Andrewes and Doctor Samuel Johnson, the poetry of Shakespeare and Milton, the fiction of Bunyan, the lyrics of Blake and Hardy are but milestones on a long and fascinating journey.

J. ISAACS.

# VIII

# THE REVISED VERSION AND AFTER

## SYNOPSIS

## I. *The Demand for the Revised Version, 1800–69*

THE previous chapter has carried down the story of the English Bible to the end of the eighteenth century. By that time the necessity for a revision of the Authorized Version had long been making itself felt. Although that Version had greatly endeared itself to the Christian public by the beauty of its language, its inadequacy as a volume for biblical study was beyond question. Not only had successive printers introduced into it numerous small alterations, so that there was no fixed standard for its wording, but it was still replete with increasingly obscure archaisms and—what was worse—inconsistencies and errors innumerable, which the progress of scholarship was rendering more and more intolerable.[1] Nor indeed was it free from the dogmatic bias to which different groups of its translators had been (perhaps in part unconsciously) subject.[2]

It is with the nineteenth century that the explicit demand for an improved version, as distinct from the earlier stages of adverse criticism and of premature attempts at revision, may really be said to begin. Early in the century Thomas Belsham and other Unitarians published through the Unitarian Fund Society *The New Testament, in an Improved Version* (1808): it was based on the revised translation of Archbishop Newcome (1729–1800), but was to some extent animated by a dogmatic humanitarianism, and as a Unitarian production was, despite its numerous good emendations, largely boycotted. In *The Eclectic Review* for January 1809, Dr. John Pye Smith, President of Homerton Congregational College, made a strong appeal for an authoritative revision; and he was followed the next year by Dr. Herbert Marsh, Lady Margaret Professor of Divinity at Cambridge, in his published *Lectures on the Criticism and Interpretation of the Bible.* Thomas Wemyss, a layman, referred in his *Biblical Gleanings* (1816) to a number of passages mistranslated in the Authorized Version. Two years later Dr. John Bellamy published, under the patronage of the Prince Regent, a new translation of the Old Testament: it was a poor performance, based on the erroneous assumption that the Authorized Version had been made chiefly from the Septuagint and the Vulgate (an error shortly afterwards exposed in Whitaker's *Historical and Critical Enquiry*). Having been vehemently criticized in *The Quarterly Review*, it was defended by Sir James B. Burges in his *Reasons in favour of a New Translation of the Scriptures* (1819)—an apologia that evoked a further attack from *The Quarterly.* The controversy also called forth a *Vindication of the Authorized Translation*, by

[1] Cf., e.g., Newth, 61–78.     [2] Plumptre, 1677.

H. J. Todd, and an anonymous pamphlet by Dr. Richard
Laurence (Canon of Christ Church, Oxford), entitled *Remarks
upon the Critical Principles . . . adopted by Writers who have . . .
recommended a new Translation of the Bible* (1820), and arguing
learnedly against the possibility of improving on the Hebrew
and Greek texts on which the Authorized Version was based.
In 1828 the Rev. H. Walter replied to the criticism levelled by
Dr. Marsh (in a new edition of his *Lectures*) at the Authorized
Version of the Old Testament as to too great an extent dependent
on earlier versions made with the aid of the Vulgate.

Fresh stimulus was given to the discussion by a scholarly
booklet entitled *Hints for an Improved Translation of the New
Testament*, produced in 1832 by the Rev. Jas. Scholefield, Regius
Professor of Greek at Cambridge, and re-edited in 1836 and (in
an enlarged form) in 1849. A few years after its first appearance,
Granville Penn, a grandson of the famous Quaker, published a
revised translation of the New Testament, 'with the aid of most
ancient manuscripts, unknown to the age in which that version
was last put forth by authority'. Some caustic remarks regarding
the archaic vocabulary and literary quality of the Authorized
Version were offered by Henry Hallam in the third volume of his
*Literature of Europe* (1839): these have been deplored by later
writers; but his allusions to the doubtfulness of its accuracy and
the extreme touchiness of its defenders were really quite justified.
Another version of the New Testament was attempted by the
Unitarian Samuel Sharpe in 1840; and one of the whole Bible
was published the following year by J. T. Conquest, a medical
doctor, purporting to contain 'nearly twenty thousand emendations' (second edition, 1846).

In 1853 two editions of the Bible divided into paragraphs
appeared. One of them was the production of the Religious
Tract Society (which had first brought out a paragraph Bible in
1838), and was furnished with corrections of the text and explanatory notes. Both Bibles were welcomed in *The Edinburgh*

*Review* (Oct. 1855) by a writer who took occasion to say that it was high time that a new revision was undertaken by authority under a Royal Commission.

The matter was broached in the Lower House of Convocation in March 1856 by Canon William Selwyn, of Ely and Cambridge, but he met with comparatively little support; and later the same year he pleaded for revision in his *Notes on the proposed Amendment of the Authorized Version* (re-edited 1857)—a plea which Dr. C. J. Ellicott was also passionately urging at this time in his commentaries on the Pauline Epistles. In July 1856 Mr. James Heywood, M.P. for North Lancashire, moved in the House of Commons an address to the Crown, praying for a Royal Commission: Sir George Grey, on behalf of the Government, opposed him, and he withdrew his motion. The Rev. S. C. Malan, Vicar of Broadwindsor, published the same year *A Vindication of the Authorized Version of the English Bible, from charges brought against it by recent writers*, 'respectfully dedicated to the Hundred Petitioners to Parliament, who pray for a new version of the Bible', and rejoicing over the failure of Mr. Heywood's motion. The latter, however, also published writings on the subject, *The Bible and its Revisers* (1857), and *The State of the Authorized Bible Revision* (1860). The hue and cry was joined by the Unitarians, Dr. J. R. Beard publishing in 1857 his *Revised English Bible the Want of the Church*. The need was felt in America also, for the same year the American Bible Union produced the first of its revised translations (Hebrews).

In England, however, a worthier effort than any hitherto put forth, to show clearly what was needed, was now made. 'Five Clergymen' (Barrow, Moberly, Alford, Humphry, and Ellicott) produced (1857–63) several sections (including John and some Pauline Epistles) of a cautious *Revision of the Authorized Version*. Mr. Malan subjected their version of St. John to a learned and respectful criticism (1862). Nor was he the only one who deprecated the attempt to launch a new version. Dr. R. C.

Trench, Dean of Westminster, published in 1858 his important work *On the Authorized Version of the New Testament, in connexion with some recent Proposals for its Revision* (second edition, 1859), in which, while acknowledging the need for a revised translation, he expressed doubt as to whether the knowledge requisite for it was as yet available. Meanwhile, valuable contributions were being made from time to time in learned commentaries, often containing fresh translations: of these it must suffice to mention the edition of the Greek Testament completed by Dr. Henry Alford, Dean of Canterbury, in 1861, and Conybeare and Howson's *Life and Epistles of St. Paul* (1852). In 1862 three Unitarian scholars produced a revised translation of the Old Testament, and a layman, Mr. Henry Highton, one of the New Testament. Next year Dr. Robert Young, widely known through his Biblical concordance, published the first edition of his new translation of the whole Bible, based (in the Old Testament) on a theory of his own regarding the Hebrew tenses.

The urge for revision naturally provoked a reaction, which was voiced by others besides Mr. Malan;[1] so that there was real timeliness in the article on 'Version, Authorised' contributed by Professor E. H. Plumptre to vol. iii of Smith's *Dictionary of the Bible* (1863): it contained a full, careful, and learned statement of the whole case for revision. The author was himself later one of the Old Testament revisers; and many of his pleas and arguments were embodied in the Revised Version. The appearance of *Essays and Reviews* in 1859 and a remark by the Speaker of the House of Commons in 1863 led to the undertaking of *The Speaker's Commentary* (1871–81), which aimed at revising the translation, and furnishing conservative criticism. As late as 1868 Dr. B. F. Westcott was still of opinion that the time for the revision of the Hebrew and Greek texts (which must precede revision of the translation) had not yet come—a

---

[1] Plumptre 1680*b*.

view which a few years later he admitted was mistaken.[1]  But the energetic Dean Alford had already published a learned article in *The Contemporary Review* (July 1868), insisting on the urgent need for an authoritative revision of the Authorized Version, and laying down certain desiderata with regard to it.  Not only so, but he himself produced the following year a revised translation of the New Testament, which was well received, though Mr. Malan once more came forward strongly deprecating (in opposition to the Dean) the idea that the Received Text underlying the Authorized Version of the New Testament could be successfully emended.

## II. *The Production of the Revised Version*

### 1. *The Undertaking.*

On 10th February 1870, after some preliminary negotiation, Dr. Samuel Wilberforce, Bishop of Winchester, moved a resolution in the Upper House of Convocation of the Province of Canterbury, to the effect that a Committee of both Houses should be appointed to confer with any Committee appointed by the Convocation of the Province of York, to consider and report upon the desirability of revising the erroneous passages in the Authorized Version of the New Testament.  Dr. Ellicott, Bishop of Gloucester and Bristol, seconded.  The Bishop of Llandaff proposed an amendment (Dr. Thirlwall seconding) including the Old Testament in the scope of the proposal; and with this addition the resolution was passed.  The Committee consisted of the Bishops of Winchester, Bath and Wells (A. C. Hervey), St. David's (Thirlwall), Llandaff (Ollivant), Gloucester and Bristol, Ely (Browne), Lincoln (Wordsworth), and Salisbury (Moberly).  The Lower House concurred (11th Feb.), appointing the Deans of Lichfield (Bickersteth), Canterbury (Alford), Lincoln (Jeremie), and Westminster (Stanley), the

---

[1]  Westcott, viii.

Archdeacons of Bedford (Rose), Exeter (Freeman), and Rochester (Grant), and nine others, to represent it on the joint Committee. The Convocation of the Province of York declined (23rd Feb.) to co-operate, on the ground that it would deplore any recasting of the text of Scripture.

The Committee met on 24th March, and agreed to report as follows:

'I. That it is desirable that a Revision of the Authorized Version of the Holy Scriptures be undertaken. II. That the Revision be so conducted as to comprise both marginal renderings, and such emendations as it may be found necessary to insert in the text of the Authorized Version. III. That in the above Resolutions we do not contemplate any new translation of the Bible, or any alteration of the language, except where in the judgment of the most competent scholars such change is necessary. IV. That in such necessary changes, the style of the language employed in the existing Version be closely followed. V. That it is desirable that Convocation should nominate a body of its own Members to undertake the work of Revision, who shall be at liberty to invite the co-operation of any eminent for scholarship, to whatever nation or religious body they may belong'.[1]

On 3rd May this report was presented to the Upper House of Convocation, where its adoption was carried unanimously. It was also unanimously decided to appoint a fresh Committee (the Bishops of Winchester, St. David's, Llandaff, Gloucester, Salisbury, Ely, Lincoln, Bath and Wells were to be its members, with power to co-opt others) to frame a scheme for effecting a revision on the lines indicated in the Joint Committee's report. Two days later this latter report was presented to the Lower House, and debated. Efforts were made to keep the work of revision exclusively in Anglican hands: but these were unsuccessful, and the House also waived its customary right of having on the Joint Committee twice the number of members

---

[1] Cf. the sage remarks of Lightfoot (214 f.) on this inclusion of non-Anglicans; also, Newth 113 f.

that represented the Upper House. On 6th May the adoption of the report was carried with two dissentients; and eight members (Bickersteth, Alford, Stanley, Blakesley, Selwyn, Rose, Jebb, and Kay) were appointed to co-operate with the new Committee of the Upper House.

The new joint Committee met on 25th May and decided to form two Companies (consisting of its own members and other specified scholars)—one to revise the Authorized Version of the Old Testament, and the other that of the New. The principles which the Revisers were instructed to follow were these:

'1. To introduce as few alterations as possible into the Text of the Authorized Version, consistently with faithfulness. 2. To limit, as far as possible, the expression of such alterations to the language of the Authorized and earlier English versions. 3. Each Company to go twice over the portion to be revised, once provisionally, the second time finally, and on principles of voting as hereinafter is provided. 4. That the Text to be adopted be that for which the evidence is decidedly preponderating; and that when the Text so adopted differs from that from which the Authorized Version was made, the alteration be indicated in the margin. 5. To make or retain no change in the Text on the second final revision by each Company, except *two-thirds* of those present approve of the same, but on the first revision to decide by simple majorities. 6. In every case of proposed alteration that may have given rise to discussion, to defer the voting thereupon till the next Meeting, whensoever the same shall be required by one-third of those present at the Meeting, such intended vote to be announced in the notice for the next Meeting. 7. To revise the headings of chapters, pages, paragraphs, italics, and punctuation. 8. To refer, on the part of each Company, when considered desirable, to Divines, Scholars, and Literary men, whether at home or abroad, for their opinions.'

Certain minor rules about procedure were also decided upon.

## 2. *The Personnel.*

Prior to the meeting on 25th May, the members of the Committee had already allotted themselves to the Old or the New

Testament Company, and a provisional list of other scholars (Anglican and Nonconformist) had been drawn up by Dr. Ellicott, with the help of Dr. W. F. Moulton of Richmond and Dr. Gotch, Principal of the Bristol Baptist College. The names suggested were agreed upon, and the invitations issued. Of those invited, Dr. S. P. Tregelles was prevented by illness from participating, and Canon F. C. Cook of Exeter, Dr. Pusey, Dr. J. H. Newman, and Dr. W. Wright declined the invitation; but the last-named later joined the Old Testament Company.

The two Companies were then constituted as follows.

*For the Old Testament.* From the members of the Upper House of Convocation on the Joint Committee were appointed the Bishops of St. Davids (Thirlwall), Llandaff (Ollivant), Ely (Browne), Lincoln (Christopher Wordsworth), Bath and Wells (Hervey), and from the members of the Lower House, Canon W. Selwyn of Ely, Archdeacon H. J. Rose of Bedford, Canon J. Jebb of Hereford, and Dr. W. Kay, formerly of Calcutta. In addition, the following Anglicans:

Mr. O. T. Chenery, Professor of Arabic, Oxford.
The Rev. F. Field, author of *Otium Norvicense.*
Dr. C. D. Ginsburg.
The Rev. B. Harrison, Archdeacon of Maidstone.
Dr. S. Leathes, Professor of Hebrew, King's College, London.
Dr. R. Payne Smith, Regius Professor of Divinity, Oxford.
Dr. J. J. S. Perowne, St. David's College, Lampeter.
The Rev. E. H. Plumptre, Professor of New Testament Exegesis, King's College, London.
Mr. W. Aldis Wright, Librarian of Trinity College, Cambridge.

Three Presbyterians:

Dr. A. B. Davidson, Free Church College, Edinburgh.
Dr. P. Fairbairn, Principal of the Free Church College, Glasgow.
The Rev. J. McGill, St. Andrews.

Two Baptists:

Dr. B. Davies, Professor of Hebrew, Regent's Park College.
Dr. F. W. Gotch, Principal of Bristol College.

And one Congregationalist:

Dr. W. Lindsay Alexander, Theological Hall, Edinburgh.

By 1881 thirteen members had been added: Mr. R. L. Bensly of Cambridge, The Rev. J. Birrell of St. Andrews, Dr. F. Chance of Sydenham, The Rev. T. K. Cheyne of Oxford, Dr. G. Douglas of the Free Church College, Glasgow, The Rev. S. R. Driver of Oxford, The Rev. C. J. Elliott of Windsor, The Rev. J. D. Geden of the Wesleyan College, Didsbury, The Rev. J. R. Lumby of Cambridge, The Rev. A. H. Sayce of Oxford, The Rev. W. Robertson Smith of the Free Church College, Aberdeen, Dr. D. H. Weir of Glasgow, and Dr. W. Wright of Cambridge and the British Museum. In the same period the Company lost seven members by death (Thirlwall, Selwyn, Rose, Fairbairn, McGill, Davies, and Weir), and three by resignation (Christopher Wordsworth, Jebb, and Plumptre).

*For the New Testament.* From the Convocation Committee: the Bishops of Winchester (Wilberforce), Gloucester (Ellicott), and Salisbury (Moberly), the Deans of Lichfield (Bickersteth), Canterbury (Alford), and Westminster (Stanley), and Canon J. W. Blakesley of Canterbury. In addition the following Anglicans:

The Rev. F. J. A. Hort of Cambridge.
The Rev. W. G. Humphry, Prebendary of St. Paul's.
The Rev. B. H. Kennedy, Canon of Ely.
Dr. W. Lee, Archdeacon of Dublin.
Dr. J. B. Lightfoot of Cambridge.
Dr. R. Scott, Master of Balliol.
The Rev. F. H. Scrivener, Vicar of St. Gerrans, later of Hendon.
Dr. R. C. Trench, Archbishop of Dublin.

Dr. C. J. Vaughan, Master of the Temple.
Dr. B. F. Westcott, Canon of Peterborough.

Three Presbyterians:
Dr. J. Eadie, Professor of Biblical Literature, Glasgow
Dr. W. Milligan, Professor of Divinity, Aberdeen.
Dr. A. Roberts, Professor of Humanity, St. Andrews.

One Baptist:
Dr. J. Angus, Principal of Regent's Park College.

One Congregationalist:
The Rev. S. Newth, Professor of Classics, New College, London.

One Methodist:
The Rev. W. F. Moulton, Professor of Classics, Richmond College.

And one Unitarian:
Dr. G. Vance Smith, later Principal of the Presbyterian College, Carmarthen.

By 1881 there had been added—Dr. Chas. Wordsworth, Bishop of St. Andrews, Dr. C. Merivale, Dean of Ely, The Rev. E. Palmer, Professor of Latin at Oxford, and Dr. David Brown, of the Free Church College, Aberdeen. Meanwhile, the Committee lost three members by death (Wilberforce, Alford, and Eadie), and one by resignation (Merivale).[1]

## 3. *The Procedure.*

On the morning of the 22nd June 1870, the members of the New Testament Company met together, by the invitation of

---

[1] Fuller particulars regarding the personnel of the Companies may be seen in Westcott 343 f., Newth, 109–13, Ellicott 25–8, 32–6, Lupton 260 f., and Moulton 217–21. For the denominational distribution, cf. Newth 113, and Skeats and Miall, *Hist. of the Free Churches of England*, 680 f. See also the last paragraph of the Revisers' Preface to the Old Testament.

Dean Stanley, in Henry the Seventh's Chapel at Westminster Abbey, and celebrated Holy Communion in preparation for their work. Inasmuch as one member, Dr. G. Vance Smith, was a Unitarian, and took advantage of the inclusive invitation to be present at the service, violent protests were raised in certain quarters. His very appointment as a Reviser was treated by some as an outrage, while his admission to the Lord's Table was felt to be an intolerable affront to His Divinity. The hubbub, however, died down; and Dr. Vance Smith remained with the Company. The Revisers began their work the same day in the Jerusalem-Chamber, which Dean Stanley allotted for their use, and which remained their normal place of meeting.[1] The Chair was taken throughout the whole period of their work by Dr. C. J. Ellicott, Bishop of Gloucester; and they secured as Secretary the Rev. J. Troutbeck, a Minor Canon of Westminster, but not himself a Reviser.

The Company sat for nearly ten and a half years, meeting regularly for four consecutive days per month, except during August and September. The average attendance was sixteen. Work began at 11 a.m. and continued (with half an hour for lunch) till 6 p.m. Members came with their own privately considered suggestions on the portion of the New Testament due to be taken. Proceedings began with three collects and the Lord's Prayer; then came minutes, correspondence, &c.; and then the work of revision. The question of textual emendations was taken first, Drs. Scrivener and Hort presenting the relevant evidence and arguments, usually on opposite sides; that settled, there came the discussion of proposed alterations of rendering, and, when needful, the voting. When it was seen how slow the rate of progress was bound to be, the question of dividing the Company into two sections (as had been done in the case of the Authorized Version) was considered; but for good reasons it was decided in the negative. The rule requiring a two-thirds majority

---

[1] See Newth 117 f., for details of the room, and how it was occupied.

for any alteration of the second revision was duly observed, with the result that the judgement of a bare majority had to be relegated to the margins. The average amount of the text covered per day was about thirty-five verses. The work was finished on 11th November 1880; and its conclusion was marked by a special service of thanksgiving in the Church of St. Martin-in-the Fields.[1]

The Old Testament Company commenced work on the 30th June 1870, their place of meeting being the Westminster Chapter Library. Dr. Thirlwall, Bishop of St. Davids, was the first Chairman: he resigned in 1871, and was succeeded by Dr. Browne, Bishop of Ely. Mr. W. Aldis Wright acted as Secretary.

The work lasted about fourteen years. The Company met for ten days every two months (except during August and September). Details regarding the method of procedure and voting are given in the Preface to the Revised Version, the rule requiring a two-thirds majority for changes adopted on the second revision being followed, as in the case of the New Testament revision. The rate of progress was more rapid than that attained by the New Testament Company, mainly because less time was in the circumstances needed for the discussion of textual problems (see below, pp. 252–4f.). But, owing to its far greater length, the revision of the Old Testament was not finished until the 20th June 1884. The Preface to it—the work of Mr. Aldis Wright—is dated the 10th July in the same year.

## 4. *The Co-operation of America.*

On 7th July 1870 the Lower House of Convocation passed a resolution requesting the Upper House to instruct the Revision-Committee to invite the co-operation of American divines in the work. This suggestion was accepted and acted on, though time passed before the actual co-operation could begin. In August

---

[1] For fuller details (attendances, &c.), see Newth 118–23, 124 f., Milligan 128, Ellicott 35 f.

1870 Dr. Angus visited New York; and it was arranged that Dr. Philip Schaff there should select and invite suitable American scholars for the purpose. In October 1871 Dr. Schaff visited England, and was present by invitation at one of the meetings of the New Testament Company. By December the arrangements were reported to be complete; but for one reason or another the American Companies (consisting mostly of non-episcopalians) did not actually hold their first meeting until the 4th October 1872.

The American Old Testament Company consisted at first of eleven members, of whom one died in the course of the work, and to whom four were added. The New Testament Company consisted of fifteen members (including Dr. Schaff and the Unitarian Professor Ezra Abbott), of whom four died and two resigned, and to whom four were added.[1] They met for work in the Bible-House, New York.

By the time the Americans began, the English Revisers had been once over the Synoptic Gospels and twice over the Pentateuch. Portions of the English revision were forwarded to them from time to time; and their criticisms were considered when the second English revision was in process. Their further criticisms were taken into account before the final revision was decided on; and such amendments or alternative renderings as they would have preferred to see adopted in this were printed as an appendix to the earlier editions of the English Revised Version (see next page). In general, it may be said that the American Revisers were less tolerant than their English colleagues of archaisms and other signs of traditional usage: in many cases they would have liked to transpose the text and the margin. Something more will need to be said presently (in connexion with the publication of the Revised Version) about the special arrangements made for the printing of the American Revisers' findings.

[1] Names and details in Westcott 347–50, Newth 114–16, Lupton 261 *ab*, Moulton 244 f., Schaff 396 f.

## 5. *The Arrangements for Publication.*

The Revisers received no remuneration for their services. Shortly after the work commenced, the Convocation-Committee of Revision was able to make an agreement (Dec. 1872) with the University Presses of Oxford and Cambridge, to the effect that these firms should have the exclusive copyright of the finished work, and should in return not only bear the expenses of production, but should jointly contribute £20,000 towards the expenses incurred by the two Companies in the course of the work.

The claims of the American Revisers were met by their undertaking (1877) to print no edition of their own for fourteen years after the appearance of the English Revision, the English University Presses agreeing in return that all published copies should contain an appendix setting forth the preferences of the American Revisers concerning points on which they had been unable to secure the concurrence of the English Companies. The American Revisers kept their organization together; and when the period of fourteen years had expired, they produced a revised Version after their own hearts, through Messrs. Nelson of New York. It bore on the title-page the words '. . . *newly Edited by the American Revision Committee A.D. 1901, Standard Edition*', and embodied, not only the preferences included in the aforesaid appendix, but about as many more additional alterations. Therewith, the printing of the appendix in the copies produced in England became unnecessary and was discontinued.[1]

## 6. *The Character of the Achievement.*

No account, however brief, of the Revised Version could be considered complete without some description of the outstanding features of the final product, as compared and contrasted with the Authorized Version which it was designed to supersede. Con-

---

[1] There is a good account of the American edition, and a selection of its special features and renderings, in Lupton 269 *a*-71 *a*.

siderations of space will allow only the barest outline of these more prominent characteristics, and will unfortunately forbid the inclusion of examples. Readers who desire fuller grounds for the description here given will need to seek them in the fuller works of reference specified in our concluding bibliography.

The Revised Version of the New Testament was first published in England on the 17th May 1881 (20th May in the United States); that of the Old and New Testaments together on the 19th May 1885.

As a whole, the Revised Version embodied the labours of a larger and more representative group of scholars than did any translation before or since. The utmost care was taken to enlist the services of the best qualified men, irrespective, largely, of their particular ecclesiastical connexions, and to prevent the domination of any sectional or partisan interest. While differences of opinion frequently emerged as a matter of course, and here and there an individual Reviser might feel aggrieved, the Companies as wholes carried through their work in a spirit of great harmony and with a humble sense of their great responsibility. When the Revised Old and New Testaments appeared, each was furnished with a useful preface explaining the principles on which the work had been carried out.

As regards externals, the contents of the Scriptures were now printed in paragraphs, according to the sense-divisions, a fresh line not being begun, as was the case with the Authorized Version, with every fresh verse, and the verse-numbers being printed down the side of each column. The Revisers found it impracticable to overhaul, as they had been asked to do, the headings of chapters and pages, and these were entirely omitted. The use of italics, which had run riot in successive editions of the Authorized Version, according to the personal choice of successive editors, was restricted and regularized. Pending experience as to how the Revised Version would be received, virtually no marginal references were included—a distinct defect where parallel passages or explicit quotations were involved. The margins were, however, very largely utilized for brief comments of all sorts, especially as regards dubious or alternative renderings. When it is remembered that a two-thirds majority was required for any rendering on the second and final revision before it could be admitted to the text, it will be realized that some of the most valuable work of the Revisers had to go into the margins; and no intelligent student of the Version can afford to disregard their contents.

As regards literary style, the Revisers aimed at being both Elizabethan and intelligible. They *revised* the Authorized Version; they did not produce a fresh translation. They retained as much of the older version as they felt was consistent with 'faithfulness' and clarity. Obscure archaisms were removed: 'its' was substituted for 'his' when referring to inanimate objects. Old Testament characters mentioned in the New Testament were designated by their more familiar Old Testament names. Technical terms were rendered as accurately as possible.

The ethics of translation, however, are a far more complicated matter than most people realize. Broadly speaking, there are two ideals, roughly corresponding (as it happens) to the characteristic tendencies of our two older Universities. The Oxford method aims at conveying the sense of the original in free idiomatic English without too much regard to the precise wording of the former: the Cambridge method is to pay meticulous attention to verbal accuracy, to translate as literally as is possible without positive violence to English usage, or positive misrepresentation of the author's meaning, and to leave it to the reader to discern the sense as well as he can from the context. For good or ill, the Cambridge genius presided over the English Revision.[1] One might plead in defence of it that English had already through the Authorized Version become largely impregnated with the idiom of the Biblical languages, and that the decision to retain

[1] Cf. W. Sanday in *The Expositor*, ii. iii. 249–52 (April 1882).

the style of the Authorized naturally involved a fairly literal method of translation. Moreover, such a method was obviously more useful for any close study of the Bible by those not conversant with the original tongues. The Authorized translators, for instance, had avowedly, for the sake of variety, refrained from rendering particular Hebrew and Greek words consistently by the same English words, even when no variation in meaning necessitated change: such a procedure naturally made Biblical study by means of an English concordance largely futile. The Revisers very properly aimed at a consistent rendering of the same word in the original when its meaning did not vary. Needless to say, an indefinite number of sheer inaccuracies in translation had to be remedied. On one ground and another, the number of changes felt to be necessary ran into thousands. The average for the New Testament has been variously computed at between two and three per verse: that for the Old Testament was somewhat lower, largely because very much less in the way of emendation of the original text was necessary, and also to some extent because, after 1881, the Old Testament Company was rendered cautious by the criticism levelled at the Revised Version of the New Testament on the score of needless alterations.

A mere revision of the translation would have been little use unless it had been accompanied by a critical scrutiny of the original texts to be translated. The Revisers were accordingly instructed to adopt that text for which the evidence was 'decidedly preponderating', and to indicate in the margin whenever a different text from that utilized in the production of the Authorized Version was accepted. This last requirement proved impracticable: but the scrutiny of the text itself was a very serious part of the Revisers' work, especially in the New Testament.

In the Old Testament, the fixity of the Hebrew Text since A.D. 200 virtually ruled out any necessity of comparing variant readings in the Hebrew manuscripts, and left only the tasks (*a*) of purely conjectural emendation when the Hebrew text was obviously corrupt, and (*b*) of the use of the ancient translations. (chiefly the Greek) for the purpose of restoring the original text.[1] On the whole, the Revisers followed the Hebrew fairly closely, and made too sparing a use of the Greek and other versions: a number of valuable improvements contributed by the versions were, however, inserted in the margins.

In the case of the New Testament, the textual problem was more serious and difficult. The 'Textus Receptus', from which the Authorized had been made, was built up in the sixteenth century from very late and imperfect manuscript sources, and was known to be in need of drastic revision. The Revisers included among their number two Cambridge scholars, Dr. B. F. Westcott and the Rev. F. J. A. Hort, who were engaged on an independent revision of the Greek text of the New Testament, and whose first volume on the subject was published a few days before the Revised Version of the New Testament appeared in English. Their theory, which cannot be explained here, was based on the best work previously done by English and Continental scholars in the same field, and was quickly recognized as marking an epoch in the study of the subject. It involved very numerous departures from the Textus Receptus, and consequent modifications in the English translation. Although Westcott and Hort undoubtedly exercised very great influence on the judgement of the New Testament Company, they did not by any means control it; and a more conservative estimate of the evidence was usually defended by Dr. F. H. A. Scrivener. While subsequent study has shown the need of occasionally modifying Westcott and Hort's text, there can be no doubt whatever that their theory on the whole was on right lines, and that the influence of their arguments on the mind of the Revisers had the effect of giving English readers a version far nearer to the meaning of the New Testament authors than any translation

[1] See above, pp. 56 ff.

based, like the Authorized Version, on the Textus Receptus could possibly have done.

### 7. *The Apocrypha.*

The first suggestion that the scheme for a Revised Version of the English Bible should include the Apocrypha (of which the 1611 version was known to have been hastily and negligently constructed) was made in the course of the negotiations with the University Presses (see above, p. 249). As a result of the agreement then reached, the New Testament Company—when its work on the New Testament was done—divided itself up into three Committees, to sit respectively in London, Westminster, and Cambridge, and to revise respectively (1) Ecclesiasticus; (2) 1 Maccabees, to which Tobit and Judith were afterwards added; and (3) 2 Maccabees and Wisdom. These portions of the work were finished at different dates between 1882 and 1892. A small committee of the Old Testament Company, to which the rest of the Apocrypha was entrusted, began its work in July 1884 (as soon as the Revised Old Testament was finished), and continued it for about ten years. The American Committee did not co-operate in the revision of the Apocrypha.

Pending its publication certain other works on the Apocrypha appeared. In 1880 E. C. Bissell produced a new translation, introduction, and commentary, as volume xv of the Lange-Schaff *Commentary*: another edition of the Authorized Version, with Introduction and notes, by W. R. Churton, appeared in 1884; and in 1888 the volume on the Apocrypha in *The Speaker's Commentary* was edited by H. Wace. The Authorized Version with a full critical apparatus of various readings and renderings was in 1892 edited by C. J. Ball as the closing section of the so-called *Variorum Bible*. Finally, in 1895, the English Revised Version was published (both separately, and later the same year bound up with the rest of the Bible), and the next year was laid before Convocation by Dr. C. J. Ellicott. It was a vast improvement on the Authorized Version; but it suffered from the want of a single co-ordinating authority to superintend the work of the four Committees. The different parts of it differ somewhat in merit; and the condition of the study of the original texts and the early versions (especially of such parts as were known to have rested on Hebrew originals) was not sufficiently advanced to render a still later and more competent version unnecessary (see below, p. 270).

## 8. *Subsequent Modifications.*

Since the first publication of the Revised Version, no changes have been made in the wording of its text and margins; but sundry variations in the manner of its production have been provided. Only the more important of these are enumerated here.

As a preliminary to the enumeration, it may be noted that in 1881, shortly after the Revised Version of the New Testament appeared, the Oxford University Press published *H KAINH ΔIAΘHKH, The Greek Testament, with the Readings adopted by the Revisers of the Authorized Version.* The Revisers' marginal readings were faithfully noted, along with the variations of the Textus Receptus, in the footnotes. It was prepared by the Rev. E. Palmer, Archdeacon of Oxford. A little later, the Cambridge University Press produced *The New Testament in the Original Greek, according to the Text followed in the Authorized Version, together with* (as footnotes) *the Variations adopted in the Revised Version.* This edition was prepared by Dr. F. H. A. Scrivener.

Comparison between the old and the new versions was further facilitated by the publication in 1882 of *The Parallel New Testament,* which contained in parallel columns (1) the English Authorized Version (with its marginal notes), (2) the Revised (with its marginal notes and readings), (3) the Greek Text underlying the Revised, and (4) a blank column for manuscript notes (which however contained the Greek readings adopted in the Authorized, and those corresponding to the Revisers' margins). A further step of the same kind was taken in 1885, when *The Parallel Bible* was produced, an edition containing the Authorized Version of the whole Bible on the left side of the page and the Revised on the right. In 1900 the Oxford University Press published *The Holy Bible: Two Version edition: being the Authorised Version with the differences of the Revised Version printed in the margins.*

In 1898 the publication of an edition of the Revised Version *with references* met a long-felt want: and still fuller references for the New Testament were furnished in 1910.[1] In 1901, with the appearance of the independent American edition, the appendix of alterations preferred by the American Revisers disappeared from the English editions (see above, p. 249). In December 1903 an edition was offered to the public containing the revised English *text* only, without the marginal comments: this permitted a useful reduction in price; but in other respects it was a retrograde step. Various other modifications in format have, of course, been tried from time to time, e.g. an edition in which each verse began on a fresh line (as in the Authorized) first appeared in 1911: but reference must be made to the booklets issued by the University Presses for fuller details of these comparatively minor changes.

Regret has sometimes been expressed that it has not been found practicable to produce the Revised Version (with margins, and in a reasonably large type) as cheaply as the Authorized Version, with the result that it has not been used so much in Day- and Sunday-Schools as it ought to have been. One cannot, of course, expect that trade-conditions and financial considerations should be entirely ignored by those responsible for publication. But it is good to know that efforts are being made to remedy, to some extent, the disproportion in price; and it is to be hoped

---

[1] Moulton, 239–43.

that the production of a cheaper Revised Version will soon lead to increased sales and wider vogue.

## 9. *Literature, 1870–81: (a) On the Revised Version*

The actual commencement of the work of Revision did not stop the flow of literature dealing with the enterprise. A paper read by Dr. J. B. Lightfoot in the spring of 1870 was published —in order to quieten the rising alarm—in 1871 under the title *On a Fresh Revision of the English New Testament* (later editions, 1872, 1891). *The Quarterly Review* for April 1870 contained an article written apparently before the decisions of Convocation were known, and urging the necessity for early and cautious revision. In May Bishop Ellicott published a small book, *Considerations on the Revision of the English Version of the New Testament*, to enlighten and interest the public, and to offer suggestions in regard to the way in which the revision should be carried out. In 1872 the Rev. J. W. Burgon, Vicar of St. Mary's, Oxford, addressed to Dr. Ellicott a strong protest (entitled, *An Unitarian Reviser of our Authorized Version, intolerable*) against the Rev. G. Vance Smith being invited to the Lord's Table in Westminster Abbey, and being included among the Revisers. The same year, in the Preface to the second edition of his *General View of the History of the English Bible*, Dr. Westcott expressed appreciation of the work being done (see above, pp. 239f.). Next year (1873) the Rev. Samuel Davidson, a Congregationalist, published a small treatise *On a Fresh Revision of the English Old Testament*, learnedly and comprehensively discussing the need, and formulating certain principles regarding the way in which the author thought it should be met. In 1875 the Rev. J. B. McClellan produced a large quarto volume containing a new translation of the Gospels (in harmonistic parallel columns), and an introduction dealing cautiously with the problem of textual criticism, in preparation against the wider changes likely to be advocated by the Revisers (see below,

p. 312). In February and March 1878 Dr. W. Milligan, one of the Revisers, published in *The Expositor* (I. vii) two articles demonstrating the need for far-reaching textual revision of the Greek New Testament.

10. *Literature, 1870–81: (b) General*

Pending the arrival of the Revised Version, efforts were made from time to time to improve on the Authorized Version by means of Paragraph and Variorum Bibles. Thus in 1870 appeared *The Reference Paragraph Bible* (see below, p. 312). In 1860 and 1872 the Religious Tract Society issued revised and enlarged Paragraph Bibles. In 1870–3 Dr. Scrivener edited for the Cambridge Press *The Cambridge Paragraph Bible*, in three volumes (see below, p. 312). In 1877 a revised Bible was published by Messrs. Eyre & Spottiswoode, the Old Testament being edited by Drs. F. W. Gotch and B. Davies, the New Testament by Drs. G. A. Jacob and S. G. Green: the text was split up into short paragraphs; a few marginal notes, chronological tables, and a few maps were provided. In 1880 a better production, *The Variorum Edition of the Holy Bible*, appeared, Drs. Cheyne and Driver having edited the Old, Dr. Sanday and Messrs. Clarke and Goodwin the New Testament: this volume incorporated a *Variorum Bible* published a few years earlier, and also substantial *Aids to the Student of the Holy Bible*. A second edition appeared in 1883, a third in 1889 (see below, p. 313).

Somewhat less ambitious projects were Dr. William Kay's translation of the Psalms (1874), Sir Edward Strachey's slightly emended transcript of the Authorized Version of Isaiah in the second edition of his *Jewish History and Politics* (1874), Matthew Arnold's somewhat more emended transcript of Isaiah xl–lxvi, &c., published for the use of school-children and other non-technical readers (1875), and Dr. Samuel Cox's translation of Job (1880).

### III. *The Reception of the Revised Version*

1. *1881–5*

On 17th May 1881, the day of its publication, Dr. Ellicott, Bishop of Gloucester, presented a copy of the New Testament, with the Revisers' final report, to the Convocation of the Province of Canterbury; and a copy was also presented to the Queen. On the following day both Houses of Convocation passed votes of thanks to the Revisers.

The first sales of the revised New Testament were enormous: and it was not long before favourable appreciation and adverse criticisms began to be heard. The discussion as to the merits and demerits of the new version soon became extensive, and was often marked by considerable acrimony on the part of the adverse critics. An enormous literature remains to bear witness to the range and duration of the debate: books of varying sizes and particularly articles in newspapers and journals appeared in plenty. Considerations of space will make it possible for us to allude here only to the more significant compositions on each side.[1]

The reader can easily imagine for himself the lines which the defenders of the Revised Version would be likely to take. The grounds on which it was attacked were numerous, and not all of them were without justification: but by far the most widely resented features were (1) the departure from the familiar and beloved wording of the Authorized in many more places than was considered by the critics necessary, and (2) the disappearance (largely in consequence of (1)) of the dignified, rhythmical, and musical *style* of the Authorized, the Revisers being accused of having no ear for good English. The New Testament was the more frequent object of attack, inasmuch as it not only came first, but was more familiar and devotionally precious than the Old.

[1] A good enumeration and survey of the literature of 1881 and 1882 may be seen in *The Church Quarterly Review* for Jan. 1883, 343–68.

One of the earliest attacks came from Canon F. C. Cook of Exeter, who published *A Protest* against the rendering 'Deliver us from the evil one' in the Lord's Prayer, in the form of *A Letter to the Bishop of London* dated 21st May 1881. Dr. J. B. Lightfoot replied in letters to *The Guardian* of 7th, 14th, and 21st Sept.: these were later reprinted in the third edition of his book *On a Fresh Revision*, &c. (see above, p. 257 and below, p. 264). Canon Cook replied in *The Guardian* for 28th September, and early the following year published a long *Second Letter to the Lord Bishop*, answering Lightfoot point by point.

On 22nd May Dr. Westcott, then Regius Professor of Divinity at Cambridge, preached at Trinity College a sermon very shortly afterwards published under the title, *The Lesson of Biblical Revision*, a temperate and sympathetic apologia in devotional terms.

The July numbers of several periodicals contained articles on the subject. *The Church Quarterly Review* had a defence of Westcott and Hort's newly published text (514–21: see above, pp. 253f.), and gave a somewhat grudging welcome to the new English Version (522–39). In *The Contemporary Review* (150–68) Dr. J. J. S. Perowne, Dean of Peterborough, expressed approval of it, coupled with some criticisms of its pedantry and its poor English. A contributor to *The Edinburgh Review* (157–88) was still more critical: his net judgement was one of qualified disappointment. A little later the Rev. S. C. Malan published *Seven Chapters of the Revision of 1881 revised*, grumbling and protesting at the new version, and supporting his complaints by detailed strictures on its rendering of Matt. i–vi and Luke xi.

Voices in defence, however, were not wanting. The Rev. W. G. Humphry, Prebendary of St. Paul's, and a Reviser, published in July *A Word on the Revised Version of the New Testament*. The same month another Reviser, Canon B. H. Kennedy, preached in Ely Cathedral three sermons, which were published early in the next year, with a dedicatory letter to Scrivener, and appendices, as *Ely Lectures on the Revised Version of the New Testament.* Somewhat more critical were the popular little volume of the Rev. A. Carter, *The Story of the New Testament* (Aug. 1881), and the very learned *Otium Norvicense (Pars Tertia)* of Dr. F. Field, an Old Testament Reviser (Sept. 1881, but reprinted with additions in 1899). Dr. Robert Young, of Concordance-fame, published at Edinburgh *Contributions to a new Revision or a critical Companion to the New Testament* (Edinburgh, Sept. 1881). *The Expositor* commenced in July 1881 and continued for many months a useful series of articles, expounding and defending (but not uncritically) the work of the Revisers. Dr. W. Sanday wrote the first 'Introductory Paper', three more the same year (Oct.–Dec.), chiefly on the Greek Text, and one next year (Apr.) on the style: others were by Dr. J. A. Beet, Canon T. S. Evans, &c.

But the doughtiest and most ruthless of all foes of the Revision now drew nigh. Dr. John William Burgon, Dean of Chichester, published three long and slashing articles in *The Quarterly Review* for October 1881 and January and April 1882 (Nos. 304–6). They were formally anonymous, but it was widely known who the author was. In 1883 they were republished under his name, with much additional matter, in a large volume entitled *The Revision Revised.* The judgements they expressed, particularly those directed against the textual theory of Westcott and Hort, were very wrong-headed; and the violence of their tone was unparalleled. Nothing the Revisers had done was right. The writer had the effrontery to suggest that these twenty-odd accomplished scholars, who for eleven years had devoted their continuous labours without payment to the production of a better English version of the New Testament, should receive from the Church 'nothing short of stern and well-merited rebuke' (Oct. 1881, 308). Dean Burgon was competently answered—especially by Dr. Sanday in *The*

*Contemporary Review* for December 1881 (985–1006), and by an anonymous writer in *The Church Quarterly Review* for January 1882 (419–51)—and the manner of his attack was generally deplored. But his emphatic style and undoubted learning secured for his arguments an influence far beyond what they deserved; and they are supposed to have hindered very considerably the acceptance of the Revised Version by the British public.

Early in 1882 Sir Edmund Beckett, Bart., published an attack on the Revised Version entitled, *Should the Revised New Testament be authorised?*: he deprecated its use in public worship as not legal, and elaborated his complaints with particular reference to Matthew, Hebrews, and the Apocalypse. He was answered by Dr. F. W. Farrar in *The Contemporary Review* for March 1882 (359–80: an article which Dr. Burgon described as 'a vulgar effusion'); and Sir Edmund published a *Reply* which the editor of *The Contemporary* had refused. Conservative criticism of the Revisers' Greek Text on the lines of Dean Burgon's articles, but less vehemently worded, was advanced by Canon F. C. Cook in his *Revised Version of the First Three Gospels considered* . . . (1882: see below, p. 314): he was answered in *The Church Quarterly Review* for October 1882 (127–39). Other volumes produced in 1882 and 1883, in defence or explanation of the Revisers' work, by Drs. Alex. Roberts, C. J. Ellicott, Prebendary Humphry, Dr. C. J. Vaughan, Master of the Temple, and Dr. Philip Schaff, are specified in the Bibliography belonging to this chapter. *The Church Quarterly Review* for January 1883 (343–68) contained a survey of the literature thus far produced, and a discriminating defence of the Revisers against the storm of criticism that had blown up against them.

Some piquancy was added to an already sufficiently brisk debate by the productions of certain Unitarians, who claimed that the new version told strongly in favour of their characteristic doctrines (see the bibliography under the names of G. Vance Smith, J. Page Hopps, Alexander Gordon, and Henry Ierson).

## 2. *Since 1885*

The long-awaited appearance of the Revised Old Testament in May 1885 marked a new stage in the discussion. It was prepared for by Dr. A. Roberts's *Old Testament Revision: a handbook for English Readers*, which appeared in 1883. Naturally it did not raise so vigorous a controversy as the New Testament had done: on the whole it was favourably received. An early volume in defence of it was Dr. T. W. Chambers's *Companion to the Revised Old Testament* (1885). It was, however, the periodicals that provided most of the discussion. *The Church Quarterly Review* for July 1885 (438–61) and October 1885 (181–213) contained two appreciative and informative articles, offering sympathetic criticism on special features. On the other hand, both *The Edinburgh Review* for October 1885 (448–94) and *The Quarterly Review* for the same month (281–329) included condemnatory articles, written from an obscurantist point of view (e.g. complaining of renderings on the ground that they disturbed regnant theological exegesis), and in particular attacking the use made of the ancient versions in emending the Massoretic text (see above, pp. 252f.) and the insertion of so many textual alternatives, &c., in the margins. *The Quarterly* article was the less accurate and the more bitter of the two, and stated of the Revisers that 'in many instances they appear to start with a prejudice against the Christian Faith' (328).

From 1885 to 1890 *The Expositor* published a series of articles written by Drs. Driver, Kirkpatrick, A. B. Davidson, Cheyne, and others, discussing the new version and providing explanatory comments on passages of special interest in all the Books of the Old Testament. Some of these articles, those namely by the Revs. Jennings and Lowe (July–Dec. 1885), criticized the reviewers for being too conservative and cautious.

An article on Westcott in *The Expositor* for January 1887 (22–38), by the Rev. W. H. Simcox, concluded with an open defence of the view that the English Bible to-day ought to include, not only what the original authors wrote, but also the orthodox glosses subsequently added and long retained by the Church. Six articles contributed by Westcott himself to *The Expositor* for February–December 1887 were re-edited in book form in 1897 as *Some Lessons of the Revised Version of the New Testament*. *The Expository Times*, between December 1889 (its third number) and January 1897, published numerous explanatory comments and articles on the Revised Version as a whole, especially expressions of opinion from ministers and schoolmasters up and down the country, from which it appeared that there was still a strong prejudice against it in many quarters.

Other episodes in the progress of the debate were: the appearance in 1891, after nineteen years, of a third edition of Lightfoot's treatise *On a Fresh Revision of the English New Testament* (see pp. 257, 260); the frequent discussion—in the course of the controversy—as to the legality and desirability of using the Revised Version in public worship in the Church of England, culminating in a resolution passed by both Houses of Convocation of the Province of Canterbury in February 1899 in favour of such use where desired by clergy and people, and leading to the actual use of it in a minority of Churches; the suggestion advanced from time to time that a fresh revision should be provided embodying only a selection of the Revisers' alterations, and preserving more of the language of the Authorized (a resolution to this effect was proposed by Dr. W. H. How, Bishop of Wakefield, in the Upper House of Convocation of the Province of York in February 1892, and was opposed by Dr. Westcott, Bishop of Durham); the Bishop of Wakefield's attack on the Revised Version in *The Expositor* for October 1892, and Dr. Ellicott's dignified and convincing reply in December; the spirited plea for still greater boldness and modernity by Mr. H. W. Horwill in *The Contemporary Review* for May 1896 (705–13); the Rev. Frank Ballard's fighting apologia for the Revised Version, *Which Bible to Read—Revised or "Authorised"?* (1897: see below, p. 313); the quiet and informative *Addresses on the Revised Version of Holy Scripture*, published by Dr. Ellicott in 1901; the decision of the British and Foreign Bible Society the same year to issue the Revised Version as well as the Authorized; and the same Society's substitution in 1904 of Nestle's edition of the Greek Testament (the text of which closely resembled that of the Revised Version) for the Textus Receptus which alone they had hitherto patronized. Critical estimates of the Revised Version are, of course, to be found in all modern histories of the English Bible which cover the nineteenth century.[1]

### 3. The Merits of the Case

No person cognizant of the facts would claim that the Revised Version was free from defects; and the growth of knowledge since the eighties has, of course, brought further defects to light. Whatever may be thought of the inherent faultiness or otherwise of its English, it would be a mistake to ignore the almost universal opinion that this is inferior in dignity and beauty to that of the Authorized, or to refuse to recognize the loss sustained by those who can no longer find in it the phrases and passages which endeared the older version to them as a devotional treasure and inspiration.

At the same time, persons sufficiently well educated to be able to read the Bible with profit may reasonably be asked to admit that the first purpose for which Christians ought to use the Bible is to inform themselves as to what its several authors really said

---

[1] Reference to Lupton, 262–6, and to Moulton, 243 f., 248–78, as examples will suffice.

and meant. Without forgetting that a passage which mis-represents the meaning of the original may yet be of devotional value to an English reader, we may claim that such a reader ought in fairness to see that truth is after all of supreme impor-tance and that the possession of it is worth some temporary sacrifice of pleasure and comfort if it cannot be otherwise secured.

Now it was said of the Authorized Version by one who knew it well that it contained hundreds of inaccuracies for every one in the Revised. Let us suppose that this statement is a rhetorical exaggeration: yet even so, the coining of it would have been impossible if it were not true that the Authorized is replete with errors, and the Revised immeasurably and unquestionably more correct. That really ought to settle the question as to which of the two Christians ought consistently to use. Give what weight you please to the arguments about rhythm, music, dignity, and the devotional value arising from long familiarity and sacred associations; these surely ought not, in the judgement of any educated and responsible Christian, to outweigh considerations of truth and falsehood.

Many Christian ministers advocate the use of both versions—the Authorized for public reading in Church, the Revised for study. But this is an unsatisfactory solution. It may spare the feelings of a small conservative section among the congregations; but it permanently keeps all who hear the Scriptures read avoidably misinformed as to what the Scriptures really say. It also lies open to the objection that a single version for all purposes has great advantages in simplicity and convenience, especially for those, young and old alike, whose contact with the Bible is to any degree educational.

As in so many human controversies, the arguments in this case are admittedly not all on one side. But to acknowledge this should not hinder us from saying that the arguments on one side, taken together, are overwhelmingly stronger than those on the other.

## IV. *Fresh English Translations produced since the Revised Version*

Most of the writers who, in the course of the discussion just summarized, advocated a further revision, wished for something in closer approximation to the Authorized Version. But there were some who felt that the Revisers had not gone far enough: and it was probably in part the interest roused by the new Version which led to the production of a series of new translations, often with the aim of rendering the Scriptures into modern English as contrasted with the customary archaic style of the Authorized and Revised Versions. An effort on these lines had been made long before by a Presbyterian Minister, the Rev. E. Harwood, who in 1768 produced *A Liberal Translation of the New Testament*—an effort which has since exposed him to general denunciation. After the appearance of the Revised Version, one of the first in the field was Mr. Ferrar Fenton, a business man, who began with a modern version of Romans in 1882, completed the Epistles by 1884, the New Testament by 1895, and the whole Bible by 1903. He displayed much originality, and made some extravagant and unwarranted claims for himself: but his works have had a very wide circulation, and a new edition of his *Holy Bible in Modern English* was published by Messrs. A. & C. Black as recently as 1938. A new *Translation of the Old Testament Scriptures from the original Hebrew* was produced by Helen Spurrell in 1885. In 1893 there began a stately series, called *The Sacred Books of the Old and New Testaments*, under the editorship of Professor Paul Haupt of Baltimore. This popularly designated *Polychrome Bible*, which never included any part of the New Testament, nor even the whole of the Old, devoted two volumes to each of several books of the Old, one containing a revised Hebrew text with brief philological notes, and one a new and scholarly translation of it into English, with fuller comments. The most eminent Old Testament scholars of England,

America, and Germany contributed to the work. A special feature of it was the use of colours to enable the reader to distinguish the various documents used in the composition of the books.

Another new experiment dates from 1896. In that year Dr. R. G. Moulton, Professor of English at Chicago, and brother of the Reviser, published a plea for greater attention to the literary form of the several parts of Scripture in his book, *The Literary Study of the Bible* (see below, p. 314). Fitting the action to the word, he began at the same time the publication of a series of small volumes, in each of which the Revised Version (occasionally improved by the incorporation of its marginal readings) of one book of the Bible was printed, arranged, and spaced in such a way as to bring out the literary articulation and form of the contents, and elucidated by an appendix of notes. These books went under the general title of *The Modern Reader's Bible*, and the whole of the Scriptures (including Tobit, Wisdom, and Ecclesiasticus) were gathered into a single volume in 1907 (see below, p. 313), the notes, &c., occupying over a fifth of the whole.

The first part of a fresh rendering of the New Testament into dignified modern English was put before the public in 1898. This was *The Twentieth Century New Testament, Part I. The Five Historical Books*. The Pauline Epistles followed in 1900, and the rest of the New Testament in 1901. A revised edition came out in 1904. The translation was based on Westcott and Hort's text. There were no notes; but useful tables of contents followed the short preface, inset headings were provided for the successive paragraphs, and the non-historical books were furnished with very brief introductions. The work was done by a group of scholars, who belonged to different sections of the Church, but whose names have not been divulged. It was favourably received, though its popularity has suffered (in the opinion of the present writer, unduly) from the rivalry of later efforts in the same field.

Of these, the first to be considered is Dr. R. F. Weymouth's *New Testament in Modern Speech*, which appeared in 1902, and has passed through numerous editions and been revised, first, by the Rev. E. Hampden-Cook, and quite recently by Professor J. A. Robertson. It was made from a special text, which was artificially constructed on the basis of the best recent editions, and was separately published by Dr. Weymouth as *The Resultant Greek Testament*. The books of the New Testament had brief introductions prefixed to them, and there were explanatory footnotes throughout. The translation is excellently done, but not markedly better than that in *The Twentieth Century New Testament*: possibly it owes its greater popularity to its slightly greater conservatism and solemnity of tone.

Both of these versions, however, have been largely eclipsed in the public eye by Dr. James Moffatt's *New Testament: a New Translation*, which was first published in November 1913. *The Old Testament* followed in 1924: a final revision of the whole Bible came out in 1935. The sales of the work have been phenomenal, especially those of the New Testament, whereof there were over seventy reprints in twenty-five years. An illustrated Jubilee edition was published in 1938. Dr. Moffatt gave himself an entirely free hand, and used a much more colloquial style than any of his predecessors since the much censured Harwood. In the New Testament, he writes as a front-rank expert, and makes large use of the new knowledge of Hellenistic Greek furnished by the papyri.[1] It is safe to say that in no version is the course of St. Paul's thought in his Epistles so easily accessible to an English reader as in Dr. Moffatt's version. When we remember that these Epistles are, except in their simplest portions, often quite unintelligible even in the rather literal Revised Version, the service conferred by these three last-named versions, and particularly by Moffatt's, is

---

[1] The Old Testament translation is regarded as much less satisfactory by Old Testament scholars in general. [Ed.]

inestimable. The rhythmical character of the poetical books and of many passages normally treated as simple prose Dr. Moffatt indicated by the use of separate lines. The violence administered by a first perusal of his work to an ear that has learned to love the diction of the Authorized Version is of course considerable, and completely puts the offence of the Revised Version in the shade: hence there are plenty of good Christians to be found who dislike 'Moffatt' as undignified and otherwise unwelcome. Yet the general popularity of the work, as shown by the sales, is evidence of the signal service that it has rendered to Bible-readers. Dr. Moffatt had as early as 1900 published his *Historical New Testament*, which contained a new translation along with much other matter.

An important contribution to the materials for Biblical study was made in 1913 by a new translation of *The Apocrypha and Pseudepigrapha of the Old Testament in English with Introductions and critical and explanatory notes to the several books edited in conjunction with many scholars* by R. H. Charles, D.Litt., D.D., and published by the Oxford University Press in two large quarto volumes. The work was done entirely by British scholars, completely meets the demands of scientific study, and supersedes all previous editions of the Apocrypha.

An interesting experiment designed for the help of a different type of reader was the series of *Books of the Old Testament in Colloquial English* published by the National Adult School Union. The series began in 1920 and ceased in 1934. Thirteen and a half books of the Old Testament were produced cheaply in ten paper-covered volumes. The style of the translation was intentionally colloquial: there were introductions and very brief footnotes where an emended Hebrew text had been followed. The sales of the volumes containing Amos, Genesis, and Jeremiah have been large enough to necessitate second editions.

The most recent effort to produce a complete translation of the Bible in modern English is that made by a group of American scholars. In 1923 Dr. Edgar J. Goodspeed published *The New Testament: an American Translation*, based on Westcott and Hort's text and using the everyday idiom of American speech. In 1935 the Old Testament having been completed in the same way, under the editorship of Dr. J. M. Powis Smith, the two appeared in one volume as *The Bible: an American Translation*. Dr. Goodspeed put the coping-stone on this undertaking by his publication of *The Apocrypha: an American Translation* in 1938, in which each of the fourteen books concerned is furnished with a short introduction and freshly translated into modern and dignified English.

Seeing that 1938 was the fourth centenary of the setting-up of the English Bible by royal authority in every Church in the country, a great number of books and booklets on the Bible have been produced: but these do not call for detailed enumeration in an account of English versions, though of course they mark an enhanced interest in the English Bible on the part of the public. Perhaps the production in 1937 of a *Bible designed to be read as Literature* (Heinemann) may be mentioned as a sign of the times. It is almost wholly in the Authorized Version (four poetical books only being in the Revised), and the contents are set out in modern literary form. One fresh version of the New Testament, however, has emerged—*The Book of Books. A Translation of the New Testament Complete and Unabridged* (Lutterworth Press). It has been produced by a number of collaborators, working under the supervision of Mr. R. Mercer Wilson, and is put forth by the United Society of Christian Literature (formerly the Religious Tract Society), of which he is Secretary. The object has been to retain the cadence and rhythm of the Authorized Version, while providing a fully intelligible modern rendering. The matter is arranged in paragraphs; and short introductions are prefixed to the several books.

Considerations of space render it impossible to include here a list either of the numerous Biblical anthologies which have

been published in order to render Bible-reading less laborious
and more helpful to those who have not time or capacity for
close and systematic study, or of special translations of particular
books by various scholars, such as T. K. Cheyne's Psalms
(1888), W. G. Rutherford's Romans, S. R. Driver's Job,
Jeremiah, &c., J. E. McFadyen's Psalms, Isaiah, &c.

Mention, however, ought to be made of certain Roman
Catholic and Jewish versions. Father F. A. Spencer published
a translation of the Four Gospels from the Greek Text in 1898.
In 1937, long after his death, his version of the whole of the
New Testament was re-edited by C. J. Callan and J. A.
McHugh and published by Macmillan. This translation, however, suffers through the effort to make it represent both the
original Greek and the Latin Vulgate at one and the same time.
A very much better scheme is that of *The Westminster Version
of the Sacred Scriptures*, produced by various Roman Catholic
scholars, edited by Fathers C. Lattey and J. Keating, and
published by Longmans. The various sections have appeared
separately, commencing in 1913; the New Testament was
complete by 1935; and of the Old Testament 'Jona' has already
been finished. The translation is made direct from the original
Greek and Hebrew into modern English; and there are introductions and explanatory footnotes which take account of modern
scholarship, though always with an eye to Catholic feeling and
custom. It is understood that a new translation of the best text
of the Latin Vulgate into modern English is being prepared by
Mgr. R. A. Knox.

The liberal-Jewish scholar Mr. C. G. Montefiore published
in two volumes in 1896 and 1899 nearly the whole of the Old
Testament in his *Bible for Home Reading*. The contents were
presented in convenient paragraphs, interspersed with devotional
comment. The basis taken was the Authorized Version; but it
was corrected wherever known to be inaccurate. The same
writer printed a version of the Synoptic Gospels on similar lines

in his two-volume commentary on *The Synoptic Gospels* (Macmillan 1911; second edition 1927).

## V. *Concluding Comments*

Little needs now to be added by way of conclusion, in view of what was said above (pp. 265f.) in regard to the merits of the case as between the Authorized and Revised Versions. The opinion was there advanced that the general adoption of the Revised Version would be an immense advantage in disseminating a knowledge of the Scriptures in a form at least roughly corresponding to the extent of modern knowledge. Yet, great as this advantage would be, the work that has been done since 1885, is a sufficient proof that, even if the Revised Version were much better than it is, neither this nor any other version can ever be quite permanent and final. Doubtless there is loss here involved, in the unattainability of a universally recognized form of words. But it is a loss that has to be faced, because the only means of avoiding it would be the petrifaction and perpetuation of error. Though it is sad to reflect that the number of habitual and devout readers of the Bible has probably in recent decades diminished, the change means that there is less damage now likely to be done by the wording of the Authorized being replaced by some other wording. Be that as it may, when once the paralysing idea that nothing but the Authorized will do has been broken down, the way is open for the giving of a better welcome to the next authoritative revision than was given to the last. Many and difficult as are the ethical and other problems that beset the task of translation, there can be little doubt that the time is ripe for the undertaking, by joint effort and official sanction from the various ecclesiastical denominations, of a new version of the whole Bible which shall embody all the knowledge that has accumulated up to the time of its production, and shall profit by all the experience gained in the course of the last half-century. The place of the Bible in our religious life is bound to be different from the place it occupied in the lives of our fathers and those who still share the position our fathers held: but all serious Christians are fundamentally at one in needing a version of the Scriptures which is as truthful as human skill, aided by the Divine grace, can make it.

C. J. CADOUX

# IX

# THE BIBLE AS THE WORD OF GOD

## SYNOPSIS

'Word' and 'Word of God'. Wide variety of God's 'words' in the Old Testament (Nature, conscience, history: the worship in the Temple and the religion of the Torah). The continuity of Christianity with some forms of Judaism. Comparison of revelation in the New Testament with that in the Old Testament. The Logos conception. Authority of Christ's teaching. The Word made flesh. Unity in variety of the New Testament. Divine purpose and election; the response of faith. The Council of Trent and the Reformers. The Canon of the Bible. The subordinate, yet necessary, place of Biblical criticism. The continued challenge of the Bible.

THROUGHOUT this book we have been thinking of the Bible as literature. We have traced the growth of that literature in its Hebrew (and Aramaic) and Greek originals. We have studied the forms it assumed in the principal versions of the ancient world. We have noticed the influence of these in shaping the successive English versions down to our own time. We have not, however, been directly concerned with the faith that created the original documents, the faith that has inspired their rendering into so many of the languages of the world. We have not considered the Bible in its claim to record or to be the true and permanent Word of God to men. Yet, without such a faith, the Bible could never have had this long and impressive history even as literature; indeed, without it, there would have been no Bible.

## 1. The 'Word of God'

What do we mean by 'a word of God'? Perhaps the best preparation for an answer is made by asking another question: what is a 'word'? It is in itself simply a sound or a combination of sounds, i.e. the sensation produced in the organ of hearing by vibrations in the air. The vocal organs which cause these vibrations are delicate but relatively simple; the receiving instrument is much more elaborate, from the tiny bones transmitting the vibrations of the outer membrane to the piano-wire structure which analyses them. But the miracle and mystery of speech, as a means of intercourse, is not in this transmitting and receiving mechanism, wonderful as it is. We may substitute touch for sound, as when the teacher of the blind and deaf Helen Keller first revealed to her the mystery of language by holding one hand under a flowing tap, and spelling into the other the touch-symbols of the word 'water'.[1] We may extend the range of speech by using telephonic or wireless electrical 'waves' as further links between the sound-waves of the speaker's voice and of the hearer's ear. This has greatly impressed the imagination of the modern man, but it is not the real miracle. Marconi was fully justified in his reply to a lady who said to him in the early days of his work, 'How wonderful this wireless is!' 'Not half so wonderful', he replied, 'as the fact that you and I are talking now.' The chief wonder is in the intelligent purpose which makes of these arbitrary sounds its servants, and in the intelligible meaning which the hearer can assign to them. The miracle is that spirit should be able to touch spirit, not that the mechanism of its operation is so elaborate. We can more or less comprehend and explain the physical and physiological mechanism, but no man can explain the spiritual control of it which includes purpose and meaning. Yet it is this spiritual fact which makes the spoken 'word' what it essentially is, one of the most universal means of human fellowship, and one of the most important characteristics of man as compared with lower animals.

The words in a printed or written book do not dispense with the essential supremacy of the spiritual fact, they simply introduce a different kind of link into the mechanism. The written or printed marks on the paper are themselves like the sound-waves in being purely arbitrary. They are secondary symbols

[1] *The Story of My Life*, by Helen Keller, p. 23.

which suggest sounds, or replace them by visual sensations. In the ancient world a book was primarily something to be read aloud by the expert, and we may still sometimes see the moving lips of inexperienced readers trying to translate the unfamiliar sight into a more familiar sound. But even when the printed page flashes its meaning at a glance to the more experienced eye, the miracle and the mystery are still there—that spirit is speaking to spirit, that two realms of unseen reality are being brought into touch with each other.

When one of those spirits is divine the same fact holds, though the quantity and quality of the operation may be enormously increased. Behind the printed page of the Bible on which we read what claims to be a word of God there is a long line of human tradition. There is the compositor who set up the type, the scholar who translated the word from its original language, the ancient scribe who first wrote down the Hebrew or Greek word, the men and women who spoke to one another of their direct experience of God, the mighty acts which revealed Him. The sheer mechanism of that long history is as wonderful as wireless, and quite as fascinating. But the supreme miracle of all is not in the invention of printing, or the achievements of scholarship, or the recording of ancient history. It lies in the spiritual fact that God's Spirit does touch man's, whether in the experiences of ancient days, or through the record of those experiences which we call the Bible, and which can still be to us the living word of the living God.

When, therefore, we turn to the Bible as the Word of God, it is essential that we put the emphasis in the right place. We are not to take the printed Bible as if it were something dictated by a voice like man's in the printing-office. The Christian should leave such formalism to the Muhammadan, who claims that God so dictated the Qur'an word by word in Arabic to Muhammad from a heavenly copy. The work of the scholar and historian in investigating the process by which the Word of God has come to us, however necessary and valuable, does not deal with the most important function of the Bible. Knowledge of that process will, however, save us from the naïve impression that God must needs employ the mechanism of *human* speech or must needs be confined to the limits of the *human* vocabulary in what His Spirit would reveal to our spirits. He who makes the winds His messengers and His ministers a flaming fire can speak in many tongues or without any. The range of means at His service is boundless, for it covers all that He has created and all that He may yet create. It covers the whole order of the physical world without us, from its tiniest happening in, say, the growth of a lily of the field to its awe-inspiring catastrophes of storm and earthquake and flood. It extends to the inner world of man's heart, his thoughts and feelings and desires, whether on the mapped coast-land of our consciousness, or in the *Hinterland* of the unexplored potentialities that exists within each of us. In that interaction of the outer and inner worlds which we call history, in the rise and course and fall of human societies, He who controls all can deliver His message without human words.

## 2. *The Old Testament*

Nowhere shall we find a greater variety of divine means to self-revelation than in the Old Testament. It records the history, and the products of the history, of a gifted people, living in a land of many natural contrasts, and affected by the fortunes of many great empires. It shows us the Jordan-jungle of primitive superstitions, as well as the Hermon-peaks of the noblest utterances about God which the world possesses. The Old Testament can be read as one of the sacred books of the east, to enable the scholar to reconstruct a phase of ancient history. It can be read as literature, whether in its original form or in the best modern versions. But we enter most fully into the inheritance which it constitutes only when we see in all its variety of form the different ways in which the Word of God has come to man, and when we still hear Him speaking through it. In such 'hearing' the personal response of faith is, of course, involved. But it was so from the beginning. The 'facts' of the Bible are without exception interpreted 'events', themselves involving the response of faith. Revelation is the unity of this duality.

The most notable illustration of God's use of Nature to reveal Himself is in the physical events connected with the Exodus. For example, we read that 'the Lord caused the sea to go back by a strong east wind all the night, and made the sea dry land, and the waters were divided' (Exod. xiv. 21). Here was a natural happening which in itself might attract no attention. But we, like Israel, may believe that it was supernaturally controlled, so as to reveal God's purpose of redemption by enabling the Israelites to escape from Egypt. The redemptive purpose so revealed became Israel's ultimate foundation of faith in its God. Again and again appeal is made to that fact in the later generations. Through the prophet Hosea God says, 'I am the Lord thy God from the land of Egypt' (xii. 9), and 'When Israel was a child, then I loved him, and called my son out of Egypt' (xi. 1). A later prophet in the time of the exile in Babylon cries to God, 'Awake, awake, put on strength, O arm of the Lord . . . art thou not it which dried up the sea, the waters of the great deep: that made the depths of the sea a way for the redeemed to pass over?' (Is. li. 9, 10). A late psalmist declares, 'He rebuked the Red Sea also, and it was dried up . . . and redeemed them from the hand of the enemy.' (cvi. 9, 10). The important thing to notice here is that the revelation lay in the mighty act of redemption itself. *That* was God's word; all that men are moved to say about it is revelation only in the secondary sense that their words point us back to and interpret God's word.

From one of the greatest events in the physical order we may turn to one of the smallest—the casting of the sacred lot. It was the faith of Israel that this could reveal the will of God: 'The lot is cast into the lap, but the whole disposing thereof is of the Lord' (Prov. xvi. 33). We may take as an example of this the occasion when Jonathan had broken, all unconsciously, the oath taken by his father (1 Sam. xiv. 41 ff). Here appeal is made to the sacred lot to decide who is the culprit. Thus, it was believed, by the sacred Urim and Thummim, administered by the priest, the decisive word of God was spoken.

When we turn from the outer events to the inner conscious-ness of man, we find a similar faith in the power of God to reveal Himself through it. 'The spirit of man is the lamp of the Lord, searching all the innermost parts of the body.' (Prov. xx. 27.) So we find that the ordinary products of man's moral conscious-ness in social relations are regarded as a revealed law of God: a man who has carelessly left a pit uncovered is responsible for the loss of the ox or ass which may be injured by falling into it (Exod. xxi. 33), and the man who sees the straying ox or ass of his enemy is to lead it back to him (Exod. xxiii. 4). From such early moral judgements we may trace the deepening consciousness of God's will for man, which finds expression at last in the prophetic summary: 'what doth the Lord require of thee, but to do justly and to love mercy and to walk humbly with thy God?' (Mic. vi. 8).

It is, however, in the combination of these two realms of revelation, that of outer events and that of the inner response to them, into the faith that Israel's history was controlled by Israel's God that we see the amplest form of the divine Word to Israel. All the great prophets testify to that faith, but it finds its clearest expression in Isaiah. When Jerusalem has been de-livered from Sennacherib, and the prophet sorrowfully sees the city given up to self-confidence and self-congratulation, he says, 'Ye looked not unto him that had done this, neither had ye respect unto him that fashioned it long ago' (xxii. 11). To those who did so look and had eyes to see, the whole course of Israel's history was the revelation of the divine purpose. Man could modify the form of its fulfilment but not annul its accomplishment. Even the mightiest of empires was but the staff wielded by God's hand. Even Cyrus, the most successful empire-builder of the Bible times, was unconsciously serving the purpose of God: 'I gird thee, though thou dost not know me' (Isa. xlv. 5). In the Old Testament as in the New, the Word of God is primarily uttered through His mighty acts in human history, and is not limited by human thought about them, or the vocabulary of human words which must describe them.

We may, then, regard these three great realms, Nature, conscience, and history, as those which are divinely controlled to utter the Word of God to man through Israel. These are the primary realms through which God speaks. But there are two other storehouses of religious experience into which the harvest of these primary realms was gathered up.

The first was the Temple and its worship. What this could mean to a true worshipper may be seen sufficiently from a single example. The familiar story of Isaiah's call (ch. vi) describes an experience of God shaped throughout in terms of the regular worship, as well as inspired by it. As with the greater Prophet in the synagogue of Nazareth, the regular worship of other days culminates in this outstanding experience. Rightly has it been said that 'He sees in vision no strange and unfamiliar scene, but a long familiar scene transfigured.'[1] The 'Holy, holy, holy' is doubtless one of the refrains of Temple psalmody itself carried over into the experience. The smoke that veils God after the moment of clear vision answers to the smoke that ascended from the altar continually. The humble confession of unworthiness is but the intenser form of what a true worshipper might at any time feel in the presence of God, as is expressed in Ps. li. To such a worshipper the 'word' of God must often have come, as the Psalms bear repeated witness: 'I cry unto the Lord with my voice, and He answereth me out of His holy hill' (iii. 4).

[1] Isaiah in *International Critical Commentary*, by G. B. Gray, p. 104.

The second sphere of religious experience through which God gave His word was that of devotion to the Law, or rather, the Torah, the 'teaching'. The Pentateuch contains many elements besides laws, and is formally a history in which are included laws, stories, poems, and sermons, of very varied dates. But, for the later post-exilic Judaism, this very varied literature was ascribed to him who figures so largely in it, viz. Moses, and it was treated as a single block of revelation given once for all on Sinai. The ancient words were reinterpreted to apply them to contemporary needs, and so arose that 'tradition of the elders' of which the New Testament speaks, the Oral Law, equally traced back to Sinai. Thus, to the Jew, God made the record of the former word into a new word, full of life and inspiration, as we may see from Ps. cxix. In this respect the attitude of the devout Jew towards the Pentateuch was, and still is, much the same as that of the devout Christian to-day to the whole Bible. Both read their Scriptures to hear in them a present and living word of God, and both are enabled to do this by a traditional interpretation amid which they have grown up, for no man can come to the Bible with a blank mind. In the centuries just before the Christian era it was the written Word which gave the chief means by which God spoke to the Jew, though not without the guidance of 'tradition'.

It was, then, under the influences and with the faith of this Jewish piety that those who were to be the first Christians grew up. The Jewish piety and faith were by no means all of one pattern. Beyond the more familiar differences of Pharisees and Sadducees there were many diverse currents, as the non-canonical literature 'between the Testaments' amply shows. There were many whose religion was of the 'apocalyptic' type, represented in the New Testament by passages in the Gospels such as Mark xiii and by the Book of Revelation. There were many who emphasized the Prophets and the Psalms in their interpretation of the Law, and were inspired by the hope of a God-given Messiah, a divinely sent representative of God, who should bring order and righteousness, joy and peace to the troubled world. This piety can be seen in the Magnificat and the Benedictus (Luke i. 46–55, 68–79). When the new faith in Jesus as the Messiah, the Christ, was born into the world, a new body of literature gradually came into being—the letters of the apostles and preachers of the new faith, the remembrances of those who had walked with Jesus in the days of His flesh. There was no consciousness of any break with the past, but the past records were reinterpreted in a new meaning, so as to make them point forward to the fullness of the time in which God had sent forth His Son. It was only very gradually, and not until a century or two had gone, when the Gospel had broken loose from its Jewish moorings and voyaged into the Gentile world, that the Christian Church became aware that it possessed a larger Bible, the Bible which includes the 'Old' and the 'New' Testaments.

### 3. *The New Testament*

The Word of God in the New Testament is as truly an historical revelation as the Word of God in the Old Testament, though it is chiefly concentrated into a single figure. It begins, though it does not end, in the days of His flesh. Here there is suggested one of the great contrasts between the Old Testament and the New. The Old Testament records what may be called a *descending* revelation. It begins with Sinai, where a God who is afar comes down to meet man in the storm-cloud, and speaks with the sound of thunder. But it descends farther, from hill to valley, onwards through the later prophets, into the religion of the psalmists, when the promise is fulfilled: 'thus saith the high and lofty One that inhabiteth eternity, whose name is Holy: I dwell in the high and holy place, with him also that is of a contrite and humble spirit' (Isa. lvii. 15). In the later religion of the Old Testament, and amongst its truest types of piety, something at least was already realized of that New Covenant which the prophet Jeremiah had anticipated, when God's teaching should be written on the hearts of individual men, and His presence and Word would be near to each. The prerogatives of the prophet become the common property of the devout, and the God of heaven has descended from heavenly palace to earthly cottage.[1]

In the New Testament the movement, considered historically, is in the other direction. It is, to men's eyes, an ascent from the lowliest of beginnings to the highest majesty. Jesus lives and teaches and heals and dies as a man amongst men. His earthly ministry, considered alone, is a failure, a failure which He Himself accepted and recognized. But from that failure, reaching its climax on the Cross, when He seems to be forsaken both by God and men, begins a new conception of God and of God's ways, signed and sealed in the Resurrection. Jesus of Nazareth, ascended into heaven, becomes the Risen Lord of life, the central figure of the New Testament faith and literature. As Moffatt has rightly said, 'In the New Testament we enter a little world of men who are doing more than looking back to Jesus; they are looking up to him, revering him as well as remembering him, and revering him as divine'.[2] Thus the descent of God from Mount Sinai to the world of men in the Old Testament is answered by an ascent of Jesus Christ from the world of men to the spiritual Mount Zion, 'the city of the living God, the heavenly Jerusalem, the general assembly and church of the first-born who are enrolled in heaven'.

This descent and ascent are combined in the highest New Testament teaching about Jesus Christ. The divine descent in the Old Testament has been paralleled in Jesus Christ Himself. To become what He did and to work what He wrought on earth He is represented as making a prior descent, hidden from

---

[1] Cf. Volz on Isa. lvii. 15, in *Kommentar zum Alten Testament*.
[2] *The Approach to the New Testament*, p. 163.

our eyes. So we get that great arc of descent and ascent which is indicated in the narrative of the washing of the disciples' feet by Jesus (John xiii): 'Jesus, knowing that the Father had given all things into His hands, and that He came forth from God and goeth unto God . . . took a towel and girded Himself.' So also, when Paul is writing to the Philippians, to inculcate lowliness of mind, he pictures Jesus in divine pre-existence, laying aside His heavenly glory to descend to earth and take the form of a servant, that He might be poured out unto death,[1] the death of the Cross. But this is the point at which the return of the arc begins: 'wherefore also God highly exalted Him, and gave unto Him the name which is above every name'—the name of Lord, the Lord of all.

It is, however, in the opening verses of the Fourth Gospel that the theme of Jesus Christ as the Word of God finds its most important expression: 'In the beginning was the Word, and the Word was with God, and the Word was divine.' Here we must remember not only what was said at the outset about the amplitude of meaning in 'Word' when applied to God, but also that this very term, in its Greek form of *Logos*, was current in contemporary thought. It meant much more than the spoken word; it meant the reason behind the word and implied the creative activity that resulted from the word. It was the highest term which the vocabulary of the age allowed, to describe the revelation of God—and that fact is significant. It is less important to know exactly what terms men apply to Jesus than that they apply to Him the highest they know, for after all, even the highest human terms are inadequate to God. The special suitability of the term *Logos* lay in its power to express both the thought behind the word and the uttered word itself. It could represent Jesus as the mediator between God and man, coming

---

[1] In *The Cross of the Servant*, p. 73 f., I have argued that the words, 'emptied himself . . . unto death' (Phil. ii. 7, 8 are derived from 'poured out his soul unto death' (Isa. liii. 12).

forth from God and becoming man. 'The Word became flesh and dwelt among us'; having seen the visible Son, men have also seen the invisible Father.

This identification of Jesus with the eternal Word has a twofold result. It does more than exalt Him to the highest place in human thought and devotion. It also adds all the warmth and reality of the human life to the eternal principle of divine activity. For the Christian, the mediator between God and man is not an abstract conception but a person. The mind of the humblest can dwell on the Person, and be rightly led, even though it cannot follow the philosophic theologian into the more abstract realms of thought.[1] The Incarnation of the Word of God thus carries with it the guarantee that our human nature is not alien to God in itself, and that there is sufficient kinship between the human and the divine for the human to utter and express the divine. With proper limitations, we may say that divine revelation had already used this principle of Incarnation in the Old Testament. The revelation of God through the prophetic consciousness was founded on the faith that human thought and experience could truly reflect the divine meaning. The finest instinct of Israel turned from the dumb idol and its oracles, to seek the living God through the consciousness of His prophets. God's highest word comes through His highest means, the means of personality, and that principle leads directly to the faith of the New Testament that Jesus Christ is the supreme Word of God to men.

With this exalted conception of Jesus as a unique Person, it is natural that His recorded teaching should have a unique claim on our attention. In all His utterances concerning eternal realities, His teaching rightly demands our faith and obedience, in accordance with His words: 'All things have been delivered unto me of my Father: and no one knoweth the Son, save the

---

[1] It is only when that humblest believer begins to imagine that his untrained thought *is* competent to deal with those realms that trouble begins.

Father; neither doth any know the Father, save the Son, and he to whomsoever the Son willeth to reveal Him' (Matt. xi. 27). But there are two ways in which this permanent Christian principle can be, and has been, abused. The first is when we seek to extend His authority to realms in which He claimed no right or desire to speak, and disregard the historical conditions of His utterances; the second is when His teaching is set in contrast with that, say, of the apostle Paul, and made the alleged basis of a Gospel without the Cross.

One example of the first specially concerns us, for it relates to our Lord's use of the Old Testament. It is plausibly said that this ought to be the rule of our own use of it, and that all critical handling of the Old Testament literature, in order to get behind the faith of Judaism to the historical religion of Israel, is therefore condemned. The answer to this is to point to the fact that the Gospels portray Him as true man, advancing in wisdom as in stature, with the language and the thought of a particular generation stamped upon His sayings, even when He most rises above it. If it had not been so, He would not have been intelligible to them or to us. When He spoke of the rising and the setting sun, there is no suggestion that He was secretly thinking in terms of the Copernican theory. His healing ministry passes beyond our comprehension, but it did not make any use of those scientific discoveries, such as anaesthetics, which in recent times have enlarged man's power to alleviate suffering and to heal disease. In one instance, as we know (Mark xiii. 32), Jesus definitely disclaimed knowledge. We have no right, therefore, to read into His words the explicit settlement of issues not then present. With this proviso, how much we have to learn from our Lord's use of the Scriptures! His personal use of them, as in withstanding temptation at the beginning of His public ministry, and in the cry of desolation from the Cross, show their profound influence upon Him through the silent years of thought and prayer. He uses the Scriptures to illustrate His work, as in the reference to the mission of Jonah to the Ninevites. He argues from the Scriptures in the accepted manner of the day. Yet he rises far above it, as when He contrasts sayings of the Old Testament with His own authoritative 'But I say unto you'. He sees the spiritual kinship of John with Elijah, and of Himself with the Suffering Servant of Isa. liii. He shows us, by His example, how to use the Old Testament spiritually, and in a Christian sense.

The other warning to be given relates to the alleged contrast of the teaching of Jesus, say in the Parable of the Prodigal Son, with the more elaborate Gospel preached by the apostle Paul. How often are we told that we should return to the simplicity of Jesus, and proclaim God's free forgiveness and welcome of the sinner when penitent, without encumbering ourselves with the subtleties of a Jewish rabbi! There is something to be learnt, of course, from this demand for simplicity. But the simplicity of Jesus is far more profound than some readers of the Sermon on the Mount recognize. It presupposes His own deep knowledge of man and of God. In that deep knowledge He offered Himself to the Cross, and His teaching must not be separated from that Cross. The Word of God to the world which the New Testament contains is not limited to the words which fell from the lips of Jesus in the days of His flesh. It is the Word of the whole history which God controls by His purpose. It is a revelation through history, just as much as is the Old Testament, though it is compressed into months instead of being extended into centuries. The *teaching* of Jesus was part of that revelation, but only part of it. As the space given in the Gospels to the Passion stories clearly shows, it was the Cross which from the beginning arrested the attention of the Church, and it was in the Cross (and its necessary sequel, the Resurrection) that the redemptive activity of God became most visible to the eye of faith.

One feature of that redemptive act, even from a purely

historical standpoint, must not be overlooked. It was a costly redemption, made in the intensest suffering, and in terms of actual living. We shall not grasp the full meaning of God's Word made flesh, unless we dwell on this and on its significance. God has translated His purpose, not into a pattern of thought or into a set form of words, but into a life and a death and a resurrection. He would have us know, in terms of actual human experience, the cost to Himself of the redemption which is His purpose. 'God so loved that He gave'; 'God commendeth His own love towards us, in that while we were yet sinners Christ died for us.' The suffering of Christ the Son must have some real counterpart in the heart of the Father, if the Gospel of the Cross is indeed rooted and grounded in eternity. However difficult it be for us to conceive of God as suffering[1]—a difficulty increased by Christian theology having yielded itself too unreservedly to the influence of Greek thought—it cannot be untrue in some deep sense to say of the Father, as well as of the Son, that 'for the joy that was set before Him He endured a Cross, despising shame.'[2]

The life and literature of the New Testament are all the richer, because they offer not one stereotyped explanation of what Jesus Christ has done for man, but many different approaches to its meaning. How could it be otherwise, when men in all the variety of their Christian experience are struggling to express what reconciliation with God means for them, and how it came about? They are one in their devotion to their Lord, one in their dependence on Him, one in their consciousness of sins forgiven and of a new life created through Christ. They have found in Him the fulfilment of the purpose which the Old Testament has revealed to them. Thus the literature of the New Testament, reflecting their varied experience, is spiritually,

---

[1] I have discussed the problem in chap. ix of my book, *Suffering, Human and Divine.*

[2] Heb. xii. 2. Nor can it be untrue that the suffering of Christ in His followers has redemptive significance in its own degree; cf. Col. i. 24 and op. cit., chap. xi.

as well as historically, continuous with the Old Testament. It enables us to take our stand with them and, if we will, to share their experience. So the Bible, from being at first the record of the Word of God uttered to the generations of old, may itself become the Word of God to a later generation, able to make it wise unto salvation.

Such, then, is the Bible when considered as the historical record of God's word to man, mediated through the history of an ancient people, and having its spiritual culmination in one supreme Personality. Is it possible to describe the unity of this revelation in a single phrase? So far as this is possible, we may think of it as the revelation of *the purpose of God*, the purpose which the Christian finds most clearly in the Gospel. It is one of the great rewards of a genuinely historical study of the Bible to be made to realize the ever-advancing movement of the revelation. It belongs to the providential order of God that the Hebrew came to conceive God chiefly in terms of the will, and will is the very heart of character. What a man aims at, that he ultimately becomes. We know a man only as we know his dominant aim. We may say that we know God only so far as we know His purpose, and enter into it. We may not know Him in His omnipotence or in His omnipresence or in His omniscience. All these are beyond our imagination and beyond our conception. When we have enumerated all we know of Him we are left saying with a Hebrew poet:

> Lo, these are but the outskirts of His ways,
> And what a whisper of a word do we hear of Him!
> But the thunder of His mighty acts who can comprehend?
>                              (Job. xxvi. 14, trans. by Driver & Gray)

But we can grasp His revealed purpose concerning man. That purpose is partially seen in the election of a people to work out the will of God in their history, an election to which racial capacity and temperament as well as the outward course of events have made their necessary contribution. Another Hebrew poet, Ben Sira, has suggestively pictured the divine Wisdom seeking a home amongst the peoples of the earth, and finding no rest for the sole of her foot, until God said:

> Pitch thy tent in Jacob,
> And in Israel take up thy inheritance. (Ecclus. xxiv. 8)

In the Old Testament, as well as in the New, God showed Himself to be righteous because He was a Saviour, a loving Father to His people who sorrows because they have rebelled against Him, a forgiving Husband though they have been faithless to Him. The God of the Old Testament is as truly the God of a redeeming purpose as the God of the New Testament. But it is, of course, in the latter that the purpose becomes clear and effectual for all mankind. Out of the New Testament there comes to us the full declaration of the Gospel of divine love at the heart of the universe, a new order of society based on a new relation of men one to another, a new conception of the kingdom of God as embracing all human history. It is a purpose still unrealized, and on the merely human level of things it often seems to us unrealizable. But the Christian faith will go on asserting and believing that it is realizable, and that it will at last, in God's own way and by God's own power, be realized.

### 4. *The Function and Authority of the Bible*

It is the momentum and dynamic of that Word of God heard in His whole purpose that has created the Church, the Church of which one supreme function and duty is to preach the Word. She does that not simply by the utterance of the evangelist and missionary, but by the tradition she creates. The Christian home and the Christian society, in which the growing child may advance in heavenly wisdom as well as in earthly stature, will always rank first amongst the evangelizing agencies of the Church. Most of those who constitute the Church of Christ have grown up in such a tradition. In our own land, it may be Roman Catholic or Anglican or that of one of the Free Churches, with all the varieties of emphasis that characterize each of these. But all are one in handing on the knowledge of the Word of God recorded in the Bible, whether directly or indirectly. We can see the faults and limitations of the other lines of tradition much more easily than those of our own. But in their several ways, each of them provides some preparation for that intimate and personal response of faith which is the goal of every variety of truly Christian education. They help to create the future lines of cleavage, along which the hammer of the Word may break the rock in pieces.

Personal and individual religion begins with the response of faith to that Word of God of which the Bible is the permanent record. This response does not depend on any particular theory of the inspiration of the Bible, though it is often associated with one. Ultimately, it is always the intrinsic nature of the truth revealed which convinces men, whether they know it or not. All authority in religion goes back to God, and springs from what God is and does. That is another way of saying the same thing. Man can know God only as God chooses to reveal Himself, and man knows God and that it *is* God acting, only by the quality and character of that which is revealed. To say this does not, of course, deny the proper place, even the necessity, of subordinate authorities. The Church, which hands on the living tradition of God's truth, does in fact exercise a very real authority, wherever its influence is operative. The Bible, as the faithful record of the historical revelation, exercises another kind of authority. It is in the different emphasis on these two subordinate authorities that the historic division of the Western Church into Catholic and Protestant began, and the nature of that difference still closely concerns our Christian life.

The Roman Catholic Church formulated its doctrine of the authority of the Bible at the Council of Trent in 1546. It deliberately placed the unwritten tradition of the Church on a full equality with the written Word of the Bible. It claimed that the oral tradition is derived from Christ or from the dictation of the Holy Spirit, and that it has been handed down through the generations of the Catholic Church in unbroken succession. The tradition of the Church is therefore to be received with a piety and reverence equal to those shown towards the Bible. No interpretation of the Bible concerning faith and morals ought to be held which is contrary to that of the Church. All this is admirably clear and definite. The Roman Catholic receives his Bible from the Church, in principle as well as in practice, and interprets it within the limits of Catholic doctrine. As a devout man, he will hear God's voice speaking in it; as a scholar he will study it in its ancient language and environment. But in both devotion and scholarship, the Church must say the last word as to God's Word.

Over against this stands the doctrine of the Reformers concerning the Scriptures. They shared the Christian faith of their opponents, and accepted the oecumenical creeds of the early Church, as well as the validity and use of human reason, within proper limits. But their criticism of certain practices of the contemporary Church led them to appeal to the Bible as the primary authority. They made the Bible in principle their supreme rule of faith and practice, though it is easy to see now how much they read into it which was not there, and how unhistorically they often treated it. We cannot to-day handle the Bible as a text-book of dogma, from any part of which proof-texts may be cited without much, if any, regard for their original meaning. The old habit may linger in certain quarters, but its results convince none who are not convinced already on other grounds. Neither do we appeal to-day to the Bible, as our fore-fathers in the faith did, to establish this or that method of Church government. We can see that the Church of the New Testament, standing at the beginning of things, had not yet worked out any formal constitution, and that the seeds of all the different Church orders, and the fruitage of none, are to be found in the New Testament. But the main contention of the Reformers, their appeal to the authority of the Bible against the authority claimed for the Church, is an essential principle of Protestantism.

The Reformers, then, recognized that the Bible carried within it its own intrinsic quality, which was sufficient proof of its divine origin and needed no testimony of man. This is sufficiently illustrated by a single quotation from Calvin's *Institutes* (I. vii. 2):

'As to the question, How shall we be sure that the Scriptures have issued from God, unless we take refuge in a decree of the Church? it is much as if one asked, How shall we learn to distinguish light from darkness, white from black, sweet from bitter?

But the Reformers were fully aware that something more than the possession of a sacred book was needed to create genuine Christian faith. So we find them formulating the important principle which may again be expressed in Calvin's words:

'Just as God alone is a fitting witness to Himself in His word, so that word will not find (the response of) faith in the hearts of men before it is sealed by the inner witness of the Spirit (*Institutes*, I. vii. 4).

'The Inner Witness of the Spirit'—that is the necessary safe-guarding principle when appeal is made to the Bible as the sufficient outer Word of God. Even so, the Protestant appeal to the Bible is liable to the charge of subjectivity; it is, in fact, open to abuse by any man who would read his own vagaries into the interpretation of the Bible. The Bible has undoubtedly suffered greatly in that way, and the mere *claim* to be guided by the Spirit of God proves nothing. Opinions are not guaranteed by providing them with high-sounding labels. But there is a deeper meaning in the appeal to the witness of the Spirit, which also does justice to the genuine truth in the appeal to the tradition of the Church.

The characteristic product of the Spirit of God, according to the New Testament, is fellowship, the fellowship of men one with another as well as with God. The Holy Spirit is represented as convincing the world of sin and righteousness and judgement, not simply by direct operation on the hearts of individual men, but chiefly by His presence in the fellowship of the Church. To claim to be guided by the Spirit of God, whilst we stand aloof from all Christ's people, is a contradiction, unless we dare to believe that all Christ's people are wrong, and we alone are right. Now and again, God may raise up an isolated witness, it may be a martyr witness, to point the rest onwards towards the truth. But these are the great exceptions. Normally, the power and presence of God's Spirit will be felt by those within a living fellowship, through which the work of the Spirit is done. This is one justification of the actual influence of the Christian tradition, to which reference has been made. But the spiritual fellowship of the Church is not confined to the present generation. There is the great company of believers throughout all the generations, in whom there has been a continuity of faith and witness, and through whom the tradition has come to us, developing in many ways, but still preserving the essential and continuous unity of man's response to the Word of God. This great consensus of faith is always the most obvious external test of the genuineness of the witness of the Spirit claimed by any individual: 'If any man preacheth unto you any Gospel other than that ye received, let him be anathema' (Gal. i. 9). If we believe that the Spirit of God is active in the life of the Church, we may also believe that the Christian consciousness, the consciousness of the whole fellowship, will sooner or later test and sift out the true from the false in the presentation and interpretation of the Word of God.

When, therefore, there is an individual response of faith to the Word of God recorded in the Scriptures, a new unity is created from the historical testimony without, and the convictive testimony within. The act of faith requires both elements—

something beyond itself, the Word of the Gospel mediated by history, and something within itself, the witness of the Spirit known in Christian conviction. Both must be examined and tested in the appropriate manner—the record of the historical facts by the scholar and the historian, the convictions by their congruence with the life of the fellowship to which they claim to belong. The witness of the past and the witness of the present combine in the unity of the faith that God has spoken to us through a veritable Word, and that His Spirit is truly in contact with our spirit. That experience is itself two-sided in what it proves. It proves our fellowship with them of old, and it proves the Bible to be a Word of God to us.

In genuine personal faith, as distinct from mere opinion or intellectual belief, there has always been this twofold aspect—the Word of God, however given, without, and the witness of God's Spirit, clothing Himself with the garb of our innermost thoughts and feelings within. For there is, as Rufus Jones somewhere says, no supernatural 'click' which would make divine guidance independent of moral conditions. The more closely we study the historical forms of revelation, the more likely are we to be convinced that this was so from the beginning, so far as the highest revelation of God is concerned. The great words of God in the Old Testament did not come by Urim and Thummim, the casting of the sacred lot, but by the historic events which the prophets interpreted, with which they linked their moral and spiritual truths. There was no infallible test to distinguish between true and false prophecy; the visions of the prophets, however sincerely believed, might be deceptive. The men who companied with Jesus had to make up their own minds, in answer to the question, 'Whom say ye that I am? What think ye of the Christ?'

Then, as now, there were moral and spiritual conditions of faith, for genuine faith is never a purely mechanical product, to which no alternative is possible. Man's opportunity to respond in faith to the Word of God, however that Word is mediated, is always the product of divine providence, acting without and within the man's own consciousness. God's Word, of course, does exercise a moral and spiritual compulsion, as it did on Jeremiah, when he declared that the Word of God was as it were a burning fire shut up in his bones, and that he was weary with forbearing and could not. But such a moral and spiritual compulsion acts only in those who are ready to be convinced morally and spiritually. Even God Himself cannot force a man into faith, for faith is itself a personal surrender springing from a genuine conviction.

We may compare such a religious conviction with the scientist's discovery of natural law or the artist's appreciation of beauty. In both realms there is something there to be discovered (and for the believer in God, that something is the work of God). But in both reactions, also, there is something contributed by the observer, whether he be scientist or artist. Each may set forth what he sees, using human language, whether it be that of the mathematical formula or that of paint and canvas. But the experience of either the scientist or the artist will be blended of that which exists independently of himself, and his own reaction to it, bearing the marks of his own personality and temperament. The human discovery is but the underside of the divine revelation.

We see, then, that there is no essential difference in the way in which the Word of God was received by them of old, as compared with ourselves. The manner of the word was sometimes peculiar to their age, but it never exonerated them from the necessity to choose whether they would hear or not; it never delivered them from the inevitable struggle of incipient faith to maintain itself against the challenge of doubts and fears. For us, there is indeed a new link in the chain, supplied by the record of *their* experiences of God. But this new link does not essentially alter the relation in which we stand to God, when, through the Bible record, His Spirit makes contact with ours.

Here, it may seem necessary to refer to the questions arising from the Canon of the Bible—its precise extent as authoritative. In the earlier chapters of this book we have seen how gradually and as it were unconsciously this particular collection of literature came into being and subsequently acquired that authority we call 'canonical'. As regards the Old Testament, we have seen that the precise limits of its later portions remained open to question even into the Christian era, and that the Canon of Palestinian Judaism, the Hebrew Scriptures, was narrower than that of Hellenistic Judaism, the Greek Bible, which passed to the Christian Church. We have seen, also, how that new literature which we call the New Testament itself came gradually into being during the first century after Christ, as the result of a selective process, and not of any formal decision by authoritative councils of the Church. It is instructive to consider such an incident as that given in a story of the African martyrs in the latter half of the second century (A.D. 180, 'The Acts of the Scillitan Saints'). A Christian named Speratus stands on trial before the Roman proconsul, who asks him, 'What have you in your case?' The reply of Speratus is, 'The Books, and the letters of a just man, one Paul'. By this he means the rolls of the four Gospels and the rolls of some at least of the Pauline epistles which have gone to make our New Testament. Such separate rolls were the nucleus of the future New Testament, and by their guidance such a Christian interpreted the Old Testament. But it was a long time before the limits were finally and universally drawn, and during that period of testing, it was the response of faith that gradually selected these particular books out of a host of others which claimed the attention of the Christians.

All this means that, whilst we may firmly believe that God's providence has led ancient believers to preserve and hand down to us all that we need as the record of His uttered Word, there can be no hard and fast line at the margins. Some of the books still preserved, lying outside of the Canon, may still witness the truth of God to us, and some of those preserved within the Canon may be of less use to us than those without it. It may make us smile, to-day, to read what Bunyan says about this in *Grace Abounding*. He tells us how, in a time of great depression, much encouragement was given to him by the words that one day crossed his mind, 'Look at the generations of old and see: did ever any trust in the Lord and was confounded?' They had a Scriptural ring about them, but Bunyan searched the Bible in vain for them. Then he asked one Christian after another where they could be found, without result. At last, a year afterwards, he writes, 'casting my eye upon the Apocrypha books, I found it in Ecclesiasticus, chap. ii. 10. This at first did somewhat daunt me, because it was not in those texts that we call holy and canonical; yet as this sentence was the sum and substance of many of the promises, it was my duty to take the comfort of it. And I bless God for that word, for it was of good to me. That word doth still ofttimes shine before my face.' We may well take John Bunyan's sanctified common sense as indicating the right attitude of the Christian towards the Canon. The proof of its authority lies in its continued power to speak, and the limits of the literary history cannot limit God's power to make use of what true word He will, in speaking to the soul of man.

Throughout this discussion of the Bible as the Word of God, comparatively little has been said of the changed conception of its nature due to Biblical criticism, though the general results of this have been assumed. The omission is deliberate, because it is important that we should realize that the truth of divine revelation will never stand or fall by the results of pure scholarship. Such scholarship will assuredly help us to interpret the record of revelation more exactly, just as improvements in the technique of wireless give us better transmitting and receiving sets, and so enable us to hear the distant voice more clearly and accurately. But we can profitably use our wireless set without ourselves understanding the technique of its construction, and we do not confuse the mechanics of transmission with the experience of hearing. We may apply the same principle to the much disputed questions of Biblical inspiration and divine revelation. Our knowledge of the way in which God speaks to us is one thing; the fact that we do hear Him speak is another. Again and again, and with the best of intentions, the truth that God speaks to man has been entangled with a particular theory of the way in which He is thought to have spoken. Claims have been made for the verbal infallibility of the Bible, for example, or its freedom from error in all matters of history or of science. It seems almost to be assumed by some that God had dictated the English record of His ancient revelation, and that if He did not, its reliability is gone. But a little reflection and a little study of the way in which the record has been made ought to show us that God's purpose was not to anticipate the discoveries of science or the investigations of historical research, for which He has endowed man with reason. It is not for us to tell God what His revelation ought to be, either in manner or in matter. It is ours humbly and reverently to study what is given, with an open mind, and to accept whatever seems to be God's way, even though it might not have been our way. Above all, it is important that we should make that distinction between what may be called the machinery of revelation and the spiritual fact which that serves. It is sheer prejudice on our part when we think that the truth of God's Word ought to be verbal truth, or that the essential message must have been spoken in Hebrew or Greek words, as though uttered by human lips. The primary feature of divine revelation is what God does. The human interpretation of this divine activity is secondary. We may believe with fullest confidence that the Spirit of God has guided men in this inter-pretation, and that the providence of God has secured for us a sufficiently faithful record of that interpretation. The proof of that confidence is that God still speaks to us through the record. But it is God who is infallible, not His human interpreter.

As to the authority of the Bible, so interpreted, no doubt there are important differences of application resulting from critical and historical study of the record. We no longer feel justified in making the battles of the Israelites a defence of war, or in using the cursing psalms against our enemies. Nor do we say, as even John Wesley did, that to give up belief in witchcraft is to give up the Bible.[1] We do not any longer believe that a particular system of Church government can be established by New Testament ordinance, whether episcopal or presbyterian or congregational. We still maintain that the Bible is our standard of faith and practice, but we look to it for great guiding principles rather than formal rules. If it be said that this puts the responsibility upon the reader, and does not deliver him from the necessity for patient thought and prayer and sanctified common sense in reading it, that is all to the good. It means that the Bible as well as the Son of God has taken to itself the form of a servant, that it may be known in its kingly authority even through the disguise of the human record. The sheep know the voice of the divine shepherd, whatever his garb. After all, God desires to be known and loved for Himself, and it is fitting that the human lover of God should make his own discovery of God through the Bible, and build up his own anthology out of those records of the past, his own favourite passages with all their hallowed associations, wherein the living God has spoken to his soul with a living voice. Those to whom the Bible has become the Word of God know that there is no cause for anxiety about the permanence of its authority, whenever and wherever it has free course to prevail. So long as human history endures, the Bible will continue to exert its intrinsic power over the hearts and lives of believers.

The Bible is the Word of God in the sense that it is an historical record, subject to the general methods of literary and historical criticism, of a unique religious experience, in which

[1] *Journal* for 25th May 1768.

God revealed Himself to man to a degree that is itself unique.[1] Because of its fidelity to this ancient experience of God, the record is capable of becoming a 'means of grace' to the modern man. But it demands from him a response of interpretative faith parallel to that by which the original experience was conditioned. The revelation of God is neither in the outer event nor in the new unity of conviction which is intuitively created through their interaction. The right view of revelation must do justice to both the 'objective' and 'subjective' elements. It must recognize both the divine control of history and the inner witness of the Holy Spirit, for both co-operate in all divine revelation.

H. WHEELER ROBINSON

[1] That a difference of degree may become a difference of kind is rightly argued by Professor John Baillie in *Our Knowledge of God*, pp. 101 ff.

# BIBLIOGRAPHY

*(Additional books are cited in the text)*

## FOR CHAPTER I

BUHL, F. *Canon and Text of the Old Testament*, Eng. trans., 1892.

BURKITT, F. C. Art. 'Text and Versions', in *Encyclopaedia Biblica*, vol. iv, 4977 ff.,1903.

EISSFELDT, O. *Einleitung in das Alte Testament*, Fünfter Teil, 1934.

GEDEN, A. S. *Introduction to the Hebrew Bible*, 1909.

GINSBURG, C. D. *Introduction to the Massoretico-Critical Edition of the Hebrew Bible*, 1897.

KAHLE, P. 'Der Alttestamentliche Bibeltext', *Theologische Rundschau*, Neue Folge, v. (1933), 227–38.

—— 'Die Masoretische Überlieferung des hebräischen Bibeltextes', pp. 71 ff., of *Historische Grammatik der Hebräischen Sprache*, by H. Bauer and P. Leander, 1922.

KENYON, F. *Our Bible and the Ancient Manuscripts*, 1939.

LEVIAS, C. Art. 'Masorah' in *The Jewish Encyclopedia*, viii, pp. 365–71, 1904.

ROBINSON, H. WHEELER. *The Old Testament: Its Making and Meaning*, 1937.

ROBINSON, T. H. *The Genius of Hebrew Grammar*, 1928.

STRACK, H. L. 'Text of the Old Testament', in Hastings's *Dictionary of the Bible*, iv. 726–32, 1902.

THOMAS, D. W. *The Recovery of the Ancient Hebrew Language*, 1939.

URBAN, W. M. 'The Problem of Translation in General Linguistics', App. II in *Language and Reality*, 1939.

WILDEBOER, G. *The Origin of the Canon of the Old Testament*, Eng. trans., 1895.

## FOR CHAPTER II

BERTRAM, G. 'Zur Septuaginta-Forschung' in *Theologische Rundschau*, Neue Folge iii (1931), 283–96, v (1933), 173–86, x (1938), 69–80, 133–59.

BURKITT, F. C. Art. 'Text and Versions', *Encyclopaedia Biblica*, vol. iv, 4977 ff., 1903.

CHARLES, R. H. (Ed.) *Apocrypha and Pseudepigrapha of the O.T.*, 2 vols., Oxford, 1913.

DEISSMANN, G. A. *Die Hellenisierung des semitischen Monotheismus*, Leipzig, Teubner, 1903.

—— *The Philology of the Greek Bible*, Hodder, 1908.

HARNACK, A. *The Origin of the N.T.*, Engl. trans., Williams & Norgate, 1925.

KENYON, SIR F. *Our Bible and the Ancient Manuscripts*, 4th ed., Eyre & Spottiswoode, 1939.

—— *The Text of the Greek Bible*, Duckworth, 1937.

KÜMMEL, W. G. 'Textkritik und Textgeschichte des Neuen Testaments 1914–1937' in *Theologische Rundschau*, Neue Folge x (1938), 206–21, 292–327, xi (1939), 84–107.

MEECHAM, H. G. *The Letter of Aristeas*, Manchester University Press, 1935.

—— *The Oldest Version of the Bible*, Holborn Publ. House, 1932.

NESTLE, E. Art. 'Septuagint', Hastings's *Dictionary of the Bible*, vol. iv, pp. 437–54, T. & T. Clark, 1902.

OESTERLEY, W. O. E. *An Introduction to the Books of the Apocrypha*, S.P.C.K., 1935.

OTTLEY, R. R. *A Handbook to the Septuagint*, Methuen, 1920.

SOUTER, A. *Text and Canon of the N.T.*, Duckworth, 1913.

SWETE, H. B. *Introduction to the O.T. in Greek*, 1st ed., 1900; 3rd ed. revised by R. R. Ottley, Cambridge, 1914.

THACKERAY, H. ST. J. *Josephus, the Man and the Historian*, New York, 1929.

—— *The Septuagint and Jewish Worship*, Milford, 1921. Lecture 4, 'Josephus and Judaism : His Biblical Text'.

TURNER, C. H. 'Historical Introduction to the Textual Criticism of the N.T.' in *The Journal of Theological Studies* x (1908), 13–28, (1909), 161–82, 354–74, xi (1909), 1–24, (1910), 180–210.

*Texts:*

SWETE, H. B. *The Old Testament in Greek*, vol. i, 4th ed., Cambridge, 1909, vols. ii and iii, 3rd ed., 1905, 1907.

RAHLFS, A. *Septuaginta*, 2 vols., Stuttgart, 1935.

SOUTER, A. *Nouum Testamentum Graece*, Oxford, 1910.

NESTLE, E. *Novum Testamentum Graece*, with critical apparatus, 16th ed., Stuttgart, 1936.

## FOR CHAPTER III

A very full Bibliography of works published up to the end of the nine-teenth century will be found in Nestle's article on the *Syriac Versions* in Hastings's *Dictionary of the Bible*, iv. 648, 651 f.

*Old Testament.* There is no satisfactory edition of the text of the Syriac Old Testament. Ceriani's facsimile of the Codex Ambrosianus (1876) is costly and rare, the editions of Lee (1823) and of the American Missionaries at Urmia (1852) are also difficult to get and reproduce a very inferior text, but the Urmia text was reprinted by the Trinitarian Bible Society in 1913. A critical edition is being prepared by the British and Foreign Bible Society; the Pentateuch has already been published. There are several good editions of the Psalms, the best being that of W. E. Barnes (1904). For the later versions we have Gwynn's *Remnants of the Later Syriac Versions of the Bible* (1909). A comprehensive survey of the field, to which a valuable Bibliography is attached, is given by L. Haefeli in *Die Peschitta des Alten Testaments* (1927). Detailed work on individual books has been done by a number of scholars, nearly all of whom write either in German or in Latin; a list will be found in Haefeli.

*New Testament*. The Diatessaron is best known through Ephrem's Commentary (Latin translation of the Armenian version, by Aucher and Moesinger, 1876). Of the numerous studies which have been published on this subject, the most important is that of J. Rendel Harris, *Fragments of the Commentary of Ephrem Syrus upon the Diatessaron* (1896). The most important survey of the relation between the Diatessaron and the versions of the separate Gospels is that of Vogels, *Die altsyrischen Evangelien in ihrem Verhältnis zu Tatians Diatessaron* (1911). See also A. S. Marmardji, *Diatessaron de Tatien*, Beyrouth, 1936.

Cureton published *Remains of a very antient recension of the Four Gospels Syriac* in 1858. Bensly, Harris, and Burkitt issued *The Four Gospels in Syriac transcribed from the Sinaitic Palimpsest* in 1894, supplemented by additional transcriptions in 1896. A definitive edition of the Old Syriac was published by Burkitt under the title *Evangelion da-Mepharreshe* (1904), where the readings of both manuscripts are recorded.

There are numerous editions of the Peshitta; the best is that of the British and Foreign Bible Society.

The Acts and the Epistles according to the Philoxenian version were published by Hall in 1884, the four 'rejected' Epistles by Pococke in 1630, and the Apocalypse by Gwynn in 1897.

White printed the Harklensian version between 1778 and 1803, though he was, apparently, under the impression that his text was that of the Philoxenian.

For the general study of the Syriac versions of the New Testament and their place in the textual criticism of the Bible, the reader will do best to refer to sections dealing with the subject in various Introductions to the New Testament, e.g.

LAKE. *The Text of the New Testament*, 6th ed., 1928, especially to be recommended for its conciseness, fullness of material, and clarity.

## FOR CHAPTER IV

BERGER, S. *De l'histoire de la Vulgate en France*, Paris, 1887.

—— *Les Préfaces jointes aux livres de la Bible dans les manuscrits de la Vulgate*, Paris, 1892.

—— *Histoire de la Vulgate pendant les premiers siècles du moyen âge*, Paris, 1893.

BILLEN, A. V. *The Old-Latin Texts of the Heptateuch*, Cambridge, 1927.

BLONDHEIM, D. S. *Les parlers judéo-romans et la Vetus latina*, Paris, 1925.

BURKITT, F. C. Art. 'Texts and Versions' in *Encyclopaedia Biblica*, vol. iv, cols. 4992 ff. and 5022 ff., London, 1903.

—— 'The Book of Rules of Tyconius' in *Texts and Studies*, vol. iii. 1, Cambridge, 1893.

—— 'The Old Latin and the Itala' in *Texts and Studies*, vol. iv. 3, Cambridge, 1896.

CHAPMAN, J. *Notes on the Early History of the Vulgate Gospels*, Oxford, 1908.

CORSSEN, P. *Bericht über die lateinischen Bibelübersetzungen*, Leipzig, 1899.

GLUNZ, H. *Britannien und Bibeltext*, Leipzig, 1930.

KAULEN, F. *Geschichte der Vulgata*, Mainz, 1868.

KENNEDY, H. A. A. Art. 'Latin Versions, the Old' in Hastings's *Dictionary of the Bible*, vol. iii, pp. 47 ff., Edinburgh, 1900.

PLATER, W. E., and WHITE, H. J. *A Grammar of the Vulgate*, Oxford, 1926.

QUENTIN, H. 'Mémoire sur l'établissement du texte de la Vulgate', *Collectanea Biblica Latina*, vol. vi, Rome and Paris, 1922.

SCHMID, O. *Über verschiedene Eintheilungen der Heiligen Schrift*, Graz, 1892.

v. SODEN, HANS. *Das lateinische Neue Testament in Afrika zur Zeit Cyprians*, Leipzig, 1909.

SOUTER, A. *The Earliest Latin Commentaries on the Epistles of St. Paul*, Oxford, 1927.

STUMMER, F. *Einführung in die lateinische Bibel*, Paderborn, 1928.

TURNER, C. H. *The Oldest Manuscript of the Vulgate Gospels*, Oxford, 1931.

VOGELS, H. J. *Vulgatastudien. Die Evangelien der Vulgata untersucht auf ihre lateinische und griechische Vorlage*, Münster, 1928.

WESTCOTT, B. F. Art. 'Vulgate, the' in Smith's *Dictionary of the Bible*, vol. iii, pp. 1689 ff., London, 1863.

WHITE, H. J. Art. 'Vulgate' in Hastings's *Dictionary of the Bible*, vol. iv, pp. 873 ff., Edinburgh, 1902.

—— 'The Codex Amiatinus and its Birthplace' in *Studia Biblica*, vol. ii, pp. 273 ff., Oxford, 1890.

ZIEGLER, L. *Die lateinischen Bibelübersetzungen vor Hieronymus und die Itala des Augustinus*, München, 1879.

Various articles in *The Journal of Theological Studies, Revue Bénédictine, Revue Biblique, Harvard Theological Review, Zeitschrift für die neutestamentliche Wissenschaft*, &c.

*Editions*: (*a*) Old-Latin:

SABATIER, P. *Bibliorum sacrorum latinae versiones antiquae seu vetus italica* . . . , Rheims, 1743–9.

JÜLICHER, A. *Itala. Das neue Testament in altlateinischer Überlieferung*: I. *Matthäus-Evangelium*, Berlin, 1938.

(*b*) Vulgate:

PAPAL COMMISSION. *Biblia Sacra iuxta latinam vulgatam versionem* (Gen.-Ruth), Rome, 1926, and following.

HETZENAUER, M., *Biblia Sacra vulgatae editionis*, Innsbrück, 1906.

WORDSWORTH, J., and WHITE, H. J. *Nouum Testamentum Domini nostri Iesu Christi latine secundum editionem Sancti Hieronymi* (Matt.–Philem.), Oxford, 1889 and following.

—— *Nouum Testamentum Latine Editio Minor*, Oxford, 1911.

## FOR CHAPTER V

The Vespasian Psalter. (1) *Anglo-Saxon and Early English Psalter*, edited by J. Stevenson, Publications of the Surtees Society, 1843–7. (2) *The Oldest English Texts*, edited by Henry Sweet, Early English Text Society, 1885, pp. 183–420.

The Paris Psalter. (1) *Libri Psalmorum Versio Antiqua Latina; cum Paraphrasi Anglo-Saxonica, partim soluta oratione, partim metrice composita. Nunc primum . . . edidit Benjamin Thorpe*, Oxford, 1835. (2) *The West-Saxon Psalms, being the prose portion . . . of the so-called Paris Psalter*, edited . . . by James Wilson Bright and Robert Lee Ramsay, Boston, 1907.

*Biblical Quotations in Old English Prose Writers*, edited with the Vulgate and other Latin originals . . . , by Albert S. Cook. London, 1898.

*The Lindisfarne and Rushworth Gospels, now first printed from the original manuscripts* . . . , edited by George Waring. Publications of the Surtees Society, 1854–65.

*The Holy Gospels in Anglo-Saxon, Northumbrian, and Old Mercian Versions, synoptically arranged . . . together with the early Latin version as contained in the Lindisfarne MS.*, edited by the Rev. Walter W. Skeat, Cambridge, 1871–87.

*The Gospels in West Saxon*, edited by J. W. Bright, Boston and London (Belles Lettres Series), 1905–10.

*The Gospels. Gothic, Anglo-Saxon, Wycliffe and Tyndale versions,* arranged in parallel columns with preface and notes by Joseph Bosworth . . . assisted by George Waring, London, 1865.

*The Old English Version of the Heptateuch, Ælfric's Treatise on the Old and New Testament, and his Preface to Genesis,* edited . . . by S. J. Crawford, Early English Text Society, 1922.

The Northern Metrical Psalter. (1) *Anglo-Saxon and Early English Psalter,* Surtees Society, 1843–7. (2) *Yorkshire Writers. Richard Rolle of Hampole and his Followers,* edited by C. Horstman, vol. ii, pp. 129–273, London, 1896.

*The Earliest English Prose Psalter,* edited from its two manuscripts by Dr. K. D. Buelbring, Early English Text Society, 1891.

*The Psalter, or Psalms of David, and certain Canticles, with a translation and exposition in English, by Richard Rolle of Hampole,* edited by H. R. Bramley, Oxford, 1884.

*A Fourteenth Century English Biblical Version,* edited by Anna C. Paues, Cambridge, 1904.

*The Pauline Epistles contained in MS. Parker 32,* . . . edited by M. J. Powell, Early English Text Society, 1916.

*The New Testament . . . translated out of the Latin Vulgat by John Wiclif . . . about 1378, to which is præfixt a History of the several Translations of the H. Bible and N. Testament &c. into English,* edited by John Lewis, London, 1731.

*The New Testament translated from the Latin in the year 1380 by John Wiclif, to which are prefixed . . . an historical account of the Saxon and English Versions of the Scriptures previous to the opening of the fifteenth century,* edited by the Rev. Henry Hervey Baber, London, 1810.

*The English Hexapla, exhibiting the six important English translations of the New Testament Scriptures, Wiclif, Tyndale* [etc.], London, Bagster & Sons, n.d. [1841.]

*The Holy Bible, containing the Old and New Testaments, with the Apocryphal books, in the earliest English versions, made from the Latin Vulgate by John Wycliffe and his followers;* edited by the Rev. Josiah Forshall and Sir Frederic Madden, 4 volumes, Oxford, 1850.

*The New Testament in English, according to the version by John Wycliffe . . . and revised by John Purvey* [With introduction by W. W. Skeat], Oxford, 1879.

*The Books of Job, Psalms, Proverbs, Ecclesiastes, and the Song of Solomon, according to the Wycliffite version made by Nicholas de Hereford . . . and revised by John Purvey* [With introduction by W. W. Skeat], Oxford, 1881.

*The New Testament in Scots, being Purvey's revision of Wycliffe's version turned into Scots by Murdoch Nisbet, c. 1520*, edited from the unique manuscript . . . by Thomas Graves Law, Scottish Text Society, 3 vols., 1901–5.

*The Lollard Bible and other Medieval Biblical Versions*, by Margaret Deanesly, Cambridge, 1920.

*John Wyclif. A Study of the English Medieval Church*, by Herbert B. Workman, Vol. ii, pp. 149–200, Oxford, 1926.

*The Bible and its Literary Associations*, edited by Margaret B. Crook (ch. xi, 'The Bible in Anglo-Saxon and Medieval England'), New York, 1937.

## FOR CHAPTER VI

ARBER, E. *The First Printed English New Testament*, London, 1871.

BAGSTER & SONS. *The English Hexapla of the New Testament Scriptures*, London, 1841.

CARLETON, J. G. *The Part of Rheims in the Making of the English Bible*, Oxford, 1902.

CHEKE, SIR JOHN. *The Gospel according to Saint Matthew*, London, 1843.

CLAPTON, ERNEST. *Our Prayer Book Psalter*, London, 1934.

COTTON, HENRY. *Editions of the Bible and Parts thereof in English*, 2nd ed., Oxford, 1852.

COVERDALE, M. *The Bible 1535*, London, 1838.

DARLOW T. H. and MOULE, H. T. *Historical Catalogue of the Printed Editions of Holy Scripture in the Library of the British and Foreign Bible Society*, London, 1903.

DEMAUS, ROBERT. *William Tindale*, London, 1886.

EARLE, JOHN. *The Psalter of the Great Bible of 1539*, London, 1894.

FORSHALL, J. and MADDEN, F. *The Holy Bible . . . John Wycliffe*, 4 vols., Oxford, 1850.

FRY, F. *The Prophet Jonas*, translated by Tindale and Coverdale, London, 1863.

LUPTON, J. H. English Versions; Hastings's *Dictionary of the Bible*, extra vol., 1904.

MOMBERT, J. I. *English Versions of the Bible*, London, 1906.

—— *Tindale's Pentateuch*. New York and London, 1884.

MOULTON, W. F. *The History of the English Bible*, 5th ed., London, 1911.

MOZLEY, J. F. *William Tyndale*. London, 1937.

POLLARD, A. W. *Records of the English Bible*, Oxford, 1911.

SKEAT, W. W. *The New Testament . . . J. Wycliffe and J. Purvey*, Oxford, 1879.
—— *The Books of Job, Psalms, Proverbs, Ecclesiastes, and the Song of Solomon, according to the Wycliffite Version*, Oxford, 1881.
HARDY WALLIS, N. *The New Testament*, translated by William Tyndale 1534, Cambridge, 1938.
WESTCOTT, B. F. *A General View of the History of the English Bible*, 3rd ed., revised by W. A. Wright, London, 1905.
WHITTINGHAM, W. *The New Testament 1557*, London, 1842.
WRIGHT, W. A. *The Hexaplar Psalter*, Cambridge, 1911.

## FOR CHAPTER VII

CARLETON, J. G. *The Part of Rheims in the Making of the English Bible*, Oxford, 1902.
DARLOW, T. H. and MOULE, H. T. *Historical Catalogue of the Printed Editions of Holy Scripture in the Library of the British and Foreign Bible Society*, London, 1903.
LOWTH, R. *Lectures on the Sacred Poetry of the Hebrews*, translated from the Latin by G. Gregory, 3rd ed., London, 1835.
MOMBERT, J. I. *English Versions of the Bible*, London, 1906.
POLLARD, A. W. *The Holy Bible*, an exact reprint in Roman type, page for page of the authorized version published in the year 1611, Oxford, 1911.
—— *Records of the English Bible*, Oxford, 1911.
SCRIVENER, F. H. *The Authorized Edition of the English Bible 1611*, Cambridge, 1884.
TRENCH, R. C. *On the Authorized Version of the New Testament*, 2nd ed., London, 1859.
WESTCOTT, B. F. *A General View of the History of the English Bible*, 3rd ed., revised by W. A. Wright, London, 1905.
WRIGHT, A. W. *The Bible Word Book*, 2nd ed., London, 1884.

## FOR CHAPTER VIII

(The place of publication is London except where otherwise stated.)

### I. HISTORIES OF THE ENGLISH BIBLE

ANDERSON, C. *Annals of the English Bible*, 2 vols., 1845. Vol. i revised, 1862.
BLUNT, J. H. Art. on 'English Bible', in *Encyclopaedia Britannica*, 9th ed., vol. viii, pp. 381–90, Edinburgh, 1878.

CARPENTER, J. E. *The Bible in the Nineteenth Century.* Eight Lectures, 1903.

DORE, J. *Old Bibles or an account of the various versions of the English Bible,* 1876 (only down to the A.V.).

—— *Old Bibles: An Account of the Early Versions of the English Bible.* 2nd ed., . . . 1888. (Only down to the A.V.)

EADIE, J. *The English Bible: an external and critical history of the various English translations of Scripture, with remarks on the need of revising the English New Testament,* 2 vols., 1876.

EDGAR, A. *The Bibles of England: a plain account for plain people of the principal versions of the Bible in English,* Paisley and London, 1889.

GOODSPEED, E. J. *The Making of the English New Testament,* Chicago, 1925.

HEATON, W. J. *Our Own English Bible, its translators and their work,* 3 vols., 1908–13.

HOARE, H. W. *The Evolution of the English Bible: an historical sketch of the successive Versions from 1382 to 1885,* 1901. 2nd ed., 1902.

—— *Our English Bible: the story of its origin and growth,* revised ed., 1911.

KENYON, F. G. *Our Bible and the Ancient Manuscripts,* 1895. Fourth ed., revised, rewritten and enlarged, 1939. Pp. 194–245.

—— Art. on 'English Versions' in Hastings's one-volume *Dictionary of the Bible,* Edinburgh, 1909.

—— *The Story of the Bible: a Popular Account of How it Came to Us,* London and New York, 1936 and 1937. Pp. 47 ff.

LOFTIE, W. J. *A Century of Bibles or the Authorised Version from 1611 to 1711* . . ., 1872.

LOVETT, R. *The Printed English Bible, 1525–1885.* 'Present Day Primers', 1894.

LUPTON, J. H. Art. on 'Versions (English)', in Hastings's *Dictionary of the Bible,* extra volume, pp. 236–71, Edinburgh, 1904 (quoted in footnotes as 'Lupton').

MILLIGAN, G. *The English Bible: a sketch of its history.* 'Guild Text-books', 1895 (quoted in footnotes as 'Milligan').

—— Art. on 'Versions, English', in Hastings's *Dictionary of the Bible,* vol. iv, pp. 855–60, Edinburgh, 1902.

MOMBERT, J. I. *English Versions of the Bible. A Handbook,* 1883. 2nd ed., 1890.

MOULTON, W. F. *The History of the English Bible,* 2nd ed., 1878. 3rd ed. (with an appendix on the R.V.), 1884. 4th ed., 1887. 5th ed., revised and enlarged, by his sons J. H. Moulton and W. Fiddian Moulton, 1911. Abridged ed., prepared by A. W. Harrison, 1937 (the 1911 ed. is quoted in the footnotes as 'Moulton').

MUIR, W. *Our Grand Old Bible; being the Story of the Authorized Version of the English Bible, told for the Tercentenary Celebration*, 1911. Pp. 199 ff. deal with the R.V.

PATTISON, T. H. *The History of the English Bible*, 1894.

PAUES, A. C. and HENSON, H. H. Art. on 'Bible, English', in *Encyclopaedia Britannica*, 11th ed., vol. iii, pp. 894–905. New York, 1910. In 14th ed., vol. iii, pp. 529–35, New York, 1929.

PLUMPTRE, E. H. Art. on 'Version, Authorised' in Smith's *Dictionary of the Bible*, vol. iii, pp. 1665–83, 1863 (quoted in the footnotes as 'Plumptre').

SMYTH, J. P. *How we got our Bible*, 1886. Later editions 1886, 1889, and 1906.

STOUGHTON, J. *Our English Bible: its Translations and Translators*, 1878.

TALBOT, R. T. *Our Bible and How it has come to us*, 1893.

WESTCOTT, B. F. *A General View of the History of the English Bible*, London and Cambridge, 1868. 2nd ed., 1872 (quoted in the footnotes as 'Westcott'). A third edition has been supervised by W. Aldis Wright.

## 2. SOME NOTEWORTHY EDITIONS OF THE BIBLE

1841. *The English Hexapla,* exhibiting in parallel columns the N.T. versions of Wycliffe, Tyndale, Cranmer, Geneva, the Anglo-Rhemish, and the A.V., with a Greek Text and other matter. Published by Bagster.

1846. *The Miniature Quarto Bible*: the whole Bible in the A.V. with introductory and concluding remarks to each book, and numerous notes. Published by Bagster.

1870. *The Reference Paragraph Bible . . . containing seventy thousand original and selected parallel references and marginal readings. Arranged in Paragraphs and Parallelisms.* The Text published by Royal Licence. London and Glasgow (Collins). (See above, p. 258).

1870–3. *The Cambridge Paragraph Bible of the Authorized English Version with the Text revised by a collation of its early and other Principal Editions, the use of the Italic type made uniform, the Marginal References remodelled, and a Critical Introduction prefixed,* by Rev. F. H. A. Scrivener. In three vols. Cambridge (University Press), 1870–3. (See above p. 258.)

1875. McCLELLAN, JOHN BROWN (Vicar of Bottisham), *The New Testament . . . a new Translation, on the basis of the Authorized Version, from a critically revised Greek text. . . . A contribution to Christian Evidence.* Vol. i (the Four Gospels) only published. London (Macmillan). (See above, p. 257).

1880, 1883 and 1889. *The Variorum Edition of the Holy Bible, . . . with various renderings and readings from the best authorities,* edited by T. K. Cheyne, S. R. Driver, R. L. Clarke, A. Goodwin, and W. Sanday. (See above, p. 258.)

1898–1904. *The Twentieth Century New Testament. Part I. The Five Historical Books,* 1898. *Part II. The Pauline Letters,* 1900. *Part III. Pastoral, Personal and General Letters, and the Revelation,* 1901. *The Twentieth Century New Testament. Revised Edition,* 1904. London, New York, and Chicago. (See above, p. 268).

1902–39. WEYMOUTH, R. F. *The New Testament in Modern Speech: an idiomatic translation into everyday English from the text of 'The Resultant Greek Testament',* 1902. Edited and partly revised by E. Hampden-Cook, 1907. Numerous editions. Popular edition, translation revised by J. A. Robertson, 1939. (See above, p. 269.)

1903–38. FENTON, FERRAR. *The Holy Bible in Modern English . . . translated . . . direct from the original Hebrew, Chaldee, and Greek,* Tonbridge. Later edition, 1938. (See above, p. 267.)

1907–1926. MOULTON, R. G. *The Modern Reader's Bible: the books of the Bible with three books of the Apocrypha presented in modern literary form.* Edited, with introductions and notes. (See above, p. 268.)

1913–38. MOFFATT, J. *The New Testament: a new translation,* 1913. *The Old Testament: a new translation,* in two vols. 1924. Numerous reprints of both. Jubilee edition of the whole, 1938. (See above, pp. 269 f.)

1935. *The Bible: an American Translation.* Chicago. (See above, p. 271.)

1937. *The Bible designed to be read as Literature.* (See above, p. 271.)

1938. *The Book of Books. A translation of the New Testament complete and unabridged.*

## 3. SPECIAL TREATISES

BALLARD, F. *Which Bible to read—Revised or 'Authorised'? A statement of the facts and an appeal to the modern Christian,* 1897. 2nd ed., revised and enlarged, 1898.

BECKETT, E. *Should the Revised New Testament be authorised?* 1882.

BURGON, J. W. *The Revision Revised. Three articles . . . to which is added a reply to Bishop Ellicott's Pamphlet. . . .* 1883.

CARTER, A. *The Story of the New Testament told in connection with the Revised Version. . . .* 1881.

CHAMBERS, T. W. *A Companion to the Revised Version,* London and New York, 1885.

COOK, F. C. *The Revised Version of the Gospels considered in its bearings upon the record of our Lord's words and of incidents in his life*, 1882.

DAVIDSON, S. *On a Fresh Revision of the English Old Testament*, 1873.

*Documentary History of the American Committee on Revision.* Prepared by order of the American Committee, New York, 1885.

ELLICOTT, C. J. *Addresses on the Revised Version of Holy Scripture*, 1901 (quoted in footnotes as 'Ellicott').

(ELLICOTT, C. J. and PALMER, E.) *The Revisers and the Greek Text of the New Testament*, by two members of the New Testament Company, 1882.

FIELD, F. *Notes on the Translation of the New Testament, being the Otium Norvicense (Pars Tertia)* . . . *reprinted with additions by the Author*, Cambridge, 1899.

GORDON, A. *Christian Doctrine in the light of New Testament Revision*, 1882.

HEATON, W. J. *Should the Revised Version of the Scriptures be further revised? A popular tract*, 1908. 2nd ed., 1908. 9th ed., 1912.

*Historical Account of the Work of the American Committee of Revision.* Prepared by a special Committee appointed for the purpose in May 1884, New York, 1885.

HOPPS, J. P. *The Revised New Testament. Two Lectures* . . . *with an Appendix containing specimens of suggestive alterations*, 1881. (A threepenny pamphlet.)

HUMPHRY, W. G. *A Commentary on the Revised Version of the New Testament*, London, Paris, and New York, 1882. New ed., revised, 1888.

IERSON, HENRY. *Notes on the Amended English Bible with special reference to certain texts in the Revised Version of the Old and New Testaments bearing upon the principles of Unitarian Christianity*, 1887.

KENNEDY, B. H. *Ely Lectures on the Revised Version of the New Testament*, 1882.

LEARY, T. H. L. *A Critical Examination of Bishop Lightfoot's Defence of the Last Petition in the Lord's Prayer*, 1882.

LIGHTFOOT, J. B. *On a Fresh Revision of the English New Testament*, 1871. 3rd ed., 1891 (quoted in the footnotes as 'Lightfoot').

MALAN, S. C. *A Plea for the Received Greek Text and for the Authorized Version of the New Testament, in answer to some of the Dean of Canterbury's Criticisms on both*, 1869.

MOULTON, R. G. *The Literary Study of the Bible: an account of the leading forms of literature represented in the Sacred Writings: intended for English readers*, 1896.

*The New Revision and its Study:* by six members of the American New Testament Company, Philadelphia, 1881.

NEWTH, S. *Lectures on Bible Revision*, 1881 (quoted in the footnotes as 'Newth').

*Revised Version* of the New Testament, *Preface* dated from the Jerusalem Chamber, Westminster Abbey, 11th Nov. 1880. *Preface* to the *Revised Version* of the Old Testament, dated from the same place, 10th July 1884.

ROBERTS, A. *The Companion to the Revised Version of the English New Testament*, London, Paris, and New York, 1882.

—— *Old Testament Revision: a handbook for English Readers*, 1883.

SCHAFF, PHILIP. *A Companion to the Greek Testament and the English Version*, published simultaneously in London (Macmillan) and New York (Harper), 1883. A solid and comprehensive handbook, with special attention to textual criticism (quoted in the footnotes as 'Schaff').

SCRIVENER, F. H. A. *Supplement to the Authorized Version of the New Testament: being a Critical Illustration of its more difficult passages from the Syriac, Latin and earlier English Versions, with an Introduction*, vol. i (all published), 1845.

—— *The Authorized Edition of the English Bible (1611), its subsequent reprints and modern representatives*, Cambridge (Univ. Press), 1884.

SKEATS, H. S. and MIALL, C. S. *History of the Free Churches of England 1688–1891*, pp. 678–82, 1891.

SMITH, G. VANCE. *Texts and Margins of the Revised New Testament affecting theological doctrine briefly reviewed*, 1881.

THORNTON, S. *The Revised Version of the Bible: our duty in regard to it*, 1902. Revised ed., 1903.

TRENCH, R. C. *On the Authorized Version of the New Testament, in connexion with some recent proposals for its revision*, 1858, 1859.

VAUGHAN, C. J. *Authorized or Revised? Sermons on some of the texts in which the Revised Version differs from the Authorized*, 1882.

WESTCOTT, B. F. *The Lesson of Biblical Revision. A Sermon*, Cambridge, 1881.

—— *Some Lessons of the Revised Version of the New Testament*, 1897.

YOUNG, R. *Contributions to a new Revision or a critical Companion to the New Testament*, Edinburgh, 1881.

## FOR CHAPTER IX

BERTHOLET, A. 'Sammlung und Kanonisierung des A.T.' *Die Religion in Geschichte und Gegenwart²*, vol. i, 975–8, 1927.

BEVAN, EDWYN. *Symbolism and Belief*, 1938.

DICKIE, E. P. *Revelation and Response*, 1938.

VON DOBSCHÜTZ E. Art. 'Bible in the Church', in *Encyclopaedia of Religion and Ethics*, vol. ii, pp. 579–615, 1909.

DODD, C. H. *The Authority of the Bible*, 1928.

GARVIE, A. E. 'Revelation', in Hastings's *Dictionary of the Bible*, extra vol., pp. 321–337, 1904.

GORE, C. 'The Authority of Holy Scripture' (Ch. VIII of *The Holy Spirit and the Church*), 1924.

HÄNEL, J. *Der Schriftbegriff Jesu*, 1919.

HEMPEL, J. *Altes Testament und Geschichte*, 1930.

IVERACH, J. Art. 'Authority', *Encyclopaedia of Religion and Ethics*, vol. ii, pp. 249–254, 1909.

LILLEY, A. L. *Religion and Revelation*, 1932.

MANSON, T. W. 'The Nature and Authority of the Canonical Scriptures', in *A Companion to the Bible*, ed. by T. W. Manson, 1939.

MARTINEAU, J. *The Seat of Authority in Religion*, 2nd ed., 1890.

PEAKE, A. S. *The Bible: its Origin, its Significance and its Abiding Worth*, 1913.

RAWLINSON, A. E. J. *Authority and Freedom*, 1924.

ROBINSON, H. WHEELER. 'Canonicity and Inspiration', in *The Expository Times*, Dec. 1935 (vol. xlvii, no. 3, pp. 119–23, 1935).

—— 'The Canon' (Ch. VIII of *The Old Testament: its Making and Meaning*), 1937.

SANDAY, W. Art. 'Bible', in *Encyclopaedia of Religion and Ethics*, vol. ii, pp. 562–579, 1909.

SCOTT, E. F. *The New Testament Idea of Revelation*, 1935.

VON SODEN, HANS. *Die Religion in Geschichte und Gegenwart*[2], vol. i, 986–93, 1927.

SÖDERBLOM, N. *The Nature of Revelation*, 1933.

TAYLOR, A. E. *The Faith of a Moralist* (Series II), 1937.

# CHRONOLOGICAL TABLE

**B.C.**

*c*. 1000– Beginnings of Hebrew Literature.
   760– Hebrew written prophecy.
   621 'Canonical' recognition of Deuteronomy.
   397 Ezra's Law-book.
*c*. 250 Greek translation of the Pentateuch (LXX).
   132 Prologue to Ecclesiasticus.
 –100 Greek Papyrus fragments of Deuteronomy (Rylands) and Codex of Numbers-Deuteronomy (Chester-Beatty)

**A.D.**

 50–63 Pauline Epistles.
   65– St. Mark's Gospel.
*c*. 100 Completion of O.T. Canon (Josephus).
*c*. 100 Syriac O.T.
100–150 Papyrus fragments of Fourth Gospel.
*c*. 150– Syriac Versions of N.T.
130–200 Aquila, Theodotion, Symmachus.
   200 Completion of N.T. Canon.
150–200 Old-Latin Versions (O.T. and N.T.)·
   240 Hexapla of Origen (186–253).
300–400 Greek Uncial MSS.
346–420 Jerome and the Vulgate.
   400– Targums.
*c*. 500– Work of the Masoretes.
   735 Bede's translation of St. John's Gospel (not extant).
895/916 Earliest Hebrew MSS. of 'Prophets'.
 1008 Earliest MS. of complete Hebrew Bible (fragments from sixth century).
  950– Anglo-Saxon glosses to Lindisfarne Gospels (700).
  992 Aelfric's translations.
 1384 †Wyclif.
 1450 First printed Latin Bible.
 1488   ,,      Hebrew Bible (Soncino).
 1516   ,,      Greek N.T. (Erasmus).
 1522   ,,      Greek O.T. (Complutensian Polyglot).
1525/6 Tindale's N.T. (†1536)
 1529   ,,      Pentateuch

A.D.
1535 Coverdale's Bible.
1537 Matthew's Bible.
1539 Taverner's Bible
1539 The Great Bible.
1557 Whittingham's N.T.
1560 The Genevan Bible.
1568 The Bishops' Bible.
1582 Rhemes N.T.
1609/10 Douai O.T.
1611 Authorized Version.
1881 Revised N.T.
1885    ,,     O.T.
1895    ,,     Apocrypha.

# INDEXES

## I. PERSONAL NAMES

Abbot, Archbp., 217.
Abbot, Ezra, 248.
Addison, Joseph, 196, 233.
Ælfric, 116, 130 ff., 137.
Æthelmer, 132.
Æthelwerd, 132.
Ainsworth, Henry, 225, 226, 227.
Akiba, Rabbi, 20, 51.
Alcuin, 118.
Alexander the Great, 19, 40.
Alexander, W. Lindsay, 244.
Alford, Henry, 238, 239, 240, 242, 244.
Alfred, 129.
Allen, John, 224.
Allen, William, 191.
Andrewes, Lancelot, 198, 234.
Angus, J., 245, 248.
Antiochus Epiphanes, 47, 64.
Aphrahat, 87, 91, 92, 93, 94.
Aquila, 51 f., 59.
Arnobius, 110 n.
Arnold, Matthew, 258.
Artaxerxes, 21.
Arundel, Archbp., 148 f.
Athanasius, 68.
Athias, Joseph, 23.
Augustine, 103, 106, 107, 109 n., 110, 113, 116, 118.
Aurogallus, 151.
Avitus of Vienne, 116.

Bacher, W., 31 n.
Bacon, Roger, 119.
Baduellus, 185.
Baer, 23.
Baillie, John, 302 n.
Ball, C. J., 254.
Ballard, F., 265.

Bancroft, Bp., 197, 199, 212.
Barker, Matthew, 203, 223.
Barnes, Robert, 154.
Barrow, 238.
Baruch, 24, 25.
Basilides, 66.
Bauer, H., 27 n.
Beard, J. R., 238.
Beckett, Sir Edmund, 262.
Bede, 129.
Bedwell, William, 199.
Beet, J. A., 261.
Bellamy, John, 236.
Belsham, Thomas, 236.
Bengel, J. A., 76, 80.
Ben Asher, 31.
Ben Chayyim, Jacob, 21, 30, 31, 160.
Ben Kalonymos, Isaac, 184.
Ben Sira, 291.
Bensly, R. L., 244.
Bentley, Richard, 227.
Bertram, 205.
Beza, Theodore, 73, 182, 183, 185, 205, 206, 224.
Bickersteth, 240, 242, 244.
Billen, A. V., 108 n.
Bilson, Bp., 201, 207
Birckman, Arnold, 152.
Birrell, J., 244.
Bissell, E. C., 254.
Blake, William, 234.
Blakesley, J. W., 242, 244.
Blayney, B., 225, 233.
Bois, John, 198, 202.
Bomberg, Daniel, 21.
Bonner, 179.
Brett, Richard, 198.
Bristow, Richard, 191.

Y 2

# II. SUBJECTS

## III. SCRIPTURE REFERENCES

### OLD TESTAMENT

Genesis (*cont.*)
xlix . . . . . . . 7
xlix. 10 . . . . . 37
l . . . . . . . 208

Exodus:
ii. 22 . . . . . 127, 164
xii . . . . . . 208
xii. 3 . . . . . . 164
xiv. 21 . . . . . . 279
xv . . . . . . . 167
xv. 4 . . . . . . 164
xv. 19 . . . . . . 106
xv. 26 . . . . . . 164
xviii. 4 . . . . . . 127
xviii. 15 ff. . . . . . 16
xx–xxiii . . . . . 130
xx. 22–xxiii. 19 . . . 8
xxi. 33 . . . . . . 280
xxiii. 4 . . . . . . 280
xxiv. 10 . . . . . 35

Leviticus:
xi. 42 . . . . . . 29
xiii . . . . . . 208
xiii. 45 . . . . . . 167
xvi. 8 ff. . . . . . 9
xvii–xxvi . . . . . 9
xix . . . . . . 11
xxi. 5 . . . . . . 163
xxiii . . . . 18, 208
xxiii. 39 . . . . . 18
xxiii. 42 . . . . . 18

Numbers:
iii. 15 . . . . . . 110
v. 11–31 . . . . . 9
x. 35, 36 . . . . . 7
xii. 1 . . . . . . 165
xviii. 26 . . . . . 18
xxi. 14 . . . . . . 8
xxiii. 7 . . . . . . 165
xxiii. 8 . . . . . . 163

Deuteronomy:
vi. 4 ff. . . . . . . 163
xi. 19 . . . . . . 163

xii–xxviii . . . . . . 8
xiv. 22 ff. . . . . . . 18
xvi. 13 ff. . . . . . . 18
xviii. 14 . . . . . . 167
xxiii. 2 . . . . . . . 194
xxiii. 18 . . . . . . 163
xxvi. 12 ff. . . . . . . 18
xxviii. 50 . . . . . . 167
xxxi. 16 . . . . . . 164
xxxi. 26 . . . . . . 106
xxxii . . . . . . . 167
xxxii. 1, 2 . . . . . . 6
xxxii. 5 . . . . . . 36
xxxii. 11 . . . . . . 164
xxxii. 20 . . . . . . 110
xxxii. 35 . . . . . 213 f.
xxxiii . . . . . . . 8
xxxiii. 8 . . . . . . 8

Joshua:
x. 13 . . . . . . . 7
xv. 18 . . . . . . . 195

Judges:
v . . . . . . . 7
v. 26, 27 . . . . . . 230
v. 31 . . . . . . 35
ix. 8–15 . . . . . . 14
xii. 6 . . . . . . . 115
xv. 8 . . . . . . . 186

Ruth:
ii. 11 . . . . . . . 28

1 Samuel:
i. 5 . . . . . . . 33
ii. 10 . . . . . . . 194
vi. 18 . . . . . . 33
ix. ff. . . . . . . 8
ix. 25 . . . . . 122 *n.*
xiii. 1 . . . . . . 33
xiv. 41 . . . . . . 57
xiv. 41 ff. . . . . . 280
xvi ff. . . . . . . 8
xviii . . . . . . 208
xix. 22 . . . . . . 56
xxiii. 28 . . . . . 115

## APOCRYPHA AND PSEUDEPIGRAPHA

## NEW TESTAMENT